About Island Press

Island Press, a nonprofit organization, publishes, markets, and distributes the most advanced thinking on the conservation of our natural resources—books about soil, land, water, forests, wildlife, and hazardous and toxic wastes. These books are practical tools used by public officials, business and industry leaders, natural resource managers, and concerned citizens working to solve both local and global resource problems.

Founded in 1978, Island Press reorganized in 1984 to meet the increasing demand for substantive books on all resource-related issues. Island Press publishes and distributes under its own imprint and offers these services to other nonprofit organizations.

Support for Island Press is provided by The Mary Reynolds Babcock Foundation, The Educational Foundation of America, The Charles Engelhard Foundation, The Ford Foundation, The George Gund Foundation, The William and Flora Hewlett Foundation, The Joyce Foundation, The J. M. Kaplan Fund, The John D. and Catherine T. MacArthur Foundation, The Andrew W. Mellon Foundation, The Joyce Mertz-Gilmore Foundation, The New-Land Foundation, Northwest Area Foundation, The Jessie Smith Noyes Foundation, The J. N. Pew, Jr., Charitable Trust, The Rockefeller Brothers Fund, The Florence and John Schumann Foundation, The Tides Foundation, and individual donors.

About the Conservation Foundation

A nonprofit organization founded in 1948, The Conservation Foundation is dedicated to improving the quality of the environment through wise use of the earth's resources. Its long-standing interest and involvement in land conservation and development issues emphasize a comprehensive approach: through public advocacy characterized by reason and balance, cooperative problem solving, and the development of new ideas, it seeks effective solutions to current and emerging environmental problems.

Resource Guide for Creating Successful Communities

Resource Guide for Creating Successful Communities

The Conservation Foundation

Michael A. Mantell
Stephen F. Harper · Luther Propst

ISLAND PRESS

Washington, D.C. □ Covelo, California

Every effort has been made to reproduce material from various units of local government in an accurate form.
Some illustrations may have been omitted because of difficulties in reproduction or repetition of content.

Grateful acknowledgment is made for permission to reprint portions of "Gifts of Land" published in
Connecticut Woodlands magazine, vol. 53, no. 1, 1988, and is reprinted here in Appendix B.

Library of Congress Cataloging-in-Publication Data

Mantell, Michael
    Creating successful communities : a guidebook to growth management
strategies / by Michael Mantell, Stephen Harper, Luther Propst.
        p.   cm.
"The Conservation Foundation"
    ISBN 1-55963-030-2 — ISBN 1-55963-014-0 (pbk.)
ISBN 1-55963-031-0 (Resource guide) — ISBN
1-55963-015-9 (Resource guide : pbk.)
    1. Community development, Urban—United States.   2. City planning—
Environmental aspects—United States.   3. Land use, Urban—United
States.   I. Harper, Stephen F.   II. Propst, Luther.
III. Conservation Foundation.   IV. Title.
HN90.C6M36   1989
307.1′216′0973—dc20   89-15473
                                                                                      CIP

Printed on recycled, acid-free paper

Manufactured in the United States of America

10   9   8   7   6   5   4   3   2   1

Contents

Preface

In growing communities across the United States, citizens, developers, and local governments are working together to foster creative development and protect sensitive land resources. This resource guide is a companion to *Creating Successful Communities: A Guidebook to Growth Management Strategies*, which examines the techniques communities are implementing and the results they are achieving. The two books have been prepared in response to the need in many communities for practical assistance in preserving important natural and cultural resources and community distinctiveness while planning for and managing growth. In both books, the emphasis is on protecting and enhancing key community assets and fostering quality development in appropriate sites.

Resource Guide for Creating Successful Communities includes reference materials and growth management and conservation ordinances designed to protect and enhance the following specific resources: farmland, rivers and wetlands, historic and culturally significant properties and districts, aesthetic resources, and open spaces. In addition, an impact fee ordinance and a moratorium (interim growth management regulation) provide widespread application in protecting all types of key local resources. Sample articles of incorporation and bylaws for local land conservation organizations demonstrate how local organizations can be structured to protect natural and cultural resources. The resource guide also contains representative conservation easements and deed restrictions for preserving land and historic buildings, which local governments and nonprofit citizen organizations have found useful.

These samples provide concerned citizens and officials innovative, proven, and effective programs and language from communities—large cities to small towns—around the country. This material is not appropriate for adoption without substantial modification and refinement based upon local circumstances, and is, perhaps, not appropriate at all in some states. Rather than models to be copied, these sample ordinances, bylaws, and deeds are ideal when utilized as foundations upon which to build.

The resource guide also includes a primer of growth management techniques to help readers understand the often arcane and intimidating growth management terminology. Such understanding is necessary to participate in shaping local land use policy. This primer briefly defines growth management terms and describes the numerous tools and techniques used by communities to manage growth. Finally, a brief overview of private and public land preservation strategies is included. This summary discussion of land preservation strategies was adapted from a matrix developed by the Regional Plan Association and the Trust for Public Land. We are grateful for their fine work in this area.

Creating Successful Communities and *Resource Guide to Creating Successful Commu-*

nities are products of the Conservation Foundation's Successful Communities Program. The program offers practical ideas and technical know-how to states and localities throughout the country to help them accommodate growth while retaining the open spaces, historic buildings, scenic views, farmlands, natural features, and other qualities that make each community distinctive. With overall guidance provided by a distinguished Advisory Committee chaired by Anne T. Bass of Fort Worth, Texas, the program has four principal components:

- Direct technical assistance to states, nonprofit organizations, and designated "leadership communities" around the country;
- Research and education, including this Guidebook, a quarterly newsletter, conferences and workshops, and actions at the state and federal levels to improve growth management policies;
- Innovation grants to catalyze and foster creative growth management actions at the local level; and
- A land trust—the Successful Communities Trust—to intervene in the real estate market to protect critical natural and historic resources.

Many people both inside and outside The Conservation Foundation worked on these materials and provided valuable insights about critical issues and places covered in them. Foremost among them are Doug Wheeler, Jack Noble, Bob McCoy, David Brower, Chris Duerksen, and Mary Means, who were key to helping conceptualize and review these materials. Many others thoughtfully reviewed individual chapters or sections and provided important insights and information along the way, including John Banta, Constance Beaumont, David Doheny, Jean Hocker, Jon Kusler, Ed McMahon, Tim Mealey, Phyllis Myers, Richard Roddewig, Tom Smith, and Ed Thompson. All of the reviewers, who bear no responsibility for the finished product, deserve much thanks and credit for the inspiring work they are doing around the country in managing growth.

At The Conservation Foundation, two former staff members—Lisa Fernandez and Abby Goldsmith—as well as current research fellow Richard Russell did the lion's share of the work. *Resource Guide for Creating Successful Communities* benefited tremendously from their strong skills and enthusiasm.

Solid administrative support was provided throughout the effort by Bonita Franklin, Jo Halfant, Rosemary O'Neill, Joy Patterson, and Marsha White. It has also been a pleasure to work with our colleagues at Island Press, particularly Karen Berger and Nancy Seidule.

A final word of gratitude is due The Andrew W. Mellon Foundation, which has supported the research component of Successful Communities from its inception, including the preparation of this book. Its leadership and insistence upon solid analysis have helped this program immeasurably.

Your comments and suggestions are encouraged. So, too, is your continued involvement, interest, and leadership in helping to achieve genuinely successful communities.

Successful Communities Program
The Conservation Foundation
September 1989

Resource Guide for Creating Successful Communities

CHAPTER 1

Agricultural Land

THIS section includes three local agricultural protection ordinances. Black Hawk County, Iowa—in the heart of the corn belt—has implemented an ordinance containing performance standards to protect prime agricultural soils. This program bases permitted development densities upon the soil productivity of a site. Tighter land use restrictions apply to parcels with superior agricultural soils, requiring a minimum lot size of 35 acres for parcels with prime agricultural soils. This approach has effectively discouraged growth on land with the best agricultural soils.

Hardin County, Kentucky, has addressed the impact of scattered development on the county's agricultural lands by adopting an innovative Development Guidance System. This ordinance uses a point system based upon soil quality and compatibility with neighboring land uses to steer growth away from farmland and into areas where development and infrastructure already exist. Although this approach provides little guidance for the long-range development of a county, it may be an effective tool for a rural area that wants to accommodate growth, while minimizing the amount that occurs on prime farmland and reducing the incidence of premature or leap-frog development.

Finally, King County, Washington, has administered an aggressive farmland acquisition program to supplement its traditional regulatory tools. The county initiated one of the nation's premier farmland acquisition programs in 1979 with a $50 million farmland acquisition bond issue. To make these funds protect as much threatened land as possible, the county designated several eligible acquisition areas to protect viable agricultural districts and developed priority categories to channel funds into lands most threatened by development. This section includes the ordinance creating the Purchase of Development Rights Program and establishing priorities for acquisition.

Black Hawk County, Iowa
Agricultural Land Preservation and Zoning Ordinance

Purpose and Objectives

This ordinance is intended and designed to meet the specific objectives of Chapter 358A.5, Code of Iowa, 1981, as amended, to preserve the availability of agricultural land; to consider the protection of soil from wind and water erosion; to encourage efficient urban development patterns; to lessen congestion in the street or highway; to secure safety from fire, flood, panic, and other hazards; to protect health and the general welfare; to provide adequate light and air; to prevent the overcrowding of land; to avoid undue concentration of population; to promote reasonable access to solar energy; and to facilitate the adequate provision of transportation, water, sewerage, schools, parks and other public improvements.

Furthermore, this ordinance is also intended and designed to meet the specific purpose of Chapter 93A, Code of Iowa, 1981, as amended, to provide local citizens and local governments the means by which agricultural land may be protected from nonagricultural development pressures. This is accomplished by the creation of the Black Hawk County Comprehensive Plan, 1980, as amended, the adoption of this Agricultural Land Preservation Ordinance and the establishment of agricultural land preservation areas, as provided for in this ordinance, so that land inside these areas shall be conserved for the production of food, fiber, and livestock, thus assuring the preservation of agriculture as a major factor in the economy of this county and state. It is further the intent of this ordinance as authorized in Chapter 93A to provide for the orderly use and development of land and related natural resources in Iowa for residential, commercial, industrial, and recreational purposes, preserve private property rights, protect significant natural and historic resources and fragile ecosystems of this county including forests, wetlands, rivers, streams, lakes and their shorelines, aquifers, prairies, and recreational areas, to provide the efficient use and conservation of energy resources, and to promote the protection of soil from wind and water erosion.

Section VI

D. "E-S" ENVIRONMENTALLY SENSITIVE OVERLAY DISTRICT MAPS

1. The boundaries of the "E-S" Environmentally Sensitive Overlay District shall be the same as shown in the Official Soil Survey of Black Hawk County, published by the

United States Department of Agriculture-Soil Conservation Service, December 1978, or from a soil map upon an aerial photograph compiled and attested by a Certified Soil Scientist or Soil Technician and on the flood boundary/floodway and the flood insurance rate maps prepared as a part of the Flood Insurance Study for Black Hawk County, dated November 17, 1982. These maps are hereby adopted by reference and declared to be the "E-S" Environmentally Sensitive Overlay District. The soil characteristics, notations, and explanatory materials contained with the Soil Survey and the flood profiles and all explanatory material contained with the Flood Insurance Study and the flood insurance rate maps are also declared to be a part of this ordinance. Subsequent amendments and supplements to the survey and the Flood Insurance Study shall be adopted automatically.

2. The Environmentally Sensitive Overlay Districts shall include the corresponding designated areas:

    a. As identified in the Soil Survey as indicated below:

        1. Poor Bearing Capacity Soils. Soils rated as severe for either building site development or sanitary facilities for requested use.

        2. Excessive Slopes. Soils identified as having a "D" or "F" class slope or the special symbol for bedrock escarpments, other than bedrock escarpments, short steep slopes, and gullies.

        3. Aquifer Recharge Areas. Soils identified as alluvial, channeled, muck, and/or marsh, or soils identified as having bedrock less than sixty (60) inches from the surface or the special symbol for marsh or swamp, spring, wet spots, depression or sink and rock outcrop.

        4. Surface Waters. Areas identified by symbols for water features including rivers and streams: perennial; double line and single line intermittent; not crossable with tillage implements, lakes, ponds and reservoirs: both perennial and intermittent, and marsh or swamps.

    b. As identified in the Flood Insurance Study for Black Hawk County, Iowa, as indicated below:

        1. Floodway (FW). The designated floodway on the flood boundary and floodway map.

        2. Floodway Fringe (FF). The designated floodway fringe on the flood boundary and floodway map.

        3. Shallow Flooding (SF). The designated "B" zone on the flood insurance rate map.

        4. General Floodplain (FP). The areas shown on the flood boundary and floodway map as being within the approximately 100 year flood boundary, but for which the floodway and the floodway fringe and base flood elevation were not determined by the Flood Insurance Study.

E. INTERPRETATION OF ENVIRONMENTALLY SENSITIVE OVERLAY DISTRICT BOUNDARIES

The boundaries of the areas of the Environmentally Sensitive Overlay District shall be determined by scaling distances on the Flood Insurance Study Maps and the Soil Survey. Where interpretation is needed to determine the exact location of the boundaries of the districts as shown on the maps, as for example where there appears to be a conflict between a mapped boundary and actual field conditions, the Administrative Officer shall make the necessary interpretation. Within flood prone areas, the regulatory flood elevation for the point in question, as reported in the Flood Insurance Study, shall be the governing factor in locating the district boundary on the land. Any person contesting the location of the district boundary shall be given a reasonable opportunity to present his case to the Board of Adjustment, as provided in Section XXVII, and to submit his own technical evidence if he/she so desires. Any person contesting the regulatory flood elevation data in the Flood Insurance Study shall submit technical evidence to the Iowa Natural Resources Council for review. The findings of the Iowa Natural Resources Council shall be the final determination as to the regulatory flood protection elevation for that location.

Section VIII. Natural Resource Protection and Preservation

A. INTENT

In accordance with the Black Hawk County Comprehensive Plan it is the intent of this section to recognize, and to preserve the natural processes of land, as land undergoes change for man's use. This ordinance identifies the functions of the land which provide important public benefits and have designed provisions to protect those functions. The public benefits arrived by the protection of natural functions of lands include:

1. Protection of public safety by reducing the risks of natural hazards, specifically flooding;
2. Protection of public resources such as water supplies and the water quality of our lakes, rivers, and aquifers;
3. Protection of public and private economic resources from expenditures and property values loss due to environmental degradation; and
4. The preservation of important productive lands and renewable resources.

For purposes of this ordinance land shall be identified by function(s) and may be further classified as either sensitive or significant. Identification and classification of lands shall be based upon the explanatory materials, notations, and maps found in (a) the official Soil Survey of Black Hawk County, Iowa, published by the United States Department of Agriculture Soil Conservation Service, December 1978, (b) The Flood Insurance Study for Black Hawk County, published by Federal Emergency Management Agency-Federal Insurance Administration, November 17, 1982, and (c) The Black Hawk County Conservation Resource Inventory, submitted to the Black Hawk County Conservation Board, March 1981. Subsequent amendments and supplements to the survey, study, and inventory shall be adopted automatically.

B. SENSITIVE LANDS

Sensitive lands are those areas where substantial evidence indicates that uncontrolled or incompatible development could result in damage to the environment, to life or to property.

1. Identification: Those lands shall include those as specified in Section VI (D), Establishment of Districts and District Boundaries: "E-S" Environmentally Sensitive Overlay District Maps. They include: (a) floodplains, (b) surface waters, (c) aquifer recharge areas, (d) excessive slopes, and (e) poor bearing capacity soils.
2. Permitted and Conditional Uses: Subject to Section XVIII, General Regulations and Provisions of the "E-S" Environmentally Sensitive Overlay District and Section XIX. Use Regulation for "E-S" Environmentally Sensitive Overlay District.
3. Performance Standards: Subject to Section XVIII, General Regulations and Provisions of the "E-S" Environmentally Sensitive Overlay District and Section XIX, Use Regulation for "E-S" Environmentally Sensitive Overlay District.

C. SIGNIFICANT LANDS

Significant lands are agricultural lands of highly productive soils, renewable resource lands, which promote the long-term productivity of an area by contributing to water, soil, or vegetation cover conservation, and fragile lands.

1. Identification.
    a. Agricultural Lands of Highly Productive Soils: Shall be defined as a parcel of land where more than twenty-five (25) percent of its area consists of agricultural lands of productive soils (having a corn suitability rating that has been rated at fifty (50) or above). Determination regarding corn suitability ratings and other soil characteristics shall be referenced from the official Soil Survey of Black Hawk County, Iowa, published by the United States Department of Agriculture Soil Conservation Service, December 1978.
    Soil boundaries shall be determined from the soil maps found in the official Soil Survey of Black Hawk County, Iowa, or from a soil map upon an aerial photograph compiled and attested by a certified soil scientist or technician.
    It shall be noted that it is the policy of Black Hawk County, Iowa, rich in fertile productive soils to maintain this nonrenewable resource for future generations to employ in the production of food and fiber; therefore, such lands shall be preserved as "A" Agricultural District, unless there are extenuating circumstances.
    b. Other Significant Lands: Shall be identified by reference from the Black Hawk County Conservation Resource Inventory. These lands shall include wetlands, recreational lakes, forest covers, forest reservations, rivers and streams, river and stream banks, open and native prairies and wildlife habitats, as designated upon the established priority list approved by the County Board of Supervisors, as amended.
2. Permitted and Conditional Uses.
    a. Agricultural Lands of Highly Productive Soils: Subject to Section II, Special Exemption; Section IX, Use Regulation for "A" Agricultural District; Section XVIII, General Regulations and Provisions of the "E-S" Environmentally Sensitive Overlay District; and Section XIX, Use Regulation for "E-S" Environmentally Sensitive Overlay District.
    b. Other Significant Lands: Lands as designated upon the established priority list approved by the Black Hawk County Board of Supervisors, as amended, shall be preserved in their natural, undisturbed state and are not to be used for economic gain, including but not limited to using land for development, the storage of equipment, machinery or crops.
3. Performance Standards.
    Shall be applicable to the appropriate section(s) of the ordinance.
4. Incentives for Preservation.
    In accordance with Chapter 427.1, Code of Iowa, as amended, the Black Hawk County Board of Supervisors may grant a tax exemption to other significant lands as designated upon the established priority list, as a mandate.

Section IX. Use Regulation for "A" Agricultural District

INTENT

The "A" Agricultural District is intended and designed to serve the agricultural community and protect agricultural land from encroachment of urban land uses. Furthermore, in accordance with Chapters 358A and 93A, Code of Iowa, 1981, as amended, it is the intent to preserve the availability of agricultural land and to encourage efficient urban development patterns. This district is not intended to be used for non-farm residential subdivisions, unless in existence at the time of adoption of this ordinance.

In the "A" Agricultural District, the following provisions, regulations, and restrictions shall apply:

A. PRINCIPAL PERMITTED USES

1. Agricultural and incidental agricultural related uses.
2. Feedlots and confinement facilities for livestock.

3. Specialized animal farms including but not limited to fowl, rabbits, mink, chinchilla, and bees.
4. Specialized horticultural operations including orchards, viticulture, truck gardens, Christmas tree farms, floriculture, wholesale nurseries, raising of tree fruits, nuts and berries, sod, private or wholesale greenhouses, and vegetable raising.
5. Stables, private. Located at least fifty (50) feet from all boundary lines of the property on which located.
6. Forest, forest preserves and environmentally significant lands.
7. Hiking and horseback riding trails.
8. Public utility structures and equipment necessary for the operation thereof.
9. Transmitting stations and towers, base of which shall be at least height of tower from any lot line.
10. Parks, recreation areas, wildlife preserves, and game refuges owned by governmental agencies.
11. Structures or methods for the conservation of soil.
12. Farm dwellings.
13. Single-family dwellings provided that the owner/occupant is actively engaged in the farming operation and is a member of the farm owner's immediate family. Only one (1) lot for this purpose shall be separated from a farm and at least thirty-five (35) acres shall remain after the transfer with the farm. This provision shall be authorized only after the recommendation of the County Planning and Zoning Commission and approval of the County Board of Supervisors.
14. Single-family dwellings in existence prior to the adoption of this ordinance.
15. Single-family dwellings upon lots of record.
16. Any use erected or maintained by a public agency.
17. Mobile homes, in accordance with Section XXIV of this ordinance.
18. Single-family dwellings provided that seventy-five (75) percent of the lot contains the following soil classifications and is in accordance with Section VII, paragraph B:

Map Symbol	Soil
110B	Lamont Fine Sandy Loam
284B	Flagler Sandy Loam

19. Kennels, private, located at least fifty (50) feet from all boundary lines of the property on which located.

B. ACCESSORY USES

1. Accessory buildings and uses customarily incidental to any of the above uses.
2. Living quarters for persons or migratory workers employed on the premises on a seasonal basis.
3. Roadside stands, offering for sale any agricultural products or other products produced on the premises.
4. Bulletin boards and signs pertaining to the lease, hire or sale of a building or premises, or signs pertaining to any material that is grown or treated within the district; provided, however, that such signs shall be located upon or immediately adjacent to the building or in the area in which such materials are treated, processed, or stored.
5. Home occupations.
6. Seed and feed dealerships provided, however, there is no evidence of showroom or other commercial activities.
7. Church directional and community recognition signs.

C. HEIGHT REGULATIONS

Any building hereafter erected or structurally altered may be erected to any height not in conflict with other existing or future ordinances of Black Hawk County, Iowa.

D. WATER AND SEWER SYSTEMS

Subject to approval of the County Department of Health.

E. MINIMUM LOT AREA, LOT FRONTAGE, AND YARD REQUIREMENTS FOR "A" AGRICULTURAL DISTRICTS SHALL BE AS FOLLOWS:

Use	Lot Area	Lot Width	Front	Side	Rear
Farm Dwelling	35 Acres	330'	50 ft.	25 ft.	50 ft.
Mobile Home	35 Acres	330'	50 ft.	25 ft.	50 ft.
Single-Family Dwelling	1.5 Acres	150'	50 ft.	25 ft.	50 ft.
Other Permitted Structures	—	—	50 ft.	25 ft.	50 ft.
Accessory Buildings	—	—	50 ft.	25 ft.[1]	50 ft.[1]

[1] Accessory buildings to be placed in the rear or side yards may reduce minimum side and rear yard requirements to four (4) feet.

Section X. Use Regulation for "A-L" Agricultural Limited District

INTENT

The "A-L" Agricultural Limited District is intended to reinforce the intent of the "A" Agricultural District and in addition to provide for those activities which may be interrelated with agriculture.

In the "A-L" Agricultural District, the following provisions, regulations, and restrictions shall apply:

A. PRINCIPAL PERMITTED USES

1. Any use permitted in the "A" Agricultural District.
2. Stables, public and riding academies, clubs, and other structures for housing horses. Any such structure shall be located at least fifty (50) feet from all boundary lines of the property on which located.
3. Grain elevators with usual accessory structures.
4. Church or other place of worship, including parish house and Sunday School building.
5. Cemeteries, including mausoleums and crematories, provided that any mausoleum and crematory shall be distant at least two hundred (200) feet from adjacent property and street and highway lines.
6. Schools, both public and private educational institutions, preschools, and day nursery or care facilities.
7. Institutions of a religious, charitable, philanthropic or similar nature.
8. Veterinary clinics, but not nearer than six hundred and sixty (660) feet from any zoned residential district, incorporated boundary line or dwelling other than the leasee or owner of the site.
9. Private airports, airstrips, landing fields, and associated facilities.
10. Sanitary landfill and solid waste facilities, as provided in Section XXI of this ordinance.
11. Private, recreational areas, including parks, playgrounds, golf courses and country clubs, boy scout, girl scout, service and church camps, hunting and fishing clubs, private gun clubs and skeet shooting ranges and similar uses. This provision shall

not be construed to mean automobile race tracks, drag strips, go-cart tracks, and/or activity areas for motorcycles, mini bikes, and snowmobiles, miniature golf courses, drive-in theaters, and similar commercial uses.

12. Private commercial campgrounds.

B. ACCESSORY USES

1. Accessory buildings and uses customarily incidental to any of the above uses.
2. Other accessory uses as allowed in "A" District.
3. Church bulletin boards.

C. HEIGHT REGULATIONS

Any building hereafter erected or structurally altered may be erected to any height not in conflict with other existing or future ordinances of Black Hawk County, Iowa.

D. WATER AND SEWER SYSTEMS

Subject to approval of the County Department of Health.

E. MINIMUM LOT AREA, LOT FRONTAGE, AND YARD REQUIREMENTS FOR "A-L" AGRICULTURAL DISTRICTS SHALL BE AS FOLLOWS:

Use	Lot Area	Lot Width	Front	Side	Rear
Farm Dwelling	35 Acres	330'	50 ft.	25 ft.	50 ft.
Mobile Home	35 Acres	330'	50 ft.	25 ft.	50 ft.
Single-Family Dwelling	1.5 Acres	150'	50 ft.	25 ft.	50 ft.
Other Permitted Structures	—	—	50 ft.	25 ft.	50 ft.
Accessory Buildings	—	—	50 ft.	25 ft.[1]	50 ft.[1]

As specified under the provisions of the "A" Agricultural District.

Section XX. Agricultural Land Preservation Area Overlay

INTENT

It is the intent of this section to provide for the establishment of voluntary agricultural land preservation areas in accordance with Chapter 93A of the Code of Iowa, 1981, as amended, and the provisions of this ordinance. Black Hawk County and the State of Iowa recognize the importance of preserving the finite supply of agricultural land. Conversion of farmland to urban development and other non-farm uses reduces future food production capabilities and may ultimately undermine agriculture as the major economic activity in Black Hawk County and Iowa.

A. CREATION OF AGRICULTURAL LAND PRESERVATION AREAS

1. An owner or owners of farmland may submit a proposal to the County Board for the creation of an agricultural land preservation area within the county. An agricultural land preservation area, at its creation, shall include at least five hundred (500) acres of farmland, however, a smaller area may be created if the farmland is adjacent to an established area.

2. The proposal shall include a description of the proposed area, including its boundaries. The territory shall be as compact and as nearly adjacent as feasible.

3. Land shall not be included in an agricultural land preservation area without the consent of the owner.

4. Agricultural land preservation areas shall not exist within the corporate limits of the city.

B. PRINCIPAL PERMITTED USES

The following uses shall be permitted in an agricultural land preservation area.

1. Farm operations as defined in Chapter 93A, Code of Iowa, 1981, as amended.

2. Residences constructed for occupation by a person engaged in farming or in a family farm operation. Nonconforming preexisting residences may be continued in residential use.

3. Property of a telephone company, city utility as defined in Section 390.1, public utility as defined in Section 476.1, or pipeline company as defined in Section 479.2.

4. Exceptions. The Board may permit any use not listed above in an agricultural land preservation area only if it finds all of the following:

   a. The use is consistent with the purposes set forth in Chapter 93A, Code of Iowa, 1981, as amended.

   b. The use is consistent with the Land Use Policies of the Black Hawk County Comprehensive Plan, does not interfere seriously with the farm operations within the area, and does not materially alter the stability of the overall land use pattern in the area.

   c. The use is located within the appropriate zoning district which authorizes said use.

C. PROCEDURES

1. Within thirty (30) days of receipt of a proposal for an agricultural land area which meets the statutory requirements, as attested by the Zoning Administrator, the County Board shall provide notice of the proposal by publishing notice in a newspaper of general circulation in the county. Within forty-five (45) days after receipt, the County Board shall hold a public hearing on the proposal.

2. Within sixty (60) days after receipt, the County Board shall adopt the proposal or any modification of the proposal it deems appropriate, unless to do so would be inconsistent with the purposes of this ordinance.

D. CERTIFICATION

1. Requirement that description of agricultural land preservation areas be filed with County Auditor and County Recorder. Upon the creation of an agricultural land preservation area, its description shall be filed by the County Board with the County Auditor and placed on record in the office of the County Recorder.

2. Upon creation, the description of the area shall be overlaid upon the Official Black Hawk County Zoning maps by the County Zoning Administrator.

E. WITHDRAWAL

1. At any time after three (3) years from the date of creation of an agricultural land preservation area, an owner may withdraw from an agricultural land preservation area by filing with the County Board a request for withdrawal containing a legal description of the land to be withdrawn and a statement of the reasons for the

withdrawal. The County Board shall, within sixty (60) days of receipt of the request, approve or deny the request for withdrawal.

2. At any time after six (6) years from the date of creation of an agricultural land preservation area, an owner may withdraw from an agricultural land preservation area by filing with the County Board a notice of withdrawal containing a legal description of the land to be withdrawn.

3. The Board shall cause the description of that agricultural area filed with the County Auditor and recorded with the County Recorder to be modified to reflect any withdrawal.

4. Said modification shall be made by the withdrawal of described boundary from the Official Black Hawk County Zoning maps by the County Zoning Administrator.

5. Withdrawal shall be effective on the date of recording.

6. The agricultural land preservation area from which the land is withdrawn shall continue in existence even if smaller than five hundred (500) acres after withdrawal.

F. INCENTIVES FOR AGRICULTURAL LAND PRESERVATION AREA CREATION

1. Limitation on power of certain public agencies to impose public benefit assessments or special assessments. The county, a political subdivision or a benefitted district providing public services such as sewer, water, or lights or for non-farm drainage shall not impose benefit assessments or special assessments on land used primarily for agricultural production within an agricultural land preservation area on the basis of frontage, acreage, or value, unless the benefit assessments or special assessments were imposed prior to the formation of the agricultural land preservation area, or unless the service is provided to the landowner on the same basis as others having the service.

2. Nuisance restriction. A farm or farm operation located in an agricultural land preservation area shall not be found to be a nuisance regardless of the established date of operation or expansion of the agricultural activities of the farm or farm operation, subject to provisions of Chapter 93A, Code of Iowa, 1981, as amended, and the Black Hawk County Right-to-Farm Ordinance.

3. Water priority. In the application for a permit to divert, store, or withdraw water and in the allocation of available water resources under a water permit system, the Iowa Natural Resources Council shall give priority to the use of water resources by a farm or farm operations, exclusive of irrigation, located in an agricultural land preservation area over all other uses except the competing uses of water for ordinary household purposes.

4. Limitation of state regulation. In order to accomplish the purposes set forth in this ordinance and Chapter 93A, Code of Iowa, 1981, as amended, a rule adopted by a state agency which would restrict or regulate farms or farm operations may contain standards which are less restrictive for farms or farm operations inside an agricultural land preservation area than for farms or farm operations outside such an area. A rule containing such a discrimination shall not for the fact of such discrimination alone be found or held to be unreasonable, arbitrary, capricious, beyond the authority delegated to the agency, or characterized by an abuse of discretion or clearly unwarranted exercise or discretion.

5. Statement of prime agricultural soils. If the damages are to be paid by the state and the land to be condemned is within an agricultural land preservation area as provided in Chapter 93A, Code of Iowa, and this ordinance a statement disclosing whether any of that land is classified as Class I or Class II land under the United States Department of Agriculture Soil Conservation Service Land Capability Classification System contained in the Agriculture Handbook Number 210, 1961 edition and, if so classified, stating that the Class I and Class II land is reasonably necessary for the work of internal improvement for which condemnation is sought.

Hardin County, Kentucky
Development Guidance System

3.1 The Terms of Compliance _____

The Hardin County Planned Growth Zone contains a limited number of uses-by-right and very few prohibited uses. Uses-by-right are considered compatible by nature and not subject to approval by way of the DEVELOPMENT GUIDANCE SYSTEM process. All other development, including all changes of developed use, not specifically prohibited is required to obtain a Conditional Use Permit issued pursuant to Articles 4, 5, and 6 of this ordinance.

3.101 USES-BY-RIGHT

The following development shall be by right in the Planned Growth Zone, subject to provisions of KRS 198B, where applicable, KRS 100.111(23), other state laws, and applicable deed restrictions or covenants:

(1) "land which is used solely for agricultural, farming, dairying, stock raising, or similar purposes . . ." [KRS 100.203(4)];

(2) construction or placement of a dwelling unit on a lot in a legally platted subdivision as permitted by the appropriately filed deed restrictions; included are additions to these units, provided those additions are for residential use;

(3) placement of a dwelling unit on a residential park lot approved prior to the original implementation date of this ordinance; included are additions to these units, provided those additions are for residential use;

(4) construction or placement of and/or addition to a dwelling unit on a lot outside a legally platted subdivision or residential park, provided this unit or addition is for residential use;

(5) placement of a second dwelling unit on a parcel of land in agricultural use;

(6) expansion of a non-residential use where the proposed floor area will not exceed 60 percent of the existing floor area;

(7) conduct of a home occupation;

(8) conduct of a temporary use;

(9) installation of on-site signs on non-residential sites up to a maximum of 80 square feet for all sign surfaces, both existing and proposed; placement of these permitted signs is pursuant to 6.618;

13

(10) installation of off-site signs not exceeding 25 square feet for each advertising surface and not greater in total height than eight feet; placement of
these permitted signs is not to occur on public rights-of-way;

(11) initiation of a use on a site or in a building which is identified within the
same four digit Standard Industrial Classification as the previous use;
and

(12) continued identical use of any development in existence and occupied
on 30 January 1984.

3.102 PROHIBITED USES

The following development shall be prohibited in the Planned Growth Zone:

(1) initiation of any development whose use of the underground water supply
or springs would have a negative impact on the amount of such water
available on adjacent property;

(2) initiation of any development which will pollute or contaminate the surface or underground water supply or which will produce noxious odors or
fumes emanating off-sites thus endangering the public health and welfare;

(3) initiation of any development which would endanger or destroy any listing
on the Kentucky Archaeological Survey maintained by the State Archae-
ologist at the University of Kentucky or any listing on the Survey of
Historic Sites in Kentucky or the National Register of Historic Places; and

(4) installation of signs, whether for temporary or permanent use, which
blink, flash, or move in any way, except informational or public service
signs.

3.103 CONDITIONAL USES

All development activities which are not uses-by-right as explained in 3.101,
nor prohibited as explained in 3.102, shall be considered conditional uses
and shall be permitted subject to the approval process included in Articles 4,
5, and 6.

3.2 The Burden of Proof

The burden of proof shall rest with the applicant in all proceedings required by this
ordinance.

3.3 The Provisions for Compliance, Uses-By-Right

Persons proposing development activities constituting uses-by-right are not required
to submit an application for approval as called for by this ordinance. Compliance
with the Kentucky Building Code (pursuant to KRS 198B), however, is strictly required.

3.4 The Provisions for Compliance, Conditional Uses

Persons proposing development activities constituting conditional uses shall obtain
approval prior to the commencement of construction activities. Approval shall be

granted only upon completion of the process included in Articles 4, 5, and 6, and subject to the development standards included in Article 6.

3.5 The Provisions for Compliance, Special Conditional Uses

Persons proposing development activities constituting special conditional uses shall obtain approval prior to the commencement of any construction or alteration activities. Approval shall be granted only within the guidelines presented below and only upon the completion of the process specified therein. Conditional Use Permits shall only be required when a change of use, the installation of a sign, a resubdivision of land, or a revision to a plat is proposed, whether or not a permit has been issued previously for that site.

3.501 CHANGING THE USE OF PREVIOUSLY DEVELOPED LAND

Proposals to change the use of land developed prior to 30 January 1984 shall obtain approval prior to the initiation of change. Approval shall be granted only upon completion of the processes included in Articles 5 and 6.

Proposals to change the use of land on which a use-by-right was established since 30 January 1984 shall obtain approval prior to the initiation of change. Approval shall be granted only upon the completion of the processes included in Articles 4, 5, and 6.

3.502 INSTALLING SIGNS

Proposals for signs not identified in 3.101(8) and (9) shall obtain approval prior to the commencement of any construction or installation activities. Approval shall be granted only upon completion of the processes included in Articles 5 and 6.

3.503 REPLATTING LAND

Proposals for replatting previously platted land shall obtain approval prior to the conveyance of land. Approval shall be granted only upon completion of the process included in Article 6.

3.504 RESUBDIVIDING LAND

Proposals for resubdividing previously platted land shall obtain approval prior to the creation of any new lots. Approval shall be granted only upon completion of the processes included in Articles 5 and 6.

3.505 REVISING PLATS

Proposals for revising plats shall obtain approval prior to the filing of such revisions with the Hardin County Clerk. Approval shall be granted only upon completion of the processes included in Articles 5 and 6.

3.506 CORRECTING PLATS

Proposals for correcting plats shall obtain approval prior to the filing of such corrections with the Hardin County Clerk. Approval shall be granted only upon completion of the processes included in Article 6.

3.507 CREATING MULTI-RESIDENTIAL DEVELOPMENT

Proposals for locating more than one dwelling unit on a lot (so long as the proposal does not meet the definition of a residential park) shall obtain approval prior to any construction or installation activities. Approval for the second dwelling unit on a lot shall be granted only upon completion of the process included in Article 5. Approval for proposals involving more than two dwelling units shall be granted only upon completion of the process included in Article 5 and the plot plan requirements of Article 6.

Proposals for locating more than two dwelling units on a parcel of land in agricultural use (so long as the proposal does not meet the definition of a residential park) shall obtain approval prior to any construction or installation activities. Approval shall be granted only upon completion of the process included in Article 5.

4.1 The Purpose

For years citizens have attempted to tell planning commissions that wise land use decisions must be based on a wide range of issues. But because most land use proposals are judged against traditional zoning ordinances which address only use and density, those citizen demands have gone largely unanswered. The Growth Guidance Assessment represents the first step taken by the DEVELOPMENT GUIDANCE SYSTEM toward addressing those demands.

Substantively, the Growth Guidance Assessment brings new criteria into the land use decision process. As such, this assessment includes social, economic, and environmental concepts not usually associated with the zoning decision making process. Such concerns are held by the public and are included in the Commission's statement of goals; thus, they are part of the DEVELOPMENT GUIDANCE SYSTEM.

Procedurally, the Growth Guidance Assessment brings two attributes to the land use approval process which are presently lacking under traditional zoning— expeditious review of sites and defensible decisions regarding the review and decision. Drawn out procedures and endless public hearings cannot be considered a substitute for sound planning. Likewise, decisions made one way for one proposal and another way for a similar proposal cannot be supported. Developers and concerned citizens alike should know, in advance, of the time it will take to achieve approval for a given site. Everyone concerned should also know all the criteria to be used in making the decision including a certainty that if all the criteria are met, the site will be approved. Similarly, everyone should be confident that if the criteria are not met, the site will be denied.

4.2 The Scope

The Growth Guidance Assessment is the only procedure to be used in determining whether a site is suitable for development. All rules and criteria to be used by the Commission in the process are presented herein; no others shall apply. Approval granted under this assessment is binding.

4.3 The Provisions for Compliance, Conditional Uses

Developers proposing development involving conditional uses are required to obtain approval prior to the commencement of construction. Approval can only be granted by the Commission upon completion of the following procedure.

4.301 THE PRE-APPLICATION CONFERENCE

Prior to submission of an application, the developer should meet with the staff for the purpose of discussing the site, the general area in which the site is located, and the goals of the DEVELOPMENT GUIDANCE SYSTEM in the Planned Growth Zone.

4.302 FILING THE APPLICATION

Developers proposing conditional uses shall submit one copy of the completed conditional use application to the staff along with the appropriate fees.

4.303 PAYMENT OF FEES, REFUNDS

Developers proposing conditional uses shall pay a fee equal to 90 dollars plus five dollars per acre of land, or fraction thereof, contained in the proposed site.

   If the site is denied at the conclusion of the Growth Guidance Assessment process, all but thirty dollars of this fee shall be refunded.

4.4 The Provisions for Commission Decisions

Upon receipt of a complete application, the staff shall work the site through the Growth Guidance Assessment, assessing points as required. Five days from the receipt of the application and fees shall be allotted for this process.

4.401 AUTOMATIC APPROVAL STATUS

Scoring 150 or more points gains automatic approval status for the site. This means that development on that location contributes to the fulfillment of enough of the goals of the COMPREHENSIVE DEVELOPMENT GUIDE and the DEVELOPMENT GUIDANCE SYSTEM to warrant prompt handling. Proposed sites earning this designation are automatically placed for scheduling in Article 5 by the staff. In such cases, the staff shall report this action to the Commission during its next meeting.

4.402 COMMISSION REVIEW STATUS

Scoring less than 150 points gains a Commission review for the site. This means that the proposal will be included on the agenda for the next Commission meeting. At that meeting, upon review of the soils and amenities assessments, the Commission shall grant approval or denial status. Compliance with goals of the COMPREHENSIVE DEVELOPMENT GUIDE and the DEVELOPMENT GUIDANCE SYSTEM shall be a determining factor in this decision.

   Achieving approval status from the Commission advances a site on for scheduling in Article 5. Achieving denial status sends the proposal back to the developer. Denial status means that development on that location does not contribute to the fulfillment of enough of the goals of the COMPREHENSIVE DEVELOPMENT GUIDE and the DEVELOPMENT GUIDANCE SYSTEM to be considered at this point in time. As amenities and characteristics in the area change, points awarded will increase. Future development, thus, remains possible.

4.5 The Soils Assessment

Every parcel of land in the Planned Growth Zone is unique in many different ways. Great differences in terrain exist, often times within short distances. Individual sites have unique aspects and different relations to surrounding sites. But, a key factor determining the relative potential of a given site is the soils that exist on that site. More than any other one natural criteria, soils portray the best use of a site. Thus, an assessment of the soils and their potential is a mandatory first step in examining any site's characteristics for development.

According to the SOIL SURVEY OF HARDIN AND LARUE COUNTIES, KENTUCKY, published by the US Soil Conservation Service, the following soil associations are found in Hardin County. Based on corn yield per acre, these associations have been divided into ten groups.

Map Symbol	Soil Series	Soil Group
As	Ashton Silt Loam	1
A1D	Allegheny-Lenberg Caneyville Complex	7
CrB	Crider Silt Loam	2
CrC	Crider Silt Loam	4
CsC	Cumberland Silt Loam	4
CrD	Crider Silt Loam	6
CsD	Cumberland Silt Loam	6
CtC3	Cumberland Silty Clay Loam	6
CtD3	Cumberland Silty Clay Loam	7
CnE	Caneyville-Rock Outcrop Complex	10
CnD	Caneyville-Rock Outcrop Complex	8
Dn	Dunning Silty Clay Loam	3
E1B	Elk Silt Loam	2
E1C	Elk Silt Loam	4
FrC	Frondorf-Lenberg Silt Loam	6
FrD	Frondorf-Lenberg Silt Loam	7
FdC	Fredonia-Rock Outcrop Complex	8
GnB	Gatton Silt Loam	5
GmE	Garmon Silt Loam	9
Gu	Gullied Land	9
HnB	Hagerstown Silt Loam	2
Hu	Huntington Silt Loam	2
HnC	Hagerstown Silt Loam	4
HnD	Hagerstown Silt Loam	6
Ln	Lindside Silt Loam	2
Lc	Lawrence Silt Loam	5
LfE	Lenberg-Frondorf Complex	7

Map Symbol	Soil Series	Soil Group
Mr	McGary Silt Loam	3
Mv	Melvin Silt Loam	5
MdC3	Markland Silty Clay	7
NcB	Nicholson Silt Loam	5
Nb	Newark Silt Loam	5
NcA	Nicholson Silt Loam	5
No	Nolin Silt Loam	2
Nv	Nolin Variant Fine Sandy Loam	5
OtB	Otwell Silt Loam	5
OtA	Otwell Silt Loam	5
PmB	Pembroke Silt Loam	2
PmC	Pembroke Silt Loam	4
RbC	Riney Loam	4
RbD	Riney Loam	6
RcD3	Riney Sandy Clay Loam	6
Rd	Robertsville Silt Loam	6
RbE	Riney Loam	7
RaE	Allegheny Complex	9
RoE	Rock Outcrop Corydon Complex	10
SdB	Sadler Silt Loam	5
SnB	Sonora Silt Loam	5
SdA	Sadler Silt Loam	5
Sg	Sensabaugh Silt Loam	3
SdC	Sadler Silt Loam	4
SnC	Sonora Silt Loam	4
SnC3	Sonora Silt Loam	6
VrC	Vertrees Silt Loam	4
VrD	Vertrees Silt Loam	6
VtD3	Vertrees Silty Clay Loam	7
VrE	Vertrees Silt Loam	7
W1B	Wellston Silt Loam	5
WbC	Waynesboro Loam	4
W1C	Wellston Silt Loam	4
WbD	Waynesboro Loam	6
WcC3	Waynesboro Clay Loam	6
W1C3	Wellston Silt Loam	6
WbE	Waynesboro Loam	7
WcD3	Waynesboro Clay Loam	7

The ten groups identified above have been assigned relative values for agriculture based on the calculation of actual corn yield per acre divided by the highest corn yield per acre. Presented below, these values will be used in the assessment that follows. Also shown are the numbers of acres of that soil group which are present in Hardin County.

Soil Group	Actual Yield Highest Yield	Soil Value	Acres in Hardin Country
1	$\frac{100}{100}$	100	795
2	$\frac{87.56}{100}$	88	74,815
3	$\frac{71.00}{100}$	71	7,875
4	$\frac{66.81}{100}$	67	87,760
5	$\frac{65.99}{100}$	66	68,750
6	$\frac{54.30}{100}$	54	37,905
7	$\frac{35.00}{100}$	35	45,630
8	$\frac{25.00}{100}$	25	27,180
9	$\frac{15.00}{100}$	15	30,910
10	$\frac{10.00}{100}$	10	10,655

4.501 THE WORKSHEET

The first ten unnumbered lines of the accompanying worksheet are to be used to identify the various types of soil found on the site proposed for development. Soil symbols, soil names, and the corresponding groups (from 4.5) are to be listed in the designated columns. The appropriate number of acres in each soil group is to be listed under the corresponding group number, one through ten. Instructions for numbered lines one through 15 are as follows.

(1) Figures placed in columns one through ten are to be added vertically. The sums are to be placed in the correct column on line one.

(2) All figures shown on line one are to be added together. The sum is to be placed on line two. This should correspond with the total acreage of the site.

(3) Relative soil values per acre are listed.

(4–6) Because improvements can be made to soils to make them more productive, lines four through six award additional points for each improvement made. If one of the indicated improvements has been made, points shown on the "Possible" lines are to be transferred to the "Earned" lines.

(7) Figures placed on lines three through six are to be added vertically. The sums are to be placed in the correct column on line seven.

(8) Maximum soil values are listed. (Note: in arriving at these values, it has been determined that soils in groups 2, 5, and 6 warrant only special combinations of the improvements; if points cannot be earned for all improvements made, the figures in line nine represent the actual value of the soils in question.

(10) Figures on line one are to be multiplied by the figures in the corresponding

columns on line nine. The products of those calculations are to be listed on line ten. These products illustrate the value of each soil group on the site.

(11) All values listed on line ten are to be totalled with the sum to be placed on line 11. This number represents the total value of the soils on the site.

(12) The assessment figure previously put on line 11 is to be divided by the figure on line two. The product of this calculation, the average value of an acre of soil on this site, is to be placed on line 12.

(13) Line 13 is included as an effort to preserve large tracts of Hardin County's important agricultural soils from early conversion to development. The main target of preservation is those tracts with over ten acres of prime soils.

After adding the figures in columns one through three on line one, refer to the following chart. The appropriate number of points as shown is to be transferred to line 13.

Acres	Points
Less than 10	0
10 – 14.9	5
15 – 20	10
Over 20	15

(14) Figures on lines 12 and 13 are to be added together and the sum placed on line 14. This represents the adjusted soils assessment for the site.

(15) Line 15 calculates the difference between the maximum points to be earned per acre and the actual points earned per acre. The points represented by this difference equal the site's non-agricultural value. To this end, subtract the figure on line 14 from 115 and enter the difference on line 15.

This number will be used later in the amenities assessment.

This completes the in-depth assessment of soils on a proposed site.

4.6 The Amenities Assessment

Assessing the various soils on a given site is an excellent way of determining that site's agricultural production capacity. The assessment process, however, does not always portray a given site in the most realistic terms. Clearly, an additional assessment is warranted to determine if outside pressures have lessened the site's long term agricultural production capacity. Amenities and site characteristics, thus, must be examined.

4.601 THE WORKSHEET

The accompanying worksheet provides a mechanism by which a site's potential for development can be assessed. Combined with the development points earned in the soils assessment, the points earned here will determine whether a given site creates the growth patterns mandated by the County's goals and policies.

Whereas the factors used in this assessment play varying roles, some being more important than others, a weighting factor is used to indicate importance. As the score is assessed on each of the lines, it is to be multiplied by the weighting factor to get the actual points earned.

Characteristics	Comments			
1. Size of the proposed site	———————		1.2	
2. Percent of adjacent development	———————		2.6	
3. Percent of surrounding development	———————		2.2	
4. Agricultural use and classification	———————		0.8	
5. Access road type	———————		1.7	
6. Distance to development . . . [A] incorporated city [B] rural community	——————— ——————— ———————		2.1	
7. Distance to public water	———————		1.7	
8. Distance to public sewerage	———————		1.5	
9. Distance to a school facility	———————		1.3	
10. Distance to a fire department	———————		1.2	
11. Distance to an ambulance station	———————		0.8	
12. Terms of ownership	———————		0.7	
13. Relation to the "growth corridor"	———————		2.2	
	14. Amenities assessment for development [add lines 1–13]			
	15. Soils assessment for development [line 15 of Soils Assessment]			
	16. Growth Guidance Assessment [add lines 14 and 15]			

(1) Line one examines the size of the proposed site.

Data published by the Kentucky Department of Agriculture have been used to determine that 78 acres of land is necessary to form an economical farming unit in Hardin County.

One hundred seventy-five subdivisions have been platted in Hardin County as of early 1983. Involving 7,768 acres, these subdivisions average 44 acres each.

Larger developments can take economically viable farming units out of production. Smaller developments, not equaling the County's average size, cannot provide development amenities expected by consumers.

The following chart assigns points to various acreages based on these factors. Points earned for a proposed site are to be placed on line one and multiplied by the weight factor. That product is to be put in the "Earned" column.

Land Area	Points
0.0 – 2.0 acres	10
2.1 – 3.0 acres	9
3.1 – 6.0 acres	8
6.1 – 7.0 acres	7
7.1 – 8.0 acres	6
8.1 – 9.0 acres	5
9.1 – 15.0 acres	4
15.1 – 20.0 acres	5
20.1 – 25.0 acres	6
25.1 – 30.0 acres	7
30.1 – 35.0 acres	8
35.1 – 40.0 acres	9
40.1 – 45.0 acres	10
45.1 – 50.0 acres	9
50.1 – 55.0 acres	8
55.1 – 60.0 acres	6
60.1 – 65.0 acres	5
65.1 – 70.0 acres	4
70.1 – 75.0 acres	2
75.1 – 78.0 acres	1
Over 78.0 acres	0

(2) Line two examines the percent of adjacent land which is developed.

Where all land adjacent to a proposed site is developed, encouragement should be given to develop that site. Conversely, where a site is surrounded by undeveloped land, discouragement should be given. For use here, the greater the percent of adjacent land that is developed, the more points the site earns.

This percentage is to be determined by measuring the length of the boundary of the proposed site on an aerial photograph. Then, the length of that boundary which is adjacent to developed land is to be measured and divided by the total length.

The following chart assigns points for this criteria. Points earned for a proposed site are to be placed in the appropriate column on line two and multiplied by the weight factor. That product is to be put in the "Earned" column.

Percent of Adjacent
Land Developed   Points

Percent of Adjacent Land Developed	Points
95 – 100	10
90 – 94.9	9
80 – 89.9	8
70 – 79.9	7
60 – 69.9	6
50 – 59.9	5
40 – 49.9	4
30 – 39.9	3
20 – 29.9	2
10 – 19.9	1
Less than 10	0

(3) Line three examines the percent of surrounding area developed.

A proposed site which is in the proximity of existing development should be encouraged for development due to the closeness of improved roads and the availability of utilities and community services. Geographical areas which are entirely undeveloped and provide for the production of agricultural products are more viable for the production of food and fiber than areas with a mixture of developed and undeveloped properties.

Aerial photograph maps used by the Hardin County Property Valuation Administrator (PVA) are used in determining the percentage needed here. After locating the site on the photograph, a planimeter is used to determine the percentage of land developed within a one square mile area (the site marks the center of the square mile). This effort also gives some indication of the density of development in the area. As the determination is made, it is converted to a percentage for use here.

The following chart assigns points for this criteria. Points earned for a proposed site are to be placed in the appropriate column on line three and multiplied by the weight factor. That product is to be put in the "Earned" column.

Percent of Surrounding
Area Developed   Points

Percent of Surrounding Area Developed	Points
95 – 100	10
90 – 94.9	9
80 – 89.9	8
70 – 79.9	7
60 – 69.9	6
50 – 59.9	5
40 – 49.9	4
30 – 39.9	3
20 – 29.9	2
10 – 19.9	1
Less than 10	0

(4) Line four examines the proposed site's classification and use as agricultural land.

Land which has received special recognition or been given special consideration based on its agricultural classification has an established value for continued agricultural use. A special tax assessment is given to agricultural property by the Hardin County Property Valuation Administrator (PVA). Similarly, state law provides for the establishment of agricultural districts which receive special consideration.

Answers to the following questions assign points for this criteria. Total points earned for a proposed site are to be placed in the appropriate column on line four and multiplied by the weight factor. That product is to be put in the "Earned" column.

Has the site received an agricultural tax assessment during any part of the past three calendar years, or been a part of a state-approved agricultural district?

Answer	Points
Yes	0
No	5

Has the property been used for agricultural production earning agricultural income or been a part of a governmental agricultural program during any part of the past three calendar years?

Answer	Points
Yes	0
No	5

(5) Line five examines the characteristics of the road on which the proposed site is located.

The availability of an adequate road and transportation network needs to be considered when proposing development. Sites with access to all weather, hard surfaced roads which are maintained by some level of government are essential for quality development. Areas with unimproved and unmaintained roads are more suited for agricultural activities.

The following chart assigns points for this criteria. Points earned for a proposed site are to be placed in the appropriate column on line five and multiplied by the weight factor. That product is to be written in the "Earned" column.

Access Road Characteristics	Points
Hard surfaced, state or city maintained road	10
Hard surfaced, county maintained, through road	8
Hard surfaced, county maintained, deadend road	6
Gravel surfaced, county maintained, through road	4
Gravel surfaced, county maintained, deadend road	2
Public or private road, not maintained by any level of government	0

(6) Line six assesses the distance the proposed site if from contiguous development within incorporated cities and rural unincorporated communities. To

encourage new growth to be contiguous, thus creating proper growth patterns and keeping down the cost to local government taxpayers, sites which are closer to contiguous development receive more development points.

Existing contiguous development has been identified on aerial photographs. For use in this criteria, the distance from the proposed site to the contiguous development line is to be measured by the most direct route using existing roads.

(A) The following chart assigns points based on the distance measured to contiguous development of the closest incorporated city (Elizabethtown, Radcliff, Sonora, Upton, Vine Grove, and West Point). Points earned for a proposed site are to be placed in the appropriate column on line 6A.

Distance to Contiguous Development of Cities	Points
Adjacent to site	10
Less than 500 feet	9
500 – 999 feet	8
1,000 – 1,499 feet	7
1,500 – 1,999 feet	6
2,000 – 2,499 feet	5
2,500 – 2,999 feet	4
3,000 – 3,499 feet	3
3,500 – 3,999 feet	2
4,000 – 5,280 feet	1
Over 1 mile	0

(B) The following chart assigns points based on the distance measured to contiguous development of the closest rural unincorporated community (Cecilia, Colesburg, Eastview, Glendale, Rineyville, Summit, and White Mills). Points earned for a proposed site are to be placed in the appropriate column on line 6B.

Distance to Contiguous Development of Communities	Points
Adjacent to Site	8
Less Than 85 feet	7
86 – 165 feet	6
166 – 330 feet	5
331 – 495 feet	4
496 – 660 feet	3
661 – 825 feet	2
826 – 1,320 feet	1
Over 1/4 mile	0

Once both parts A and B of line six are scored, the larger of the points scored is to be multiplied by the weight factor. That product is to be written in the "Earned" column.

(7) Line seven determines the distance the proposed site is from a public water system line.

Where a public water line exists, areas adjacent to that line should be encouraged for development before areas without access to public water. For use in this criteria, the distance the proposed site is from a water distribution line is to be measured on aerial photographs.

The following chart assigns points based on the distance measured above. Points earned for a proposed site are to be written in the appropriate column on line seven and multiplied by the weight factor. That product is to be placed in the "Earned" column.

Distance to a Public Water System Line	Points
Adjacent to Site	10
Less than 85 feet	9
86 – 165 feet	8
166 – 330 feet	7
331 – 495 feet	6
496 – 660 feet	5
661 – 825 feet	4
826 – 990 feet	3
991 – 1,115 feet	2
1,156 – 1,320 feet	1
Over 1/4 mile	0

(8) Line eight examines the distance the proposed site is from a public sewerage line.

Where a public sewerage line exists, areas adjacent to that line should be encouraged for development. For use in this criteria, the distance the proposed site is from a sewerage line is to be measured on aerial photographs.

The following chart assigns points based on the distance measured above. Points earned for the proposed site are to be written in the appropriate column on line eight and multiplied by the weight factor. That product is to be placed in the "Earned" column.

Distance to a Public Sewerage Line	Points
Adjacent to Site	10
Less than 85 feet	9
86 – 165 feet	8
166 – 330 feet	7
331 – 495 feet	6
496 – 660 feet	5
661 – 825 feet	4
826 – 990 feet	3
991 – 1,155 feet	2
1,556 – 1,320 feet	1
Over 1/4 mile	0

(9) Line nine examines the distance the proposed site is from a public school.

The cost of transporting students to school is an expense paid by the collection of taxes. The Hardin County School District spent over $1.7 million for transporting students during the 1984–85 school year. The further development occurs from a public school, the greater the annual transportation cost is to the taxpayers.

Using aerial photographs, the distance a proposed site is from the nearest school facility is to be measured. The most direct route is to be followed using existing roads.

The following chart assigns points based on the distance measured above. Points earned for a proposed site are to multiplied by the weight factor. That product is to be placed in the "Earned" column.

Distance to a Public School Facility	Points
Less than 1 mile	10
1 to 2 miles	5
Greater than 2 miles	0

(10) Line ten looks at the distance the proposed site is from a fire department facility.

Fire protection in Hardin County is a service operated by community volunteers with financial assistance from County government. The Fiscal Court spends tax dollars to upgrade the local vehicles and equipment. The net result of this is that insurance rates for buildings within a five mile driving distance of each fire station are eligible and may receive reduced rates. Future development is therefore encouraged to be located within this five mile driving distance so that proper fire protection can be provided.

Similarly, insurance rates may also be reduced if the building is located near a fire hydrant. This provides for the possible use of fire hoses and the ability to refill fire vehicle water tanks.

Using aerial photographs, the distance a proposed site is from the nearest fire department facility and hydrant is to be measured. The most direct route is to be followed using existing roads.

The following charts assign points based on the distances measured above. Points earned in the two charts are to be totalled (ten points maximum) and written in the appropriate column on line ten and multiplied by the weight factor. That product is to be placed in the "Earned" column.

Distance to a Fire Department	Points
Less than 0.5 miles	10
0.5 – 0.9 miles	9
1.0 – 1.4 miles	8
1.5 – 1.9 miles	7
2.0 – 2.4 miles	6
2.5 – 2.9 miles	5
3.0 – 3.4 miles	4
3.5 – 3.9 miles	3
4.0 – 4.4 miles	2
4.5 – 5.0 miles	1
Over 5 miles	0

Distance to a Fire Hydrant	Points
500 feet or less	2
500 – 1,000 feet	1

(11) Line 11 examines the distance the proposed site is from one of the County's ambulance stations.

Emergency medical service in Hardin County is a service provided by County government. The Fiscal Court has spent tax dollars to locate three ambulance stations in the County so as to provide quick response as necessary. Future development is therefore encouraged to be located within a distance of an ambulance station that allows for quick response time.

Using aerial photographs, the distance a proposed site is from the nearest ambulance station is measured. The most direct route is to be followed using existing roads.

The following chart assigns points based on the distance measured above. Points earned are to be written in the appropriate column on line 11 and multiplied by the weight factor. That product is to be placed in the "Earned" column.

Distance to an Ambulance Station	Points
0.0 – 1.0 miles	10
1.1 – 2.0 miles	9
2.1 – 3.0 miles	8
3.1 – 4.0 miles	7
4.1 – 5.0 miles	6
5.1 – 6.0 miles	5
6.1 – 7.0 miles	4
7.1 – 8.0 miles	3
8.1 – 9.0 miles	2
9.1 – 10.0 miles	1
Over 10 miles	0

(12) Line 12 reviews the terms of ownership for a proposed site.

Where private investors have invested in land as speculative development sites, points are to be assigned to recognize such investment. To receive points in the first part, the site must have been purchased prior to the original adoption of the DEVELOPMENT GUIDANCE SYSTEM (9 January 1984) and held purely for speculative reasons without income producing activities occurring on it. Income producing activities include, but are not limited to agricultural production, timber harvesting, earth excavation, mineral extraction, and/or any other type of commercial or agricultural enterprise. To receive points in the second part, the year in which the property was purchased is to be determined.

Answers to the following questions assign points based on the above criteria. Points earned in the two parts are to be totalled and placed in the appropriate column on line 12 and multiplied by the weight factor. The product is to be written in the "Earned" column.

If this property was purchased prior to 9 January 1984, has it produced any income?

Answer	Points
Yes, it has produced income.	0
No, it has not produced income.	5

In what year was the property acquired?

Year	Points
1984 to date	0
1982 or 1983	1
1981	2
1980	3
1979	4
1978	5
1977	4
1976	3
1975	2
1974	1
Prior to 1974	0

(13) Line 13 looks at the proposed site's location in relation to Hardin County's growth corridor.

"Growth corridor" is a term that has been used for years to describe the territory laying between Elizabethtown and Radcliff-Vine Grove. In its effort to guide development into this general vicinity, the Commission has defined limits for the growth corridor. Those limits are to be used in this criteria.

To earn points in this classification, the proposed site must be in the growth corridor. As such, it must have access to either Rineyville Road (KY 1600) from Elizabethtown to the Meade County Line, or Shepherdsville Road (KY 251) from Elizabethtown to the Fort Knox Military Reservation, or anyplace between.

The following chart assigns points based on the location of the proposed site. Points earned are to be placed in the appropriate column on line 13 and multiplied by the weight factor. The product is to be written in the "Earned" column.

Criteria	Points
The proposed site is located in the growth corridor.	10
The proposed site is located outside the growth corridor.	0

(14) All weighted points earned on lines one through 13 are to be totalled. That sum is to be written on line 14.

(15) Points earned in the soils assessment (see line 15 of that worksheet) are to be entered on line 15.

(16) Figures on lines 14 and 15 are to be added together and the sum placed on line 16. This number represents the growth guidance assessment of the proposed site.

This completes the in-depth assessment of amenities and site characteristics of the proposed site. It also concludes the overall procedure for determining whether a site's soils and amenities are conducive to development at this time.

King County, Washington
Development Rights Ordinance

ORDINANCE NO. 4341
BE IT ORDAINED BY THE COUNCIL OF KING COUNTY:

Section 1. Repeal _____

Ordinances 3871, 3872 and 3918 are hereby repealed and replaced with this ordinance.

Section 2. Findings and Declaration of Purpose _____

The Council finds that:

(1) King County is a desirable place to live and visit because of the quantity, variety and natural beauty of its open space which contributes a vital ingredient to the quality of life of the people of the County. These open space resources presently include more than fifty thousand acres of land suitable for farming, and other woodlands, wetlands and open lands adjacent to these farmlands. Such lands provide natural separation between urban areas, furnish unique, aesthetic and economic benefits to the citizens of the County and are an important part of our heritage.

(2) Land suitable for farming is an irreplaceable natural resource with soil and topographic characteristics which have been enhanced by generations of agricultural use. When such land is converted to urban and suburban uses which do not require those special fertility and landscape characteristics, an important community resource is permanently lost to the citizens of King County.

(3) The agricultural industry in King County provides the citizens of the County with the opportunity to harvest locally grown berries, fruit and vegetables at u-pick farms and to purchase locally produced food and dairy products through the Pike Place Market, farmers markets, roadside stands and other local outlets throughout the County.

(4) It is the policy of the State of Washington and King County to protect, preserve and enhance agricultural and open space lands as evidenced by the King County Comprehensive Plan of 1964 as amended by Ordinance 1096, establishing open space policies in King County, Ch. 84.34 RCW and Ordinance 2537, authorizing current use taxation of agricultural and open space land, Ch. 84 Laws of 1979 limiting and deferring road and utility assessments on farm and open space land, Ordinance 3064, as amended, establish-

ing King County's agricultural lands policy and County and city ordinances regulating land use by zoning.

(5) However, these policies and regulations, by themselves, have not been effective to provide long-term protection of farm and open space lands under the pressure of increasing urban development. The amount of land in agricultural use in King County has declined from more than 100,000 acres in 1959 to approximately 50,000 acres in 1979, with much of this loss having been caused by actual or prospective urban development.

(6) Generally, farm and open space lands which are close to urban centers have a greater market value for future urban development than their market value for commercial farming or other open space uses. This fact encourages the speculative purchase of these lands at high prices for future development, regardless of the current zoning of such lands. Farm lands which have a market value greater than their agricultural value do not attract sustained agricultural investment and eventually these lands are sold by farmers and removed from commercial agricultural uses.

(7) The permanent acquisition by the County of voluntarily offered interests in farm and open space lands within the County, as provided in this ordinance and as authorized by the Constitution and statutes of the State of Washington, will permit these lands to remain in farm and open space uses in a developing urban area and provide long-term protection for the public interests which are served by farmlands and open space lands within the County.

(8) The acquisition of interests in farm and open space lands as provided in this ordinance is a public purpose of King County and financing such acquisition requires that the County issue its general obligation bonds in the principal amount of not to exceed $50,000,000.

Section 3. Definitions

(1) "Full Ownership" means fee simple ownership.

(2) "Agricultural Rights" means an interest in and the right to use and possess land for purposes and activities related to horticultural, livestock, dairy and other agricultural and open space uses.

(3) "Development Rights" means an interest in and the right to use and subdivide land for any and all residential, commercial and industrial purposes and activities which are not incident to agricultural and open space uses.

(4) "Value of Development Rights" means the difference between the fair market value of Full Ownership of the land (excluding the buildings thereon) and the fair market value of the Agricultural Rights to that land.

(5) "Owner" means the party or parties having the fee simple interest, a real estate contract vendor's or vendee's interest, a mortgagor's interest or a grantor of a deed of trust's interest in land.

(6) "Farmland" means a) "Farm and Agricultural Land" as now defined in RCW 84.34.020(2), or b) land which is in a single ownership of twenty or more contiguous acres, at least 80% of which is open or fallow and which has produced a gross income from agricultural uses of $100.00 or more per acre per year for three of the ten calendar years preceding the date of the owner's application. The "date of application" as used in a) or b) above shall be the date of the owner's application for purchase by the County.

(7) "Food Producing Farmland" means Farmland which has been used for the commercial, soil-dependent cultivation of vegetables, berries, other fruits, cereal grains and silage corn.

(8) "Open Space Land" means "Open Space Land" as now defined in RCW 84.34.020(1) and "open space use" shall mean any of the uses provided in such definition.

(9) "Eligible Land" means Farmland and Open Space Land for the purchase of which bond proceeds are authorized to be used pursuant to this ordinance.

(10) "Selection Committee" means the Committee formed pursuant to Section 6 of this ordinance to advise the Council in the selection of Eligible Lands for purchase.

(11) "Bonds" means the general obligation bonds of the County described in Section 12 of this ordinance.

(12) "Council" means the King County Council.

(13) "Executive" means the King County Executive.

(14) "Governmental Agency" means the United States or any agency thereof, the State of Washington or any agency thereof, any County, City or municipal corporation.

(15) "Appendices A, B, C, D, E and F" of this ordinance mean the maps which describe designated areas of Eligible Lands for purposes of priority of acquisition as provided in Section 5 of this ordinance. Official large scale maps describing such areas in detail are hereby filed with the Administrator-Clerk of the Council and incorporated herein by this reference. Smaller scale maps generally illustrating such areas are appended to this ordinance for more readily accessible public reference.

Section 4. Authorization

(1) The County is hereby authorized to issue its general obligation bonds to acquire the Farmlands and Open Space Lands described and prioritized in Section 5 of this ordinance. The property interest acquired may be either the Development Rights, Full Ownership or any lesser interest, easement, covenant or other contractual right. Such acquisition may be accomplished by purchase, gift, grant, bequest, devise, covenant or contract but only at a price which is equal to or less than the appraised value determined as provided in this ordinance. The proceeds of the Bonds shall be used to acquire such property interests only upon application of the Owner and in a strictly voluntary manner.

(2) If the Owner so elects, the Executive is authorized to pay the purchase price in a lump-sum single payment at time of closing, or to enter into contracts for installment payments against the purchase price consistent with applicable federal arbitrage regulations. When installment purchases are made, the County is authorized to pay interest on the declining unpaid principal balance at a legal rate of interest consistent with prevailing market conditions at the time of execution of the installment contract and adjusted for the tax-exempt status of such interest.

(3) The Executive is further authorized to contract with other Governmental Agencies to participate jointly in the acquisition of interests in Eligible Lands on such terms as shall be approved by the Council consistent with the purposes and procedures of this ordinance.

(4) The County may acquire Full Ownership in Eligible Lands of First Priority only where the Owner will voluntarily sell only the Full Ownership of the property. The County shall acquire only Development Rights or interests which are less than Full Ownership in Eligible Lands of Second and Third Priority.

(5) After County acquisition of Development Rights or some interest less than Full Ownership in any Eligible Lands, the County may purchase the remaining Agricultural Rights or other property interests in such land only when requested by the Owner and when such acquisition is necessary to maintain agricultural or open space uses of the property.

(6) If the County shall acquire Full Ownership in any Eligible Lands the Executive shall as soon as practicable offer the Agricultural Rights to such land for public sale at a price not less than the appraised value of such rights. If no offer for such rights is received at the appraised value, the Executive may, with the approval of the Council, either reoffer the agricultural rights for public sale or lease such land for agricultural or open space use or make such land available for publicly owned open space uses consistent with the purposes of this ordinance.

(7) Interests which the County owns in property other than Eligible Lands may be ex-

changed for property interests in Eligible Lands on an equivalent appraised value basis. If the County has acquired Full Ownership of any Eligible Lands the Agricultural Rights in such lands may be exchanged for the Development Rights to other Eligible Land of equal or higher priority on an equivalent appraised value basis. If the property interests exchanged are not exactly equal in appraised value, cash payments may be made to provide net equivalent value in the exchange.

Section 5. Eligible Lands and Priority of Acquisition

The proceeds of the Bonds shall be used to purchase property interests in the following lands in the following order of their numbered priority group. The lands described within each numbered priority group shall be deemed of equal priority regardless of the order of designation within such group.

FIRST PRIORITY

(a) Farmlands and Open Space Lands located within the designated areas of the Sammamish, Lower Green or Upper Green River Valleys as shown respectively on Appendix A, Appendix B and Appendix C of this ordinance.

(b) Food Producing Farmlands located anywhere within the County *except those lands removed from the Agricultural District by the King County Council in its affirmative action on Ordinance No. 3326** generally described but not limited to those lands on Appendix "F" but outside of the designated areas of the Sammamish, Lower Green, Upper Green and Snoqualmie River Valleys and Enumclaw Plateau.

SECOND PRIORITY

(a) Farmlands in designated areas in the Snoqualmie Valley as shown on Appendix D of this ordinance.

(b) Farmlands in designated areas of the Enumclaw Plateau as shown on Appendix E of this ordinance.

(c) Approximately 1,500 acres of Farmlands which are larger than 40 contiguous acres located anywhere within the County outside of the areas described in Appendices A to E inclusive of this ordinance.

THIRD PRIORITY

All other Farmlands located within presently established Agricultural Districts of the County and designated to be Agricultural Lands of County Significance.

Section 6. Selection Committee

(1) A seven-member Selection Committee shall be appointed within ninety (90) days following the approval of the Bonds by the voters. The Selection Committee shall advise the Council in the selection of Eligible Lands offered for acquisition by their owners. Members shall be appointed by the Executive and confirmed by the Council and shall comply with the King County Code of Ethics. No member may have an ownership interest in any of the lands eligible for purchase pursuant to this ordinance.

(2) The Selection Committee shall consist of two members each of whom shall have at least five years experience in the operation and management of commercial farms; two

* Amended by Ordinance No. 4373, July 12, 1979.

members each of whom shall have five years of experience in the management of either a construction or land development or real estate business; and three members who shall be lay citizens from different geographic areas of the County. One of the lay members shall be appointed by the Executive to serve as chairman. Committee recommendations shall be made by a majority of its members.

(3) Members shall serve three-year terms, except that the initial term of three members shall be two years and of four members shall be three years. Members may be removed by the Executive only for good cause shown. Members shall not be compensated for their services but shall be reimbursed for expenses actually incurred in the performance of their duties. Members may be reappointed to successive terms but the Selection Committee shall be terminated when the proceeds of the Bonds have been spent and in any event no later than eight years after the Bond election.

Section 7. Selection Process

Beginning in the first year following the Bond election and continuing at least once a year for a period of six years or until all Bond proceeds have been expended whichever date is sooner, the Executive shall conduct a voluntary property selection process (herein called "Selection Round") generally as follows:

(1) In the first and second Selection Rounds all properties offered in Priority One shall be eligible for purchase. In the third Selection Round all properties offered in Priority One and Priority Two shall be eligible for purchase, and in all subsequent Selection Rounds all properties offered in Priorities One, Two and Three shall be eligible for purchase. In all Selection Rounds properties of higher priority shall be purchased with available funds before properties of lower priority are purchased.

(2) The Executive shall begin each Selection Round by giving notice in one newspaper of general circulation in each area where Eligible Lands are located which may be acquired in that Round. The notice shall describe the properties eligible for purchase in that Selection Round, the procedure to be followed in the selection process, including an estimated time schedule for the steps in the process, and shall invite the Owners of such properties to make application for purchase by the County and to describe the property interest which the Owner is willing to sell.

(3) Upon closing of the application period, the County Executive shall review each application which has been received to determine the eligibility and priority classification of each property interest and to verify ownership by title search.

(4) For those applications which meet the requirements of (3) above, the Executive shall cause an appraisal of the applicant's property interest to be made. Two appraisals shall be made to determine the Value of Development Rights. One appraisal shall determine the fair market value of Full Ownership of the land (excluding buildings thereon) and one shall determine the fair market value of the Agricultural Rights only. Appraisals of the fair market value of Full Ownership or of a property interest other than Development Rights shall be made by independent appraisers selected by the Executive from a list of not less than ten qualified persons recommended by the County Assessor. Such persons shall be deemed qualified if they have been certified to be professionally competent appraisers by a recognized professional appraisal certification organization, shall have had at least five years experience as a professional appraiser and shall not have a property interest in Eligible Lands. Appraisals of the fair market value of Agricultural Rights shall be made by independent appraisers selected by the Executive with at least five years experience in the appraisal of agricultural land and who shall not have a property interest in Eligible Lands.

(5) Appraisals shall be in writing and shall be furnished to the respective owners for review. Errors of fact in any appraisal may be called to the attention of the appraiser by

the County or by Owners of the property appraised but corrections of the appraisal may be made only by the appraiser. If an Owner of property believes it has not been adequately appraised such Owner may, within the time allowed therefor on the selection schedule, request that a review appraisal be made at the Owner's expense. The Selection Committee shall appoint the review appraiser or appraisers in the same manner as the original appraiser or appraisers are appointed by the Executive. The review appraisal shall become the final appraisal.

The appraisal shall then be filed with the Executive.

(6) Terms and conditions of sale and information on the effect of the sale may be discussed by the Executive with Owners prior to the submission of written offers.

(7) Sealed, firm, written offers by all applicants who desire to have their property purchased by the County shall then be submitted on forms provided by the County to be opened by the County Executive on a day certain.

(8) The Executive shall review all offers and make recommendations thereon to the Selection Committee and the Council.

(9) The Selection Committee shall review all offers and the recommendations of the Executive and make recommendations to the Council.

(10) Upon receiving the recommendations of the Selection Committee, the Council shall take final action on such recommendations.

Section 8. Criteria for Selection within Same Priority

Only in the event that funds are not adequate in any Selection Round to purchase all Eligible Lands of equal priority for which valid offers shall have been received by the County, the following criteria shall be considered in determining which offers to accept within such priority group:

(1) An offer which is below appraisal shall be favored over an offer which is at appraisal.

(2) An offer of Development rights in land shall be favored over an offer of Full Ownership.

(3) An offer of farmland producing in the 12 months preceding application shall be favored over an offer of land which lies fallow;

(4) An offer of land which is more threatened by urban development shall be favored over an offer of land which is less threatened;

(5) An offer of land which will form a contiguous farming area with other offered or acquired Eligible Land shall be favored over an offer of land which is separated;

(6) An offer of land which will serve the dual purpose of urban separation and agricultural production shall be favored over an offer of land which will serve only one of such purposes;

(7) An offer of Farmlands in commercial production shall be favored over an offer of non-commercial Farmlands.

The weight to be given to each of the above criteria shall be determined finally by the Council for each parcel of property and such good faith determination shall be conclusive.

Section 9. Duration of Acquired Interests

(1) Development Rights acquired pursuant to this ordinance shall be held in trust by the County for the benefit of its citizens in perpetuity. Except as provided in Section 4 of this ordinance and Subsection 2 of this Section and except as found necessary by the Council to convey public road and utility easements, the County shall not sell, lease or convey any land or interest in land which it shall acquire with the use of Bond proceeds.

(2) If the Council shall find that the public farm and open space purposes described in Section 2 of this ordinance can no longer reasonably be fulfilled as to any land or interest in land acquired with Bond proceeds, the Council shall submit to the voters of the County a proposition to approve of the disposition of such land or interest. Only upon a majority vote approving such proposition can such land or interest be disposed of by the County and the proceeds of such disposition shall be used to acquire other Farmlands or Open Space Lands in the County as provided in this ordinance.

Section 10. Related Costs

The costs of appraisal, engineering, surveying, planning, financial, legal and other services lawfully incurred incident to the acquisition of interests in Eligible Lands by the County and incident to the sale, issuance and delivery of the Bonds shall be paid from the proceeds of the Bonds.

Section 11. Supplemental Funds

Supplemental or matching funds from other Governmental Agencies or private sources may become available to pay a portion of the cost of acquiring Development Rights, Full Ownership or some lesser interest in Eligible Lands or to supplement or enlarge such acquisition. The Executive is hereby authorized to utilize such funds to purchase interests in Eligible Lands or to otherwise supplement the proceeds of the Bonds in the manner provided by this ordinance and in accordance with the applicable laws or terms governing such grant.

It is the intention of the Council that the proceeds of Bonds available for the acquisition of interests in Farmlands in the Snoqualmie Valley be used in a manner consistent with the adopted multi-jurisdiction agreement affecting the uses of the Snoqualmie River.

Section 12. County Purpose

The Council finds and declares that the use of County funds for the purpose of paying in whole or in part the cost of acquisition of interests in Eligible Lands as set forth herein, including any costs necessarily incident to such acquisition, to the sale, issuance and delivery of the Bonds, or to participation with any Governmental Agency for such purposes will promote the health, welfare, benefit and safety of the people of King County and is a strictly County capital purpose.

Section 13. Terms of the Bonds

For the purpose of providing funds necessary to pay the cost of carrying out the acquisition authorized by this ordinance, the County shall issue the Bonds in the principal amount of not to exceed $50,000,000. The Bonds shall be sold at public sale in the manner required by law, shall bear interest payable at such times, shall be issued in such series from time to time out of such authorization over a period of up to six years, and shall mature serially commencing in from two to five years from the date of issue of each series and maturing in a period which may be less than but shall not exceed thirty years from the date of issue of each series, all as hereafter authorized by the Council and as provided by law. Both the principal of and interest on the Bonds shall be payable out of annual tax levies to be made upon all of the taxable property within the County in excess of constitutional and statutory limits and from any other money which may become legally available and used for such purposes. Any series of the Bonds may be combined with other authorized general obligation bonds of the County and issued and sold as single issues of County bonds. The exact date, form, terms, redemption options and maturities of each series of the Bonds shall be as hereafter fixed by ordinance of the Council.

Section 14. Farmland and Open Space Acquisition Fund

The principal proceeds of sale of the Bonds shall be deposited in a Farmland and Open Space Acquisition Fund to be hereafter created in the office of the Comptroller of King County (hereinafter "Acquisition Fund"), except that any premium and accrued interest on the Bonds received at the time of their delivery shall be paid into a fund of the County to be used for the redemption of the Bonds. Money in such Acquisition Fund may be temporarily deposited in such institutions or invested in such obligations as may be lawful for the investment of County money and may be temporarily advanced to the fund for the redemption of the Bonds to pay Bond interest pending receipt of taxes levied therefor.

The principal proceeds from the sale of the Bonds and any interest received from the deposit or investment of such proceeds shall be applied and used solely for the purposes set forth in this ordinance, and none of such proceeds shall be used for other than a strictly county capital purpose.

CHAPTER 2

Rivers and Wetlands

THIS chapter includes a model stream corridor protection ordinance and two wetlands protection ordinances that represent two different methods for regulating the loss of inland wetlands.

Several New Jersey watershed associations, state agencies, and conservative organizations produced a model stream corridor ordinance for use in New Jersey's Raritan River basin. The purpose of this ordinance is to protect a vegetative buffer along stream corridors. The model ordinance includes numerous useful standards and mechanisms that communities should consider when seeking to protect stream corridors.

Concord, Massachusetts, has created a wetlands conservancy district integrated into its zoning ordinance and has adopted detailed wetlands maps as a component of the official zoning map. The Wetlands Conservancy District applies as an overlay zone to these mapped wetland areas. The ordinance also authorizes a waiver if the local board determines, on a site-specific basis, that an area is not, in fact, a wetland. This ordinance demonstrates an uncomplicated method of incorporating wetlands protection measures into an existing zoning ordinance.

The Freshwater Wetlands and Drainage Ordinance from Yorktown, New York, represents a local ordinance enacted independently of the town's zoning authority, pursuant to the state's Freshwater Wetlands Act. This ordinance represents a more detailed approach than the Wetlands Conservancy District implemented in Concord, Massachusetts.

Raritan, New Jersey, River Basin
Pilot Project Stream Corridor Protection Ordinance

Intent and Purpose

The loss of stream corridors, those undeveloped land areas immediately adjacent to seeps, springs and small and large streams in developing areas has contributed to the inability to such streams, to absorb pollution impacts and the impacts of increasing stormwater run-off. The result is water of poor quality, the destruction of habitats for vegetation, fish and other wildlife in the stream and floodplain; increased erosion; increased flooding downstream through the loss of floodplain area; and scouring of the natural stream channel. From a fiscal standpoint the failure to preserve stream corridors results in increased costs for taxpayers to provide for more complex stormwater and flood control facilities. Indirect financial impacts result to municipalities who lose property tax income from the reduction in value of flood prone properties and the decline in the quality of neighborhoods experiencing such problems.

The protection of stream corridors, and related areas such as wetlands and headwater ephemeral stream areas contributes to community stability and protection of water resources, including water supplies. These benefits more than justify efforts to implement such a program on a basinwide basis.

An adequate vegetative buffer along streams is the one most effective means of filtering pollutants from nonpoint runoff discharge, mainly by trapping silt.

The purpose of stream corridor protection ordinance provisions is to treat streams in a holistic manner to

(1) coordinate surface water management plans with stream corridor functions

(2) to provide a reasonable set of criteria as an adjunct to the stream encroachment permitting process

(3) to provide a policy within which criteria and standards can be applied individually since no two stream corridors will be exactly alike

(4) to take into account land use mitigation measures that can offset maximum natural protection needs

It is intended that the corridor shall remain in its existing or enhanced, vegetative condition as an integral part of the related watercourse.

Permitted Uses

The following shall be permitted uses or activities in stream corridors provided they do not disturb the indigenous character of the area:

(1) conservation of soil, vegetation, water, fish and wildlife

(2) fishing, swimming, boating, hunting

40

(3) boat anchorage or mooring

(4) trail access to the stream and trails in linear parks

The following shall be allowed with appropriate permit:

(1) discharge of controlled or dispersed flow of water

(2) removal of noxious weeds, in channel debris, fallen trees

(3) stream crossing with a stream encroachment permit in accordance with "project of special concern" criteria.*

(4) forestry practices approved by a certified forester.

The following are specifically prohibited within the corridor:

(1) soil disturbance except as part of a permit

(2) cutting or removing woody vegetation or undergrowth plants or trees except as part of a permit

(3) placing fill or debris on or immediately adjacent to the corridor

(4) use as pastureland except for a limited watering access

(5) channel modification or relocation

(5) mining

Criteria for Functional Protection of Stream Corridors

The corridor shall have sufficient width and vegetation to trap a major percentage of silt, to detain the overland flow for possible recharge and to decrease velocities for dispersed discharge to the stream.

The corridor buffer areas related to seeps and springs and to trout production streams shall exceed the minimum requirements.

Wet soils in excess of the minimum buffer width shall be evaluated for their water quality enhancing value as well as plant and animal habitat values.

The buffer vegetation should provide shading of the stream for water temperature modification wherever possible.

Final determination and mapping of a stream corridor shall be based upon geographic and ecologic facts.

Delineation and regulation of the stream corridor shall be primarily for protection of the water resource. This does not preclude consideration of other compatible benefits that may be derived.

Provisions shall be made for alternative protection measures when it is necessary to intrude upon a corridor.

Standards

STANDARD NUMBER 1

Alluvial soils are depositions of soils carried by flood waters. Vegetation on these soils serves to trap additional sediments and aid in preventing in-channel mud bars. The alluvial soil areas are highly erodible if vegetative cover is disturbed. They are a most important element of the stream protection plan and shall be kept in a vegetated state.

STANDARD NUMBER 2

The presence of *wet soils* immediately adjacent to or bordering within 50 feet of the stream channel are considered as hydrologically related to the waterway.

The most important wet soils for stream corridor protection are those encompassing

---

* "Technical Manual—Stream Encroachments," Division of Water Resources, New Jersey Department of Environmental Protection.

seeps, springs and intermittent and perennial small streams. These constitute the origins of the base flow of the river. Intrusions shall be completely avoided. All other wet soils with borders occurring within 50 feet of a waterway should be included in the stream corridor in their entirety in most instances. Where this is not feasible, municipal regulations concerning wet soils shall govern the use of such areas beyond the designated stream corridor.

STANDARD NUMBER 3

Steep slopes. When the toe of a steep slope is 50 feet or less from the stream channel or the stream is within a ravine, the corridor shall extend to the top of the steep slope plus 20 feet of moderate or lesser slope.

The concern with steep slopes is erosion. The slope shall be protected from concentrated runoff discharge from adjacent land, except for natural streams. The 20 foot buffer may be waived where a wall or berm will protect the slope. There shall be no intrusions on steep slopes that will disturb the vegetative cover. On delineated streams, steep slopes adjacent to the floodway shall be included in the stream corridor. Municipal regulations concerning slopes shall govern the use of such areas beyond the stream corridor.

STANDARD NUMBER 4

Woodlands adjacent to streams and those containing seeps and springs are particularly critical. Woodlands play a significant role in retarding and filtering runoff and increasing infiltration of rainwater to recharge springs. It has been found that as much as 95% of rainfall can be retained by woodland. Woodlands also serve as important habitat for many plants and animals and modify stream temperatures by shading the channel. Wooded wetlands are critical to the water regimen. Woodlands shall be altered with extreme care in relation to the corridor and with particular regard for retaining their water related functions.

STANDARD NUMBER 5

Minimum buffer. Where critical areas do not exist, a vegetated buffer of at least 50 feet either side of the stream channel shall be established. This width will sustain shrubs or mature trees to shade the watercourse, provide linear habitat and travel way for wildlife and filter sediment and a large percentage of pollutants with minimum danger of windthrow of large trees.*

On delineated streams a buffer shall be established immediately adjacent to the floodway when the floodway is confined by steep slopes, using the same standard as for steep slopes adjacent to non-delineated streams.

STANDARD NUMBER 6

Because the occurrence of *trout production waters* is extremely limited, they shall be regarded as treasures and given every possible protection. The minimum buffer shall be expanded. All runoff discharged from roads and adjacent properties shall be dispersed to the vegetated buffer at low velocities. Stream crossings shall be avoided and done with great care where crossings are absolutely necessary.

STANDARD NUMBER 7

Determining *stream corridor boundaries.* The total extent of critical areas adjacent to the stream shall be considered in determining the boundaries of the stream corridor area.

* "Technical Basis for 25-foot-wide and 50-foot-wide Buffer Strips," New Jersey Department of Environmental Protection-Division of Water Resources, Bureau of Planning and Standards, Dec. 1983.

Using soil maps, aerial photos, U.S.G.S. maps, Fish and Wildlife wetlands maps, the critical areas should be mapped as overlays on a base map.

Using this basic data, a stream corridor protection map shall be developed subject to field verification.

Implementation

The stream corridor shall be established at time of subdivision or application for development if there is no subdivision involved. A property owner may voluntarily apply for establishing a stream corridor at any time.

When established, the corridor shall be described by metes and bounds, and monumented prior to development. An easement covering the corridor area shall be recorded with the property deed to run with the lands.

The easement shall be held by the municipality with the environmental commission assigned as the monitoring agent to implement a monitoring plan. In the event that a municipality does not have an environmental commission, this responsibility should be assigned to the municipal park, recreation or planning agency.

The environmental commission shall recommend approval or denial of requests for permits to the municipal governing body. Municipal approval shall not waive necessity to obtain the assent or permit required by any other agency, ordinance or statute before proceeding with the proposed activity or use. Other approval or permits which may be required is solely the responsibility of the applicant. No operations or uses shall be initiated by the applicant until such other approvals or permits as may be required are obtained or issued.

Violations and Penalties

The standard violation clause can apply. Additionally, where construction is involved, the municipality shall issue a "stop work" order until the deficiencies are corrected. Restoration or mitigation should be part of any penalty.

Definitions

STREAM CORRIDOR. The stream channel and those linear lands either side of the channel designated as critical areas or a vegetated buffer strip of predetermined width adjacent to the waterway.

CHANNEL. A watercourse with definite bed and banks which confine and convey continuously or intermittently flowing water. For purposes of determining "corridor," the channel shall be regarded as the area occupied by bankful flow as indicated by the first appreciable drop into the waterway from adjacent land.

PERENNIAL STREAM. A channel carrying flowing water most of the time.

INTERMITTENT STREAM. A natural channel carrying water during the wet seasons and having at least one critical area factor.

VEGETATIVE BUFFER. A linear area adjacent to a spring, seep, or stream—not necessarily related to the presence or extent of a critical area—heavily vegetated for the primary purpose of filtering pollutants from non-point sources.

CRITICAL AREAS. Those kinds of areas considered environmentally sensitive because of their ecological functions. For the purposes of this ordinance they are: alluvial soils, wet soils, steep slopes, woodlands.

WOODLAND. Forested land having a predominance of trees four inches or greater in diameter at breast height.

Concord, Massachusetts, Wetlands Conservancy District

7.3 Wetlands Conservancy District

7.3.1 Definition. Wetlands are wet meadows, marshes, swamps, bogs, and areas of flowing or standing water. Wetlands are characterized by the presence of wetland soils or the presence of plant communities which require the presence of water at or near the ground surface for a significant portion of the growing season or for seven (7) to nine (9) months of the year. The Wetlands Conservancy District consists of areas within the Town which are wetlands.

7.3.2 Purpose.

7.3.2.1 To protect persons and property against the hazards of flood water inundation by assuring the continuation of the natural flow pattern of streams and other watercourses within the Town and by preserving natural floodwater storage areas;

7.3.2.2 To maintain the quality and level of the groundwater table and water recharge areas for existing or potential water supplies; and

7.3.2.3 To protect the Town against unsuitable use or development of wetlands such as streams and other watercourses, swamps, marshes, bogs, ponds and areas subject to flooding.

7.3.3 Uses permitted without review by the Board. The following uses are permitted within the Wetlands Conservancy District:

7.3.3.1 Wildlife management, boating, fishing and hunting where otherwise legally permitted;

7.3.3.2 Construction and maintenance of sidewalks, boat landings and docks, duckwalks, bicycle, equestrian and foot paths or bridges, and unpaved recreation areas which do not alter the existing topography;

7.3.3.3 Flower and vegetable gardens, lawns, pastures, soil conservation, forestry, grazing and farming, including nurseries, truck gardening and harvesting of crops;

7.3.3.4 Construction and maintenance of a single accessory structure and improvement of existing structures, provided that the total wetland area covered by such construction and improvements shall not be more than one hundred (100) square feet;

7.3.3.5 Construction and maintenance of public and private water supplies, and maintenance or improvement of ponds, brooks, ditches and other water bodies;

7.3.3.6 Construction and maintenance of roads, driveways, utilities and other associated roadway facilities when access to land which is not situated in the Flood Plain or Wetlands Conservancy districts is not possible because of own-

ership patterns or the provisions of the Subdivision Rules and Regulations of
the Planning Board;

7.3.3.7 Construction and improvements of public sewers including accessory facilities used for their operation and maintenance, and improvements to existing
roads and systems used in the service of the public including drainage, electric
power (including conversion to underground facilities), gas, telephone, tele-
graph and other telecommunication devices; and

7.3.3.8 Repairs to septic disposal systems (SDS), including leaching facilities, but
excluding any expansion of SDS capacity beyond the minimum design flow for
the existing use of the property as required by applicable Board of Health regulations.

7.3.4 *Uses permitted subject to review by the Board.* The following uses may be permitted by the Board after notice and a public hearing:

7.3.4.1 Any use permitted in the underlying district in which the land is situated,
including dumping, filling, excavating, permanent storage of materials or construction of a building or structure, subject to the same use and development
regulations as may otherwise apply thereto, provided that the Board shall find
that the proposed use will not significantly conflict with the purpose set forth
in subsection 7.3.2 of this Bylaw.

7.3.4.2 Any use permitted in the underlying district in which the land is situated,
subject to the same use and development restrictions as may otherwise apply
thereto, provided that the land designated as being within the Wetlands Conservancy District is found by the Board not, in fact, to be a wetland.

7.3.5 *Procedure for review by the Board.*

7.3.5.1 Any person who desires to use land within the Wetlands Conservancy District for a use permitted subject to review by the Board shall submit a written
application for a special permit to the Board, with copies to the Planning
Board and Natural Resources Commission. Each such application shall be accompanied by the following submissions:

(a) A written statement meeting the requirements of a site evaluation statement
under the Subdivision Rules and Regulations of the Planning Board or a
completed environmental data form in such form as the Board shall require;

(b) Development plans consisting of site plans meeting, to the extent applicable, the requirements set forth for a definitive plan in the Subdivision
Rules and Regulations of the Planning Board; and

(c) Such additional information as the Board may require.

7.3.5.2 The Planning Board and Natural Resources Commission shall submit to the
Board written recommendations including at least:

(a) An evaluation and opinion of the site evaluation statement or environmental data form accompanying the application to the Board;

(b) An evaluation of the proposed use, including its probable effect or impact
upon: the Town's water supply, the quality of water in the area, the natural
flow pattern of watercourses, nearby or pertinent floodwater storage areas
or other areas subject to seasonal or periodic flooding, and the general
health, safety and welfare of the inhabitants of the Town; and

(c) A recommendation as to whether the special permit should be granted and
whether any restrictions should be imposed upon the proposed use as a
condition of such permit.

7.3.5.3 If a special permit is granted, the Board shall impose such conditions and
safeguards as public safety, welfare and convenience may require. The Board
shall give due consideration to the reports of the Planning Board and Natural
Resources Commission, and, where the decision of the Board differs from the
recommendations of either, the reasons therefor shall be stated in writing.

Yorktown, New York
Freshwater Wetlands and Drainage Ordinance

89-1 Title and Purpose

This local law shall be known as the "Freshwater Wetlands and Drainage Law of the Town of Yorktown." It is a local law regulating the dredging, filling, deposition or removal of materials; diversion or obstruction of water flow; placement of structures and other uses in the ponds, lakes, reservoirs, natural drainage systems and wetlands in the Town of Yorktown and the requirement of permits therefor, providing for the protection and control of wetlands, water bodies, water courses and flood hazard areas.

89-2 Legislative Intent

A. The Town Board of the Town of Yorktown has determined that the public interest, health, safety and the economic and general welfare of the residents of the Town of Yorktown will be best served by providing for the protection, preservation, proper maintenance and use of its ponds, lakes, reservoirs, water bodies, rivers, streams, water courses, wetlands, natural drainage systems and adjacent land areas from encroachment, spoiling, polluting or elimination resulting from rapid population growth attended by commercial development, housing, road construction, and/or disregard for natural resources.

B. The remaining Wetlands (as defined in this Chapter) in Yorktown are a valuable natural resource which serve to benefit the entire Town and the surrounding region by performing one or more of the following functions:

(1) Providing drainage and flood control through hydrologic absorption, natural storage and flood conveyance;

(2) Protecting subsurface water resources, watersheds and groundwater recharge systems;

(3) Providing a suitable living, breeding, nesting and feeding environment for many forms of wildlife, including but not limited to, wildfowl, shorebirds and rare species especially endangered and threatened species;

(4) Treating pollution through natural biological degradation and chemical oxidation;

(5) Controlling erosion by serving as sedimentation areas and filter basins, absorbing silt and organic matter;

(6) Providing sources of nutrients in freshwater food cycles;

(7) Serving as nursery grounds and sanctuaries for freshwater fish;

(8) Providing recreation areas for hunting, fishing, boating, hiking, bird watching, photography, camping and other uses;

(9) Serving as an educational and research resource; and

(10) Preserving much needed open space which serves to satisfy man's psychological and aesthetic needs.

C. Wetlands protection is a matter of concern to the entire Town and the establishment of regulatory and conservation practices for these areas serve to protect the Town by insuring review and regulation of any activity on Wetlands that might adversely affect the Town's citizens' health, safety and welfare.

D. Wetlands in Yorktown and other areas form an ecosystem that is not confined to any one property owner or neighborhood. Experience has demonstrated that effective Wetlands protection requires consistency of approach to preservation and conservation efforts throughout the Town.

E. Loss of Wetlands can cause or aggravate flooding erosion, diminution of water supply for drinking and waste treatment and may pose a threat to the health, safety and welfare of the people of Yorktown and the surrounding region.

F. Regulation of Wetlands is consistent with the legitimate interests of farmers to graze and water livestock, make reasonable use of water resources, harvest natural products of Wetlands, selectively cut timber and fuel wood and otherwise engage in the use of land for agricultural production.

G. The State of New York has enacted legislation titled the Freshwater Wetlands Act, found in Article 24 of the Environmental Conservation Law, which authorizes local governments to establish their own procedures for the protection and regulation of wetlands lying within their jurisdiction. The New York State Department of Environmental Conservation has promulgated implementing regulations for local government adoption of Article 24 authority, found in Part 665 of Title 6 of the Official Compilation of Codes, Rules, and Regulations of the State of New York (6 NYCRR Part 665).

H. This chapter is enacted pursuant to the above referenced law and any and all applicable laws, rules and regulations of the State of New York and nothing contained herein shall be deemed to conflict with any such laws, rules or regulations.

89–3 Intent

A. It is declared to be the intent of the Town of Yorktown to control, protect, preserve, conserve and regulate the use of Wetlands (as defined below) within the Town of Yorktown to insure that the benefits found to be provided by Wetlands as set forth in Section 89–2 hereof will not be lost and to protect the important physical, ecological, social, aesthetic, recreational and economic assets of the present and future residents of the Town, so as to protect the broader public interest.

B. These regulations are enacted with the intent of providing a reasonable balance between the rights of the individual property owner's to the free use of their property and the rights of present and future generations.

C. It is the intent of this Chapter to incorporate the consideration of Wetlands protection into the Town's land use and development approval procedures.

89–4 Definitions

A. Except where specifically defined herein, all words used in this chapter shall carry their customary meanings. Words used in the present tense include the future and the plural includes the singular. The word "shall" is intended to be mandatory.

B. As used in this chapter, the following terms shall have the meanings indicated: Administrative Permit—A permit issued by the Town Engineer for the conduct of regulated activities in Wetlands or Controlled Areas where such conduct of regulated activities is limited in scope and limited in potential impact as determined by this Chapter.

Applicant—Any individual, or individuals, firm, partnership, association, corporation, company, organization or other legal entity of any kind including municipal corporations, governmental agencies or subdivisions thereof, who has a request for a permit to conduct a regulated activity before the Approval Authority or who has an application pursuant to Section 89–5 of this Chapter before the Town Board.

Approval Authority—The administrative board or public official empowered to grant or deny Permits under this local law, to require the posting of bonds as necessary and to revoke or suspend a permit where lack of compliance to the Permit is established. The Approval Authority shall be:

(1) The Planning Board of the Town of Yorktown for Permit applications relating to regulated activities that also require subdivision or parking plan approval by the Planning Board except as specified in (2) and (3) below. Notwithstanding the foregoing, the Planning Board shall have no power to act as Approval Authority under the provisions of this Chapter except in conjunction with final Subdivision or Parking Plan approval.

(2) The Town Engineer of the Town of Yorktown for Permit applications relating to regulated activities permitted with an Administrative Permit as specified in Section 89–6 of this Chapter, subject to the limitations placed upon the Town Engineer's authority to deny such applications as set forth in Section 89–6 (c) of this Chapter.

(3) The Town Board of the Town of Yorktown shall act as the approval authority on all Permit applications not covered by (1) or (2) above and be the Approval Authority for projects that come under the Soil Removal Ordinance.

Aquiculture—Aquiculture means cultivating and harvesting products, including fish and vegetation, that are produced naturally in freshwater wetlands, and installing cribs, racks and other in-water structures for cultivating these products, but does not include filling, dredging, peat mining, or the construction of any buildings or any water-regulating structures such as dams.

Clear Cutting—The cutting of more than one half of the existing living trees measuring more than 6 inches in diameter at breast height in an area 1/4 acre or more over the period of 2 consecutive years within a specified area.

Conservation Board—The duly appointed Conservation Board of the Town of Yorktown as created pursuant to Section 239 of the General Municipal Law.

Controlled Area—The Controlled Area is an additional buffer area surrounding a Wetland that is also subject to the regulations for Wetlands as defined in this Chapter. The exact size of the Controlled Area shall be determined as follows:

(1) Except as provided in paragraph (3) of this definition of "Controlled Area," for all Wetlands greater than 1 acre, the Controlled Area shall extend 100 feet away from the edge of the Wetland.

(2) Except as provided in paragraph (3) of this definition of "Controlled Area," for all Wetlands less than 1 acre, the Controlled Area shall extend beyond the Wetlands, on all sides thereof, a distance of one-half of the width of the Wetland at that point, except that the extension shall not be greater than 100 feet, nor less than 50 feet.

(3) The Controlled Area of Natural Drainage Systems includes all adjacent surfaces for 100 feet as measured from the bank of the water course, or all adjacent surfaces which have an elevation of less than three feet above the normal water line, whichever is more.

DATE OF RECEIPT OF APPLICATION BY APPROVAL AUTHORITY or RECEIPT OF APPLICATION BY APPROVAL AUTHORITY.
An Application shall be deemed "Received" by the Approval Authority on the date of the first regular meeting of the Approval Authority following the filing of the Applica-

tion and supporting plans with the Town Clerk pursuant to the provisions of Section 89–9 (A) of this Chapter.

Dams and Water Control Measures and Devices—Barriers used to obstruct the flow of water or to raise, or lower, or maintain the level of water in Wetlands.

Deposit—to fill, place, eject or dump any Material or the act thereof, but not including storm water.

Environmental Clerk—An employee of the Town of Yorktown, or an independent contractor engaged by the Town of Yorktown, designated to perform, inter alia, the duties of the Environmental Clerk as set forth in this Chapter.

Freshwater Wetlands Map—The final freshwater Wetlands map promulgated by the New York State Department of Environmental conservation as defined in the Freshwater Wetlands Act as may be amended from time to time.

Material—Liquid, solid or gaseous substances including but not limited to: soil, silt, gravel, rock, sand, clay, peat, mud, debris and refuse; any organic or inorganic compound, chemical agent, or matter (excluding pesticides, herbicides, algaecides and agricultural or radioactive wastes to the extent that same are exempt or regulated exclusively by the State of New York); sewage, sewage sludge or effluent; and industrial or municipal solid waste.

Natural Drainage System—Natural Drainage System means rivers, streams and brooks which contain running water at least six months of the year.

Permit or Wetlands Permit—That form of Town approval required by this chapter for the conduct of a regulated activity within any Wetland or Controlled Area.

Person—See Applicant.

Planning Board—The duly appointed Planning Board of the Town of Yorktown as created pursuant to Section 271 of the Town Law.

Pollution—The presence in the environment of human induced conditions or contaminants in quantities or characteristics which are or may be injurious to human, plant or animal life or to property.

Remove—to dig, dredge, suck, bulldoze, dragline, blast or otherwise excavate or regrade or the act thereof.

State Environmental Quality Review Act (SEQRA)—The law pursuant to Article 8 of the New York Environmental Conservation Law providing for environmental quality review of actions which may have a significant effect on the environment.

Structure—Structure means anything constructed or erected, the use of which requires location on or in the ground or attachment to something having location on the ground. The term structure includes, but is not limited to, tennis courts and swimming pools.

Town Board—The duly elected Town Board of the Town of Yorktown.

Town Clerk—The duly elected Town Clerk of the Town of Yorktown.

Town Engineer—Any person employed by the Town of Yorktown as the Town Engineer.

Waterbody—Any natural or artificial pond, lake, reservoir or other area which ordinarily or intermittently contains water and which has a discernible shoreline, but not including a Natural Drainage System as defined in this Chapter.

Wetlands—

(1) All Waterbodies over 1000 square feet in area, or
(2) All geographic areas of one-quarter acre or more characterized by any or all of the following:
    (a) Marshes, swamps, bogs, or other areas of permanent water retention fed by springs or Natural Drainage Systems or

(b) Soil types that are poorly drained, very poorly drained, alluvial or flood plain soils as defined by the U.S. Department of Agricultural Soil Conservation Service and the Westchester County Soil and Water Conservation District including but not limited to the following:

25	Sun silt loam (includes formerly 291 Alden)
27	Sun extremely stoney silt loam
28	Fredon loam
35	Raynham silt loam (formerly Wallington)
101	Carlisle muck
103	Freshwater marsh
108	Uderthents wet substratum
251	Ridgebury loam (formerly Massena)
252	Ridgebury very stony loam
311	Fluvaquents (formerly Cohoctah; includes formerly Rippowam and 31 Rumney)
1011	Palms Muck
1251	Leicester loam (former 26 Leicester)
1252	Leicester very stoney loam, or

(c) Lands and submerged lands supporting a prevalence of aquatic or semi-aquatic vegetation of the following vegetative types as listed in the New York Freshwater Wetlands Act (Section 24-0107 of the Environmental Conservation Law):

  (i) Wetland trees, which depend upon seasonal or permanent flooding or sufficiently water-logged soils to give them a competitive advantage over other trees;
 (ii) Wetland shrubs, which depend upon seasonal or permanent flooding or sufficiently water-logged soils to give them a competitive advantage over other shrubs;
(iii) Emergent vegetation;
(iv) Rooted or floating-leaved vegetation;
 (v) Free-floating vegetation;
(vi) Wet meadow vegetation, which depends upon seasonal or permanent flooding or sufficiently water-logged soils to give them a competitive advantage over other open land vegetation;
(vii) Bog mat vegetation;
(viii) Submergent vegetation; or

(3) Natural Drainage Systems
(4) All areas designated on the most recent New York State Freshwater Wetlands Map as filed by the Commissioner of the Department of Environmental Conservation

General Note—The Yorktown Topography and Surface Hydrology Map, defined below, is intended to provide general guidance in locating and determining those areas which constitute Wetlands, as defined herein. Finite boundaries of Wetlands shall be established by the approval Authority when necessary, on its own initiative or upon the request of the Applicant, the Wetlands owner or the Commissioner of the New York State Department of Environmental Conservation following appropriate field survey work by qualified individuals which may include, but shall not be limited to, representatives of the Westchester County Soil and Water Conservation District and the Conservation Board.

Yorktown Topography and Surface Hydrology Map—The Yorktown Wetlands and Drainage Map dated May 1987 prepared by Frederick P. Clark Associates and the Yorktown Conservation Board, adopted by the Town Board and as from time to time updated, that shows the approximate location of areas that can be classified as Wetland.

89–5 Non-Wetlands Declaration

A. Notwithstanding any other provision of this Chapter, where a geographic area is defined as a Wetland <u>solely</u> by reason of the presence thereon of one or more of the following soil classifications:

27	Sun extremely stony silt loam
108	Uderthents wet substratum
251	Ridgebury loam
252	Ridgebury very stony loam
1251	Leicester loam
1252	Leicester very stony loam

An Applicant may petition the Town Board for a determination as to whether or not said geographic area shall be deemed a Wetlands within the meaning of this Chapter. Notwithstanding any other provision of this Chapter, no Applicant may petition the Town Board for a Non-Wetland Declaration unless said Applicant concurrently has an application for Subdivision Approval, Site Plan Approval, Parking Plan Approval or Wetlands Permit Approval before the Town Board, Planning Board or Town Engineer.

B. The Applicant shall file five copies of his application for a non-Wetlands declaration with the Environmental Clerk, along with an application fee in the amount of thirty-five ($35.00) dollars. The application shall contain such maps and details as are required by the Town Board. The Town Board shall notify the Applicant within forty-five (45) days of receipt of an application of the maps and details that are required. The Town Board may request a recommendation from the Conservation Board as to what maps and details are necessary in order to review the application.

C. Upon receipt of an application and all required maps and plans the Town Board shall refer such application and maps and plans to the Conservation Board. The Conservation Board shall review the application and file a written report with the Town Board concerning the application.

D. Within 30 days after receiving the written report from the Conservation Board, the Town Board shall hold a public hearing on the application, public notice of which shall be given at least ten (10) days prior to the date set for such hearing in a newspaper having general circulation in the Town. The Applicant shall provide prior notice of such hearing to Interested Parties pursuant to the provisions of Chapter 63 of the Code of the Town of Yorktown. All applications, maps and documents relating thereto shall be open for public inspection at the offices of the Environmental Clerk. At such hearing any person or persons having an interest may appear and be heard.

E. Within 45 days after the closing of the public hearing the Town Board shall issue a determination as to (1) whether or not the geographic area in question is defined as a wetland <u>solely</u> by reason of the presence thereon of one or more of the soil classifications set forth in paragraph A of this Section 89–5; and (2) whether or not the geographic area in question performs none of the Wetland functions set forth in Section 89–2(B) of this Chapter. The Applicant shall have the burden of proof with regard to both of the above determinations.

F. If the Town Board makes affirmative findings with regard to both of the determinations set forth in subsection (E) above, the Town Board shall approve the application before it and declare that the geographic area in question is not a Wetland within the meaning of this Chapter. If the Town Board makes a negative finding with regard to either of the determinations set forth in subsection (E) above, the Town Board shall deny the application before it. The Town Board shall state in writing findings and reasons for all approvals and denials of applications under this section 89–5. Following action by the Town Board to approve or deny an application under this Section 89–5, the written decision shall be filed in the office of the Environmental Clerk.

G. No provision of this Section 89–5 shall be construed to prevent a geographic area, determined <u>not</u> to be a Wetland, from being regulated pursuant to this Chapter as a Controlled Area.

89–6 Prohibited, Regulated and Permitted Acts

A. PROHIBITED ACTS

It shall be unlawful to place or deposit chemical wastes or to introduce influents of sufficiently high thermal content as to cause deleterious ecological effect in any Wetland or Controlled Area.

B. REGULATED ACTS WHICH REQUIRE A WETLANDS PERMIT

Except as provided in Section 89–6(c) of this Chapter, it shall be unlawful, in the absence of a specific written Permit issued by the Approval Authority, to do any of the following activities in any Wetland or Controlled Area:

(1) Place or construct any Structure.
(2) Conduct any form of draining, dredging, excavation or removal of Material either directly or indirectly.
(3) Conduct any form of dumping, filling or depositing of Material either directly or indirectly.
(4) Install any service lines or cable conduits.
(5) Introduce any form of Pollution, including but not limited to, the installing of a septic tank, the running of a sewer outfall, or the discharging of sewage treatment effluent or other liquid wastes into or so as to drain into a Wetland.
(6) Alter or grade natural features and contours, alter drainage conditions or divert any flow of a Natural Drainage System, Waterbody, marsh or swamp.
(7) Construct docks, dams, other water control devices, pilings or bridges whether or not they change the ebb and flow of the water.
(8) Install any pipes or wells.
(9) Construct a driveway or road.
(10) Clear cut any area of trees.
(11) Remove or cut more than three live healthy trees over eight inches in breast-height diameter, within a six month period.
(12) Deposit or introduce organic or inorganic chemicals (e.g. fertilizers).
(13) Conduct any other activity that substantially impairs any of the functions that Wetlands perform as described in Section 89–2(B) of this Chapter.
(14) Graze one or more horses or other animal(s).

C. REGULATED ACTS PERMITTED WITH AN ADMINISTRATIVE PERMIT

The following regulated activities are determined by this Chapter to be limited in scope and limited in potential impact. The Approval Authority for applications to conduct these regulated activities shall be the Town Engineer, except in the event the Town Engineer determines that the granting of an Administrative Permit would be inappropriate in light of the standards set forth in Section 89–7 of this Chapter, the Town Engineer shall neither approve nor deny the application, but rather, shall return the application to the Environmental Clerk for processing in accordance with the procedures set forth in Section 89–8 (B) (iii) of this Chapter. If the Town Engineer determines that the granting of an Administrative Permit would be appropriate in light of the standards set forth in Section 89–7 of this Chapter the Town Engineer shall grant the application in accordance with the provisions of 89–8 (B) (iv) of this Chapter. Notwithstanding the foregoing, the Town Engineer, in his sole discretion, may return any application for an Administrative Permit to the Environmental Clerk for processing in accordance with the provisions of Section 89–8 (B) (iii) of this Chapter. Proposed regulated activities within Wetlands or Controlled Areas for which an Administrative Permit may be granted are:

(1) The performance of a Regulated Act, as set forth in Section 89–6(B) (1), (2), (3) or (4), which does not require subdivision approval, site plan approval or the issuance of a special permit by either the Town Board or the Planning Board, and where any deposition or removal of Material from the Wetland or Controlled Area is not in excess of 20 cubic yards over a one year period.

(2) Construction of a driveway when the length of a Wetland or Controlled Area crossing or intrusion is less than 225 feet and, if a Natural Drainage System Crossing is proposed, where a single culvert of less than twenty-five feet in length and eighteen inches in diameter is required.

(3) The application of non-polluting chemicals and dyes for the purpose of maintenance that does not change the character of the Wetland (such as Health Department testing).

Notwithstanding the foregoing, no regulated activity shall be permitted with an Administrative Permit when such activities are proposed for areas designated—Wetlands—on the most recent New York State Freshwater Wetlands Map.

D. ACTS PERMITTED BY RIGHT

The following acts are permitted by right within Wetlands, without Permit, provided they do not constitute a pollution or erosion hazard or interfere with proper drainage or adversely affect reasonable water use by others. Such permitted acts must conform to the Town of Yorktown Zoning Ordinance and any and all other applicable laws and statutes.

(1) Normal ground maintenance including mowing, trimming of vegetation and removal of dead or diseased vegetation around a residence.

(2) Repair of walkways and walls.

(3) Decorative landscaping and planting, excluding those items regulated in Section 89–6-(B) (12) which regulates the use of fertilizers.

(4) Operation and maintenance of existing dams and water control devices in lakes, excluding the adjustment of water elevations over 18″ in height for the periods of less than 1 week after which the water level is returned to its previous level.

(5) Public health activities, orders and regulations of the Department of Health for emergencies only.

(6) The depositing or removal of the natural products of Wetlands through recreational or commercial fishing, aquiculture, hunting or trapping where otherwise legally permitted.

89–7 Standards for Permit Decisions

A. CONSIDERATION

In granting, denying or conditioning any Permit, the Approval Authority shall consider the following:

(1) All evidence offered at any public hearing;

(2) Any reports from other commissions and/or federal, county, state or town agencies;

(3) Additional requested information by the Approval Authority;

(4) All relevant facts and circumstances, including but not limited to the following:

    (a) the environmental impact of the proposed action;

    (b) the alternatives to the proposed action;

    (c) irreversible and irretrievable commitments of resources that would be involved in the proposed activity;

    (d) the character and degree of injury to, or interference with, safety, health, or the reasonable use of property that is caused or threatened;

    (e) the suitability or unsuitability of such activity to the area for which it is proposed; and

    (f) the effect of the proposed activity with reference to the protection or enhancement of the several functions of Wetlands and the benefits they provide which are set forth in 89–2 of this Chapter and in Section 24-0103 of the Environmental Conservation Law.

(5) The availability of preferable alternative locations on the subject parcel or, in the case of activity of sufficient magnitude, the availability of the reasonable locations;

(6) The availability of further technical improvements or safeguards that could feasibly be added to the plan or action;

(7) The possibility of further avoiding reduction of the Wetlands' or water course's natural capacity to support desirable biological life, prevent flooding, supply water, control sedimentation and/or prevent erosion, assimilate wastes, facilitate drainage, and provide recreation and open space; and

(8) The extent to which the exercise of property rights and the public benefit derived from such use may or may not outweigh or justify the possible degradation of the inland Wetland or water course, the interference with the exercise of other property rights, and the impairment or endangerment of public health, safety or welfare.

B. FINDINGS

(1) Permits will be issued by the Approval Authority pursuant to this Chapter only if Approval Authority shall find that:

    (a) The proposed regulated activity is consistent with the policy of this Chapter to preserve, protect and conserve Wetland functions and the benefits they provide, as set forth in Section 89–2 of this Chapter, by preventing the despoliation and destruction of Wetlands and regulating the development of such Wetlands consistent with the general welfare and development of the Town, and

    (b) The proposed regulated activity is consistent with the land use regulations governing Wetlands applicable in the Town of Yorktown pursuant to 6 N.Y.C.R.R. Section 665.7 if any, and

    (c) The proposed regulated activity is compatible with the public health and welfare, and

    (d) The proposed Regulated Activity cannot practicably be relocated on the site so as to eliminate or reduce the intrusion into the Wetland and/or Controlled Area.

    (e) The proposed regulated activity minimizes the degradation to, or loss of, any part of the Wetlands and the Controlled Area and minimizes any adverse impacts on the functions and benefits that said Wetland provides as set forth in Section 89–2 of this Chapter, and

    (f) The proposed regulated activities are in compliance with the standards set forth in 6 N.Y.C.R.R. Section 665.7(e) and 665.7(g).

(2) The applicant shall have the burden of proof with regard to the required findings set forth in paragraph one of this Section 89–7.

C. WETLAND ACQUISITION

Duly filed notice in writing that the State or any agency or political subdivision of the State is in the process of acquiring any Wetland by negotiation or condemnation authorizes but does not require denial of any permit, but only if both the affected landowner and the local government have been so notified.

(1) The written notice must include an indication that the acquisition process has commenced, such as that an appraisal of the property has been prepared or is in the process of being prepared.

(2) If the landowner receives no offer for the property within one year of the permit denial, this bar to the permit lapses. If its negotiations with the applicant are broken off, the State or any agency or political subdivision must, within six months of the end of negotiation, either issue its findings and determination to acquire the property pursuant to Section 204 of the Eminent Domain Procedure Law or issue a determination to acquire the property without public hearing pursuant to Section 206 of the Eminent Domain Procedure Law, or this ban to the permit lapses.

89–8 Permit Procedure Town Engineer's Review of Wetland Permit and Application for Administrative Permit

A. APPLICATION FOR WETLANDS PERMIT OR ADMINISTRATIVE PERMIT

The Applicant shall file five copies of his application for a Wetlands Permit or Administrative Permit with the Environmental Clerk which application shall contain the following information:

(1) Name and post office address of owner and applicant.
(2) Street address and tax map designation of property covered by the application.
(3) Statement with consent from owner for any agent making application.
(4) Statement of proposed work and purpose thereof.
(5) Applications affecting the water retention capacity, water flow or other drainage characteristics of any Wetland shall include a statement of the impact of the project on upstream and downstream areas giving appropriate consideration to flood or drought levels of water courses and amounts of rainfall.
(6) Copies of all applicable county, state or federal permits or permit applications that are required for such work or improvement, unless such permits are conditioned upon obtaining a Permit under this Chapter.
(7) An application fee in the amount of seventy-five ($75.00) dollars.

B. REVIEW OF APPLICATION BY TOWN ENGINEER

(i) Unless the Applicant shall request, in writing, that his application not be considered for an Administrative Permit, the Environmental Clerk upon receipt of an application prepared in accordance with Subsection A above, shall forward one copy of the application and supporting plans and documentations to the Town Engineer. The four additional copies shall stay in a central Wetlands file in the Environmental Clerk's office available for public review and inter-departmental referral.

(ii) The Town Engineer shall review the application and any supporting plans and documentation for the purpose of determining whether or not the application is eligible for treatment under the provisions of Section 89–6 (C) (Regulated Acts

Permitted with an Administrative Permit). If the Town Engineer requires additional information, plans or specifications in order to make such determination, he shall so notify the Applicant within fifteen (15) days after receipt of the application by the Town Engineer.

(iii) If the Town Engineer determines that the application is not eligible for treatment under the provisions of Section 89–6 (c) of this Chapter, or if the Town Engineer, in his discretion, elects not to process the application pursuant to the provisions of Section 89–6 (C) of this Chapter, he shall so notify the Applicant and the Environmental Clerk, in writing, return the application to the Environmental Clerk and the application shall be processed by the appropriate Approval Authority pursuant to the provisions of Section 89–9 and other provisions of this Chapter.

(iv) If the Town Engineer determines that the application is eligible for treatment under the provisions of Section 89–6 (C) of this Chapter and if the Town Engineer, in his discretion, elects to process the application pursuant to the provisions of Section 89–6 (C) of this Chapter he shall grant the application in accordance with the provisions of this Chapter, with the exception of Section 89–9.

89–9 Additional Permit Procedures (Wetlands Permit Only)

A. ADDITIONAL SUBMISSIONS

If the application is returned to the Environmental Clerk by the Town Engineer pursuant to the provisions of Section 89–8 (B) (iii) of this Chapter or if the Town Board reverses the decision of the Town Engineer granting an Administrative Permit pursuant to the provisions of Section 89–15 (A) (2) (c) of this Chapter or if, at the time of the initial application, the Applicant requests, in writing, that his application not be considered for treatment under the provisions of Section 89–6 (C) of this Chapter, the Applicant shall file with the Environmental Clerk, in addition to the information required pursuant to the provisions of Section 89–8 (A) of this Chapter, five copies of the following:

(1) Plans for the proposed regulated activities which shall be submitted drawn to a scale of not less than one inch equals fifty feet (unless otherwise specified by the Approval Authority) and prepared by a licensed engineer or landscape architect or other qualified professional. Plans shall show the following: (The Approval Authority may determine that less detailed plans are required.)

   (i) Location of construction or area proposed to be disturbed and its relation to property lines, buildings, roads and watercourses within two hundred fifty (250) feet.

   (ii) Estimated quantities of Material of excavation or fill.

   (iii) Location of any well and depth thereof and any sewage or wastewater disposal system within one hundred (100) feet of the area to be disturbed in the Wetland or Controlled Area.

   (iv) Existing and adjusted contours at two, five or ten foot intervals as determined by the Approval Authority in the proposed disturbed area and to a distance of one hundred (100) feet beyond.

   (v) Details of any drainage system proposed, both for the conduct of the work and after completion thereof, and measures proposed to control erosion and siltation both during and after the work.

   (vi) Where creation of a lake or pond is proposed, details of the construction of any dams, embankments and outlets or other water control devices.

   (vii) Other details as may be determined to be necessary by the Approval Authority. The Approval Authority shall notify the Applicant within 60 days of receipt if an application of such additional information is necessary.

(2) An additional application fee in the amount of Three Hundred Fifty ($350.00) Dollars.

B. REFERRAL OF APPLICATION

The Environmental Clerk upon receipt of the additional materials prepared in accordance with Subsection A above, shall forward one copy of the Application and supporting plans and documentations to the Conservation Board, one copy to the Town Engineer and two copies to the appropriate Approval Authority for such application. The fifth copy shall stay in a central wetlands file in the Environmental Clerk's Office available for public review. The Conservation Board shall review the application and shall file a written report with the Approval Authority with its recommendations concerning the application. Such report shall evaluate the proposed regulated activity in terms of the findings, intent and standards of this Chapter.

C. PUBLIC HEARING AND NOTICE

(1) No sooner than thirty (30) days and not later than sixty (60) days after receipt of a complete application by the Approval Authority, the Approval Authority shall hold a public hearing on such application, public notice of which shall be given at least ten (10) days prior to the date set for such hearing in a newspaper having general circulation in the Town. The Applicant shall provide prior notice of such hearing to Interested Parties pursuant to the provisions of Chapter 63 of the Town of Yorktown. All applications, maps and documents relating thereto shall be open for public inspection at the offices of the Approval Authority and Environmental Clerk. At such hearing any person or persons having an interest may appear and be heard.

(2) The provisions of Subsection (C) (1) above, notwithstanding, to the greatest extent practicable, such hearing shall be incorporated with any other public hearing conducted by the Approval Authority in connection with the activity for which approval is sought.

D. ACTION BY THE APPROVAL AUTHORITY

Unless an additional application is pending before the Approval Authority with regard to the proposed regulated activity (Subdivision, Site Plan, Special Permit), the Approval Authority shall, within seventy-five (75) days after receipt of the report of the Conservation Board, or within forty-five (45) days of the date of the closing of any public hearing held pursuant to Subsection (C) above, render a decision to approve, deny or approve with modifications the application. If additional applications are pending before the Approval Authority, the Approval Authority may render its decision at the same time as its decision on any additional application. The Approval Authority may extend the time limitations for decision rendering only when awaiting a wetland boundary or classification decision from the New York State Department of Environmental Conservation. A decision should be rendered no later than 45 days after the receipt by the Approval Authority of such requested information. The Approval Authority shall state upon the record findings and reasons for all approvals or denials taken.

89-10 Conditional Approval; Performance Bond; Insurance

A. In approving any application, the Approval Authority may impose such conditions or limitations as it determines necessary to insure compliance with the intent, purposes, standards and public policy of this Chapter.

B. The Approval Authority may require posting of a performance bond or collateral as a condition of approval, the amount and surety of such bond or collateral to be approved by the Town Board. Such bond is intended to insure the proper completion of the proposed activity in accordance with the approved plans, the restoration of the area to its natural condition as far as practicable and protection of adjoining property owners from damage resulting therefrom. It shall remain in effect until the Town Engineer certifies that the work has been completed in compliance with the terms of the permit and the bond is released by the Town Board or a substitute bond is provided and approved by the Town Board.

C. The Applicant may be required to certify that they have insurance against liability which might result from the proposed operation or use covering any and all damages which might occur in an amount to be determined by the Approval Authority commensurate with the projected operation.

89–11 Post-Decision Procedure

A. APPROVAL/CONDITIONAL APPROVAL

Following action by the Approval Authority to approve or approve with conditions any application, the written decision of the Approval Authority shall be filed in the office of the Environmental Clerk and a Wetland Permit form shall be issued by the Approval Authority to the Applicant as it was so decided and filed with the Environmental Clerk. Said Permit Form shall record:

(1) The assigned application number.
(2) Name and address of the Applicant.
(3) Name and address of property owner (if different from applicant).
(4) Address and tax map designation of property.
(5) Date of approving Authority's action on application.
(6) All conditions placed on the regulated activity.
(7) Date by which work is to be completed.
(8) Expiration date of permit.

B. DENIAL

Following action by the Approval Authority to deny an application, the written decision of the Approval Authority shall be filed in the office of the Environmental Clerk.

89–12 Expiration of Permit

(1) All permits, unless otherwise indicated, shall expire on completion of the acts specified and, unless otherwise indicated, shall be valid for a period of one (1) year. Upon good cause shown, the Approval Authority may extend the period of validity for an additional one (1) year period. Permits may be transferred to new legal owners of the affected property so long as the conditions and plans as approved remain unchanged. Notice of such transfer of permit must be filed with the Environmental Clerk within thirty (30) days of the transfer.

(2) The Approval Authority or the Town Engineer may suspend or revoke a permit in the form of a stop work order if it finds that the applicant has not complied with any of the conditions or limitations set forth in the Permit Form or has exceeded the scope of

the activity as set forth in the application. The Approval Authority may revoke the Permit if such Approval Authority finds and determines after a public hearing held in the manner provided for in this Chapter that the applicant has failed to comply with any of the terms and conditions set forth in the application and/or Permit.

89–13 Inspection

Work conducted under a Permit shall be open to inspection at any reasonable time, including weekends and holidays, by the Town Engineer, the Building Inspector or by members of the Town Board, Conservation Board, the Approval Authority or their designated representatives.

89–14 Other Permits

Conformance to this Chapter does not eliminate the necessity of any Applicant to obtain the approval or permits required by any other agencies prior to construction in accordance with the permit. Obtaining such approval or permits is the responsibility of the Applicant. No operations shall be initiated until such approvals or permits have been issued.

89–15 Appeal and Judicial Review

A. (1) Any person or agency aggrieved by the decision of the Town Engineer in granting an application for an Administrative Permit may take an appeal to the Town Board within twenty (20) days from the filing of said decision with the Environmental Clerk. Upon receipt of the Notice of Appeal, the Town Board shall refer a copy of the notice to the Town Engineer. The Town Engineer shall promptly file a copy of his file pertaining to the subject application with the Town Board. The Town Board shall set a time and date, not more than forty-five (45) days after receipt of the Notice of Appeal, when a hearing on the appeal shall be heard. At such hearing any interested person or agency, including, but not limited to, the appellant and the Town Engineer, may appear and give testimony.

(2) Within thirty (30) days after the close of the hearing the Town Board shall issue a decision providing for one of the following:
(a) Affirming the grant of the Administrative Permit; or
(b) Affirming, with modifications, the grant of the Administrative Permit; or
(c) Reversing the grant of the Administrative Permit and directing that the application shall be processed by the appropriate Approval Authority pursuant to the provisions of Section 89–9 and other provisions of this Chapter.

(3) The filing of a Notice of Appeal pursuant to the provisions of this Section 89–9 (A) shall automatically affect a stay in the decision of the Town Engineer to grant the Administrative Permit and such stay shall remain in effect until the appeal has been acted upon by the Town Board as provided for in paragraph (A) (2) above.

B. Any decision or order of the Approval Authority, except the Town Engineer, made pursuant to or within the scope of this Chapter may be appealed by any person aggrieved by such decision or order in accordance with the provisions of Article 78 of the New York State Civil Practice Law and Rules. Where permitted by law, such aggrieved person may appeal such decision or order of the Approval Authority to the Freshwater Wetlands Appeals Board pursuant to the provisions of Title 11 of Article 24 of the New York Environmental Conservation Law.

C.   In the event that the Court finds the action reviewed constitutes a taking without just compensation, and the land so regulated merits protection under this article, the court may, at the election of the Town Board, either (i) set aside the order or (ii) require the Town Board to proceed under the Eminent Domain Law to acquire the Wetlands or such less than fee rights therein as have been taken.

89–16 Penalties, Enforcement and Corrective Action

A. CRIMINAL SANCTIONS

Any Person found to have violated or disobeyed any provision of this Chapter, any order of the Approval Authority or any condition duly imposed by the Approval Authority in a Permit granted pursuant to this Chapter shall, for the first offense, be guilty of a violation punishable by a fine of not less than five hundred dollars ($500.00) nor more than one thousand dollars ($1,000.00). For each subsequent offense, such Person shall be guilty of a violation punishable by a fine of not less than one thousand dollars ($1,000.00) nor more than two thousand dollars ($2,000.00) and/ or a term of imprisonment of not more than fifteen (15) days. Each consecutive day of the violation may be considered a separate offense.

B. INJUNCTIVE RELIEF

In addition to any method of enforcement provided above, the Town of Yorktown is specifically empowered to seek injunctive relief restraining any violation or threatened violation of the provisions of this Chapter and/or compelling the restoration of the affected Wetland to its condition prior to the violation of the provisions of this Chapter.

89–17 Validity and Separability

If any clause, sentence, paragraph, section or part of this Chapter shall be adjudged by any court of competent jurisdiction to be invalid, such judgment shall not affect, impair or invalidate the remainder thereof but shall be confined in its operation to the clause, sentence, paragraph, section or part thereof directly involved in the controversy in which such judgment shall have been rendered.

89–18 Applicability

A. NEW PROJECTS

This Chapter shall be applicable to any proposed Regulated Activity for which no application to conduct such Regulated Activity has been filed with the appropriate department of the Town of Yorktown as of the effective date of this Chapter.

B. CURRENT PROJECTS

Those proposed Regulated Activities for which Applications have been so filed shall continue to be governed by the present Chapter 89 of the Code of the Town of Yorktown. Notwithstanding the above, if an applicant, or successor, fails to commence construction of a Regulated Activity within two years after obtaining final approval for such project, any Wetlands Permit obtained in connection with said project shall expire and the provisions of this Chapter shall be applied to the proposed Regulated Activity.

CHAPTER 3
Historic and Cultural Resources

THIS section includes two innovative regulatory approaches, both of which fuse traditional historic preservation authority with growth management and landscape protection provisions.

The first ordinance is the Historic and Cultural Conservation Overlay District ordinance enacted by Loudoun County, Virginia. This innovative ordinance is designed to conserve rural historic and cultural districts and village landscapes from the rapid residential subdivision development occurring throughout the county. The county's approach could be useful to jurisdictions attempting to integrate tra-ditional historic preservation objectives and efforts to protect the scenic characteristics of rural and village landscapes.

The second ordinance in this section is the Historic Preservation and Urban Design District ordinance enacted by Lubbock, Texas. This ordinance creates an urban design and historic preservation commission and vests it with both historic preservation and urban design responsibilities. This approach could be useful to cities attempting to integrate traditional historic preservation objectives and urban design objectives.

Loudon County, Virginia
Historic Site Districts/Historic and Cultural Conservation Districts

750.1 Designation and Intent

750.1.1 DESIGNATION

Historic districts may hereafter be created, in accordance with Section 15.1-503.2 of the Code of Virginia, as amended, which shall be designated as either Historic Site (HS) districts or as Historic and Cultural Conservation (HCC) districts.

Historic site district shall apply to landmarks, buildings or structures which meet the requirements for designation set out in the following sections. Historic and cultural conservation districting shall apply to areas, including rural areas, as opposed to specific landmarks, buildings or structures, which meet the requirements for designation set out in the following sections.

Historic Site Districts and Historic and Cultural Conservation Districts shall be created by amendment of the Zoning Ordinance as provided in Article 12.

750.1.2 INTENT

HS and HCC districts are intended to effect and accomplish the protection, enhancement and perpetuation of especially noteworthy examples or elements of the County's cultural, social, economic, religious, political or architectural history in order to:
A. Foster civic pride and preserve an appreciation for the historic values on which the County and the Nation were founded;
B. Maintain and improve property values;
C. Protect and enhance the County's attraction to tourists and visitors;
D. Provide for the education and general welfare of the people of the County; and
E. Otherwise accomplish the general purposes of this ordinance and the provisions of Chapter 11, Title 15.1, Code of Virginia of 1950, as amended.

750.2 Criteria for Designating Historic Site Districts and Historic and Cultural Conservation Districts

750.2.1 CRITERIA FOR DESIGNATING HISTORIC SITE DISTRICTS

The Board of Supervisors may create HS districts provided such districts meet one or more of the following criteria, as well as meet one or more of the purposes set forth in Section 750.1.2, above:

A. Such district contains a landmark, building or structure on the National Register of Historic Places or the Virginia Landmark Register, or

B. Such district meets one or more of the following local determination criteria:

   1. Is closely associated with one or more persons, events, activities, or institutions that have made a significant contribution to local, regional, or national history; or

   2. Contains buildings or structures whose exterior design or features exemplify the distinctive characteristics of an historic type, period or method of construction, or which represent the work of an acknowledged master; or

   3. Have yielded, or are likely to yield, information important to local, regional or national history.

750.2.2 CRITERIA FOR DESIGNATING HISTORIC AND CULTURAL CONSERVATION DISTRICTS

The Board of Supervisors may create HCC districts provided such districts meet the standards of Section 15.1-430(b), Code of Virginia (1950), as amended; meet one or more of the purposes set forth in Section 750.1.2, above; and meet one or more of the following criteria:

1. Is closely associated with one or more persons, events, activities, or institutions that have made a significant contribution to local, regional or national history; or

2. Contain buildings or structures whose exterior design or features exemplify the distinctive characteristics of one or more historic types, periods or methods of construction, or which represent the work of an acknowledged master or masters; or

3. Have yielded, or are likely to yield, information important to local, regional or national history; or

4. Possess an identifiable character representative of the architectural and cultural heritage of Loudoun County.

750.3 Boundaries of Historic Site Districts and Historic and Cultural Conservation Districts

750.3.1 BOUNDARIES OF HISTORIC SITE DISTRICTS

The boundaries of HS districts shall be drawn to include all lands which are adjacent to the landmark, building, or structure for which the historic site district was established and which are reasonably related to the essential historic character of said district.

750.3.2 BOUNDARIES OF HISTORIC AND CULTURAL CONSERVATION DISTRICTS

The boundaries of HCC districts shall be drawn to include all such land therein as meets the purposes of Section 750.1.2, above, and the criteria of Section 750.2.2, above.

750.4 Effect of Historic Designation on Existing Zoning Classifications and Regulations

Historic district designation, both HS and HCC, shall be an overlay zone and as such shall be in addition to existing zoning designations and the regulations appropriate thereto.

750.5 Application for Designation as Historic Site District or Historic and Cultural Conservation District

Application for historic site or historic and cultural conservation district designation shall be made by the owner, Board of Supervisors, Planning Commission or Historic District Review Committee on a form provided by the Zoning Administrator. No fee shall be required.

In addition to the above, the Planning Commission may initiate amending action to create an Historic Site district whenever there exists a national or state recognized historic landmark not encompassed by a Historic Site District designated on the zoning map.

The following information shall be required for consideration for Historic Site or Historic and Cultural Conservation district designation and shall be submitted with the application:

A. An inventory which lists each building or structure within the district which itself has historic merit or which contributes to the overall historic character of the district.
B. A graphic representation of the location of landmarks, sites, buildings or other structures of particular historic value as well as the boundaries of the total proposed area to be included within the designation.
C. A written statement documenting the particular historical attributes of the territory proposed to be designated.

750.6 Action by the Planning Commission

An application filed with the Zoning Administrator shall be advertised for public hearing as provided for in Article 12. The Planning Commission shall determine that the application either has apparent merit or does not have apparent merit in relation to the purposes set forth in Section 750.1, above, and the criteria set forth in Section 750.2, above. In either case the application shall be forwarded to the Board of Supervisors along with a statement of the findings of the Planning Commission relative to such purposes and criteria. If the application is approved by the Planning Commission, transmittal of said approval shall be accompanied by a map depicting the approved boundaries of said district, as well as a copy of the inventory of buildings and structures submitted with the application under Section 750.5 (A), which the Commission shall have reviewed and approved after any necessary additions, deletions, or changes. Before acting on any such application the Planning Commission may consider comments solicited from such local and state agencies as deemed appropriate, including the Historic District Review Committee, as established in accordance with Section 750.15, below.

750.7 Action by the Board of Supervisors

Upon receipt of a recommendation from the Planning Commission, the Board of Supervisors shall consider the application as provided for in Article 12, hereinafter, and approve or disapprove the application under the same standards as applied by the Planning Commission, above. If the application is approved by the Board of Supervisors, the Board shall also specifically approve the boundaries of said district, and the inventory of buildings and structures submitted under Section 750.5 (A) as may be amended by the Board of Supervisors.

750.7.1 MAINTENANCE OF INVENTORY OF BUILDINGS AND STRUCTURES

Following the creation of each Historic Site or Historic Cultural Conservation District, the Zoning Administrator shall maintain in his office the inventory of buildings and structures approved by the Board of Supervisors. Requests for any additions, deletions, or other changes to such inventory shall be made to the Zoning Administrator, and may only be made by him with the concurrence of the Historic District Review Committee.

750.7.2 RECORDATION OF RESOLUTIONS CREATING HISTORIC DISTRICT

Following the creation of each Historic Site or Historic and Cultural Conservation District, a copy of the resolution creating such district, and a boundary description of such district, shall be filed by the Zoning Administrator with the Clerk of the Circuit Court for Loudoun County.

750.8 Certificate of Appropriateness

In order to promote the general welfare through the preservation and protection of historic places and areas of historic interest in the County, no building or structure, including signs, shall be erected, reconstructed, substantially altered, moved or restored within a designated Historic Site or Historic and Cultural Conservation District unless and until an application for a Certificate of Appropriateness shall have been approved by the Historic District Review Committee, as provided below. Provided, however, that no Certificate of Appropriateness shall be required in cases of buildings primarily used or to be used for agricultural or horticultural purposes in which the requested change would not have a clear and substantial detrimental impact on the character of the district as determined by the Zoning Administrator. Provided further that no Certificate of Appropriateness shall be required in cases of ordinary repair or maintenance of any exterior feature which does not involve a significant change in design, material, or outer appearance thereof, as determined by the Zoning Administrator. Notwithstanding any other provision of this Ordinance, appeal from any determination made by the Zoning Administrator pursuant to this section shall be by petition to the Historic District Review Committee by any party directly aggrieved thereby.

750.9 Permit for Razing or Demolition

In order to promote the general welfare through the preservation and protection of historic places and areas of historic interest in the County, no building or structure within an historic district which is listed on the inventory of buildings and structures for such district maintained in the office of the Zoning Administrator, shall be razed or demolished without a permit being obtained from the Historic District Review Committee, except as otherwise provided in Section 750.13 or Section 750.14, below. Notwithstanding provisions of this section and Section 750.12, the Board of Supervisors may issue a permit to raze a structure upon recommendation of the Planning Commission at the time of establishment of a district.

750.10 Applications and Procedures—Certificate of Appropriateness, Permit for Razing or Demolition

Applications for Certificates of Appropriateness and Permits for Razing or Demolition shall be made to the Zoning Administrator on forms supplied by him.

The Zoning Administrator shall refer all applications to the Historic District Review Committee.

All actions taken in pursuance of the above requirements shall be preceded by at least one public meeting by the Committee, at which time any interested party, including the applicant or his representative, shall be heard.

All approvals or disapprovals by the Committee shall include a statement of the reasons for such approval or denial and the conditions to be met, where applicable, whereby the applicant could make his application acceptable to the Committee.

No reapplication for essentially the same purpose shall be reviewed by the Historic District Review Committee within one year of denial of any applications hereunder except in cases where the applicant purports to have brought himself into compliance with the conditions for approval set forth by the Committee in an earlier denial of said application.

750.11 Certificates of Appropriateness—Criteria

In passing upon applications for Certificates of Appropriateness the Historic District Review Committee shall not consider interior arrangement.

750.11.1 HISTORIC SITE (HS) DISTRICT

In reviewing an application in an HS District, the Committee shall base its decision on whether the proposals therein are architecturally compatible with the building, structure, or landmark in said district. In applying such standard, the Committee shall consider, among other factors:
A. Exterior architectural features, including all signs.
B. General design, scale and arrangement.
C. Texture and material.
D. The relationship of a, b, c, above, to other structures and features of the district.
E. The purposes for which the district was created.
F. The extent to which denial of a Certificate of Appropriateness would constitute a deprivation to the owner of a reasonable use of his property.
G. The extent to which the proposal adheres to the Historic District Guidelines adopted by the Board of Supervisors, which are incorporated herein by reference. Further, the Historic District Review Committee shall make findings stating the reason why an application conforms or fails to conform with those guidelines.

750.11.2 HISTORIC AND CULTURAL CONSERVATION (HCC DISTRICT)

In reviewing an application in an HCC District the Committee shall base its decision upon whether the proposals therein are compatible with the established architectural character of the district. In applying such standard the Committee shall consider, among other factors:
A. Exterior architectural features, including all signs.
B. General design, scale and arrangement.
C. Texture and material.
D. The relationship of a, b, c, above, to other structures and features of the district.
E. The purposes for which the district was created.
F. The relationship of the size, design and siting of any new or reconstructed structure to the landscape of the district.
G. The extent to which denial of a Certificate of Appropriateness would constitute a deprivation to the owner of a reasonable use of his property.

H. The extent to which the proposal adheres to the Historic District Guidelines adopted by the Board of Supervisors, which are incorporated herein by reference. Further, the Historic District Review Committee shall make findings stating the reason why an application conforms or fails to conform with those guidelines.

750.12 Rights to Raze or Demolish—Conditions and Procedures

The owner of a building or structure, the razing or demolition of which is subject to the provisions of this article, shall, as a matter of right, be entitled to raze or demolish such building or structure provided that:

A. He has applied to the Historic District Review Committee.

B. The owner has for a period of time set forth in the time schedule hereinafter contained and at a price reasonably related to its fair market value, made a bona fide offer to sell such building or structure and the land pertaining thereto to any person, firm, corporation, government, or agency thereof, or political subdivision or agency thereof, which gives reasonable assurance that it will preserve and restore the building or structure and the land pertaining thereto.

C. No bona fide contract, binding upon all parties thereto, shall have been executed for the sale of any such building or structure, and the land pertaining thereto, or the building or structure alone without the land pertaining thereto, prior to the expiration of the applicable time period as set forth in the time schedule below. Any appeal which may be taken to the Court, in accordance with Section 750.16 of this Ordinance shall not affect the right of the owner to make a bona fide offer to sell. Offers to sell shall be made within one year of the date of application to the Historic District Review Committee. The time schedule for offers to sell shall be as follows:

Property Valued At	Minimum Offer to Sell Period
$25,000	3 months
$25,000 – $40,000	4 months
$40,000 – $55,000	5 months
$55,000 – $75,000	6 months
$75,000 – $90,000	7 months
$90,000 or more	12 months

750.12.1 BONA FIDE OFFER TO SELL; PROCEDURES FOR FILING NOTICE OF OFFER AND QUESTIONING PRICE

Before making a bona fide offer to sell as provided for in this section, an owner shall first file a statement with the Historic District Review Committee. The statement shall identify the property, state the offering price, the date the offer of sale is to begin and name and address of the listing real estate agent, if any. The statement shall provide assurances that the building or structure shall be preserved. No time period set forth in the time schedule contained in Section 750.12 shall begin to run until said statement has been filed. Within five days of receipt of a statement, copies of the statement shall be delivered to the Historic District Review Committee.

750.12.2 QUESTION AS TO PRICE

The fact that a building or structure has been offered for sale at a price reasonably related to fair market value may be questioned, provided there is filed with the Historic District Review Committee, on or before 15 days after the offer of sale has begun, a petition in writing signed by at least five persons owning real estate in the vicinity of property offered for sale. Alternatively the Committee may question said price on their own motion. Upon receipt of such petition, or upon its own motion, the Committee shall, at the expense of the County, appoint three disinterested real estate appraisers, familiar with property values in Loudoun County, who shall forthwith make an appraisal of the building or structure in question and file a written report with the Committee stating whether or not the offer to sell the building or structure is at a price reasonably related to its fair market value. The opinion of any two of the three appraisers shall be final and binding. In the event the opinion is to the effect that the offer to sell the building or structure is at a price reasonably related to its fair market value, the owner may continue to offer the property for sale pursuant to Section 750.12. In the event the opinion is to the effect that the offer to sell the building or structure is not at a price reasonably related to its fair market value, the date of the offer to sell first established pursuant to Section 750.12 shall be void and the owner, if he wishes to take advantage of the right provided in said section, must refile the notice provided for above. Notwithstanding an adverse opinion by the appraisers if an owner has entered into a binding bona fide contract as provided in Section 750.12 prior to the date the appraisers have filed their report with the Board, the price shall be deemed reasonably related to the fair market value.

750.13 Right to Raze or Demolish

The right to raze or demolish a building, structure or landmark within an historic district shall not be subject to the foregoing conditions of offer to sell where the applicant for a Permit to Raze or Demolish can establish either:

A. The loss of such building, structure or landmark would not substantially impair the goals sought to be achieved by the establishment of such district, or

B. The forced sale of such building, structure or landmark would be economically infeasible in relation to its effect on the remaining property of the applicant. Such a claim shall be heard by the Historic District Review Committee, upon the petition of the owner of the property. Such hearing shall be public and any interested party shall be heard.

750.14 Hazardous Buildings or Structures

Nothing in this article shall prevent the razing or demolition without consideration of said Committee, of any building or structure within an historic district which is in such an unsafe condition that it would endanger life or property as determined in accordance with the provisions of the Virginia Uniform Statewide Building Code (Section 124 of the BOCA Basic Building Code, 1975, as amended).

750.15 Historic District Review Committee

For the purposes of Section 750 of this Ordinance, the Board of Supervisors shall Appoint an Historic District Review Committee. The Committee shall be composed of five members. Where possible, the membership shall include, but not necessarily be limited to, the following: an architect with experience dealing with historic structures, an architectural historian, an owner of property listed on either the state or national register of historic landmarks or an owner of property within an Historic Site District, and an owner of property within an Historic and Cultural Conservation District. The members of the Committee shall serve a two year term or until their successors are appointed. The Committee shall meet on a regular basis as their workload requires and shall adopt such operating procedures as they deem appropriate in keeping with the requirements of law, including a procedure for maintaining records of their proceedings. All decisions of the Committee shall be by majority vote of those present and voting and no action shall be effective unless those present and voting constitute at least a quorum of the members of the Committee.

750.16 Right of Appeal

Any applicant aggrieved, or other party economically injured, by any final decision of the Historic District Review Committee may appeal such decision to the Board of Supervisors. The Board of Supervisors shall render its final decision on such appeal after consultation with the Historic District Review Committee. Any applicant aggrieved, or other party economically injured, by any final decision of the Board of Supervisors may appeal to the Circuit Court for the County of Loudoun, in accordance with Section 15.1-503.2 of the Code of Virginia of 1950, as amended. The filing of a petition of appeal with the Circuit Court shall stay the decision of the Board pending the outcome of the appeal to the Court, except that the filing of such petition shall not stay the decision of the Board if such decision denies the right to raze or demolish a historic landmark, building or structure.

Lubbock, Texas
Historical Preservation and Urban Design District

Sec. 29–25. (a) *Purpose.* The purpose of this district is to provide means by which citizens can initiate action to preserve archeological, historical, cultural, architectural and landscape architectural landmarks as part of the heritage of this city. This district provides all standards, rules, regulations and other administrative procedures necessary for its implementation as part of this section.

(b) *Definitions.*

(1) *Building official.* The building official shall be the building inspection administrator of the City of Lubbock.

(2) *Exterior architectural feature.* The style, design, general arrangement, and components of all the outside surfaces of a structure which characterize the landmark or district.

(3) *Historic landmark.* Any building, structure, site, area, or land or architectural, landscape architectural, historical, archeological or cultural importance or value, as may be designated for preservation by the City Council.

(4) *Historic landmark district.* That area within the boundaries of a historic landmark plus such lands, structures, and landscape architectural features adjacent thereto as may be designated by the City Council as being necessarily regulated for the preservation and utilization of that landmark.

(5) *Landscape architectural feature.* The general arrangement of the grounds, within a historic landmark district, including but not limited to the topographic grade, water pooling and runoff, types and sites of plant materials, types and sites of surface materials such as decorative bark, rock, stone, gravel, concrete, asphalt, brick, and the types and sites of constructions not otherwise deemed to be structured per se, such as fences, retaining walls, decks and other miscellaneous fixtures.

(c) *Declaration of policy.* The City Council hereby finds and declares as a matter of public policy that the protection, enhancement, preservation and use of historic landmarks and historic landmark districts to be a public necessity and required in the interest of the culture, prosperity, education and general welfare of the people. The purposes of this chapter [section] are:

(1) To protect, enhance and perpetuate historic landmarks which represent or reflect distinctive and important elements of the city's and state's architectural, landscape architectural, archeological, cultural, social, economic, ethnic and political history, and to develop appropriate settings for such places.

(2) To safeguard the city's historic and cultural heritage, as embodied and reflected in such historic landmarks by appropriate regulations.

(3) To stabilize and improve property values in such locations.

(4) To foster civic pride in the beauty and accomplishments of the past.

(5) To protect and enhance the city's attractions to tourists and visitors and provide incidental support and stimulus to business and industry.

(6) To strengthen the economy of the city.

(7) To promote the use of historic landmarks and historic landmark districts for the culture, prosperity, education, and general welfare of the people of the city and visitors to the city.

(d) *Designation of historic landmarks and historic landmark districts.*

(1) The City Council may designate buildings, structures, sites, areas, and land in the city as historic landmarks and define, amend and delineate the boundaries thereof. The territory within such boundaries shall also be a historic landmark district, and when necessary for the preservation or utilization of the historic landmark, the City Council may extend the historic landmark district into adjoining lands by defining, amending and delineating new boundaries therefor without having to amend the boundaries of the historic landmark.

(2) The "Design-historic" zoning designation, as indicated by the suffix "DH," shall apply to all historic landmark districts in addition to their other zoning designations. The "Design-historic" zoning designation shall be indicated on the official zoning maps through the use of a map overlay, which is identified in the map legend. Said zoning designation shall indicate conditions placed on said property by the City Council.

(3) The zoning ordinance in which any building or structure is designated as a historic landmark shall incorporate by reference (a) photographs, (b) drawings, (c) renderings, (d) written standards, or any combination thereof which illustrate the exterior architectural features to be maintained, regulated and preserved.

(4) The zoning ordinance, in which any territory is designated as a historic landmark district, shall incorporate by reference (a) photographs, (b) drawings, (c) renderings, (d) written standards, or any combination thereof which illustrate any architectural feature of nonlandmark buildings or structures or landscape architectural feature to be maintained, regulated and preserved. Said photographs, drawings or renderings shall also illustrate the location of any buildings or structures within a historic landmark district, but which are not designated as historic landmarks, or landscape architectural features, and shall include notations for each such building or structure identifying its size, use, and location. The minimum number of standards, necessary to achieve the objectives of landmarks and districts, shall be required.

(5) In the event that any standard established for any "DH" district conflicts with any previously established zoning standards, the "DH" district standards shall be controlling.

(e) *Criteria for historic landmark designation.* In making historic landmark designations as set forth in section 22A.3 [29-25(d)], the City Council shall consider, but shall not be limited to, one or more of the following criteria:

(1) Character, interest or value as part of the development, heritage or cultural characteristics of the City of Lubbock, State of Texas, or the United States.

(2) Recognition as a Recorded Texas Historic Landmark, a National Historic Landmark, or entry into the National Register of Historic Places.

(3) Embodiment of distinguishing characteristics of an architectural type or style.

(4) Identification as the work of an architect, landscape architect, or master builder whose individual work has influenced the development of the city.

(5) Embodiment of elements of design, detail, materials or craftsmanship which represent a significant architectural or landscape architectural innovation.

(6) Relationship to other distinctive buildings, sites or areas which are eligible for preservation based on architectural, landscape architectural, historic or cultural motif.

(7) Portrayal of the environment of a group of people in an area of history characterized by a distinctive architectural or landscape architectural style.

(8) Archeological value in that it has produced or can be expected to produce data affecting theories of historic or prehistoric interest.

(9) Exemplification of the cultural, economic, social, ethnic or historical heritage of the city, state, or the United States.
(10) Location as the site of a significant historic event.
(11) Identification with a person or persons who significantly contributed to the culture and development of the city, state or the United States.
(12) A building, structure, or landscape development that because of its location has become of value to a neighborhood, community area, or the city.
(13) Value as an aspect of community sentiment or public pride.

(f) *Urban design and historic preservation commission created.*

(1) There is hereby created a commission to be known as the urban design and historic preservation commission of the City of Lubbock, hereinafter called the "urban design commission," composed of eleven (11) members appointed by the City Council within ninety (90) days from the effective date of this amendment. This commission shall include at least one representative for each of the following:

   a. Architecture;
   b. Urban planning;
   c. History or political science;
   d. Archeology or paleontology;
   e. Sociology or anthropology;
   f. Building construction;
   g. Landscape architecture.

Each of the seven (7) representatives shall possess special interest, knowledge or expertise in the field which he or she represents on the commission, but does not have to practice in that field as a profession. The fact that one or more representatives from the seven (7) fields of expertise may not at any given point in time be a member of the commission, for whatever reason or reasons, or is absent when a vote is taken by a quorum of the commissioners, shall not affect the validity of any decision or act of the commission.

(2) The other members of the urban design commission shall be appointed from such other individuals and organizations as the City Council may in its discretion wish to consult or consider. All members shall have knowledge and experience in the architectural, landscape architectural, archeological, cultural, social, economic, ethnic or political history of Lubbock. No one business or professional interest shall constitute a majority membership of the commission.

(3) Three (3) of the original representatives from the seven (7) fields of expertise shall serve for one year, two (2) shall serve for two (2) years, and the remaining two (2) shall serve for three (3) years. Thereafter they shall each serve for a term of three (3) years. All other members of the urban design commission and subsequent members from these fields of expertise shall serve a term of two (2) years. Vacancies in an unexpired term shall be filed by the City Council for the remainder of the term.

(4) Any appointed voting member of the urban design commission who fails to attend three (3) consecutive regular meetings of the urban design commission or fails to attend at least eighty (80) percent of all such regular meetings during any six-month period shall lose membership on the commission, unless such failure to attend was the result of illness. Verification of attendance shall be based exclusively on the minutes of each meeting as filed with the city secretary. The vacancy shall be filled by the City Council pursuant to section 22A.5-3 [29-25(f)(3)].

(5) In addition to the eleven (11) members appointed by the City Council, the following persons or their designates [designees] shall sit on the urban design commission as ex officio members:

   a. The director of planning for the City of Lubbock;
   b. The building inspection administrator for the City of Lubbock;
   c. The zoning administrator for the City of Lubbock.

(6) The following persons or their designates [designees] shall be asked to sit on the urban design commission as ex officio members:

    a. The chairperson of the Lubbock County Historical Commission;
    b. The chairperson of the West Texas Museum Association;
    c. The chairperson of the Lubbock Historic Society;
    d. The chairperson of the Lubbock Historic Foundation;
    e. The president of the Lubbock Board of Realtors;
    f. The president of the Lubbock Chamber of Commerce;
    g. The chairperson of the Lubbock Association of Mortgage-Lending Institutions;
    h. The president of the Lubbock Chapter of the A.I.A.;
    i. The judge of the County Commissioner's Court of Lubbock County;
    j. The president or chairperson of the Ranching Heritage Center.

(7) The City Council may draw on the knowledge, experience and expertise of any person or entity by appointing such person or entity to the urban design commission as a special advisor.

(g) *Urban design commission; administration.*

(1) The urban design commission shall meet at least once each month, if there are agenda items, with additional meetings upon call by the chairperson or upon petition of a simple majority of the commissioners.

(2) None of the ex officio members or special advisors shall have any voting power, authority to call a meeting by petition pursuant to section 22A.6-1 [29-25(g)(1)], or serve to make a quorum. Ex officio members and special advisors shall serve to assist the commission in its other various functions.

(3) The commission shall adopt appropriate rules and regulations for the conduct of its business and the election of its chairperson and other officers.

(4) Minutes shall be taken for each meeting and filed with the city secretary's office. Each meeting shall also be tape recorded and said recording shall be incorporated by reference into the official minutes. The absence or inaudibility of any recording, however, shall not serve to invalidate any meeting or the minutes of any meeting.

(5) Six (6) commissioners present shall constitute a quorum, and all issues shall be decided by a simple majority vote of the members present. Any members voting on recommendations may submit, either individually or collectively, written opinions to the planning and zoning commission or City Council whenever such member or members feel that the voted motion does not adequately represent their expert opinion on the matter under consideration.

(h) *Urban design commission plans review.* The urban design commission shall thoroughly familiarize itself with buildings, structures, sites, districts, areas and lands within the city which may be eligible for designation as historic landmarks and historic landmark districts. Included in this review shall be the historic site survey, architectural survey, and urban image analysis in the comprehensive plan of the City of Lubbock. These shall be updated as needed.

(i) *Action by the urban design commission.*

(1) Any citizen or citizen's group may request the urban design commission to recommend to the planning and zoning commission ordinances designating certain buildings, structures, sites, districts, areas and lands in the city as historic landmarks and historic landmark districts. The urban design commission shall hold a public hearing on all proposed ordinances.

(2) The urban design commission shall render a decision on the request within ninety (90) days after the request is made. In the event the urban design commission fails to render a decision within the prescribed time limitation, such failure shall be deemed a decision to not recommend [that] the property be designated as a historic landmark or historic landmark district, in which case said property shall not be reconsidered upon request originating from the urban design commission, for

recommendation as a historic landmark or historic landmark district, for at least one year, in the absence of an alteration of material conditions affecting the case.

(3) If the urban design commission finds that buildings, structures, sites, districts, lands or areas recommended for designation as historic landmarks or historic landmark districts cannot be preserved without acquisition, the commission shall recommend to the City Council that the fee or a lesser interest of the property in question be acquired by gift, devise, purchase, eminent domain or otherwise, pursuant to the charter, and state and federal law.

(4) Where there are conditions under which the required preservation of a historic landmark or historic landmark district would cause undue hardship on the owner or owners, district changes may be recommended by the urban design commission to the planning and zoning commission.

(5) The designation of a historic landmark or historic landmark district may be amended or removed using the same procedure provided in this article for the original designation.

(6) A notice of said zoning shall be placed by the secretary of the planning and zoning commission in the deed records of Lubbock County for each property designated as a historic landmark or historic landmark district.

(j) *Alterations and changes; certificates of appropriateness; ordinary repair or maintenance; appeal.*

(1) Landscape architecture, buildings, and other structures as landmarks. No person or entity shall construct, reconstruct, alter, change, restore, remove or demolish any exterior architectural feature or landscape architectural feature of a designated historic landmark unless application be made to the urban design commission for a certificate of appropriateness, and such a certificate be granted.

(2) [Blank].

a. *Nonlandmark landscape architectural feature in historic landmark district.* No person or entity shall construct, reconstruct, alter, change, restore, remove or demolish any nonlandmark landscape architectural feature as may be designated by the City Council for preservation in a designated historic landmark district unless application be made to the urban design commission for a certificate of appropriateness, and such certificate be granted. The normal maintenance of plant material through mowing, trimming, pruning, weeding and thinning shall be permitted, but shall not include the total elimination, either literally or effectively, of such plant material.

b. *Nonlandmark buildings and other structures in historic landmark district.* No person or entity shall construct, reconstruct, alter or change any exterior feature of a nonhistoric landmark building or structure that may be located in a designated historic landmark district, unless application be made to the urban design commission, for a certificate of appropriateness and such a certificate be granted; excluded from regulation in this paragraph shall be the total demolition and removal of a nonhistoric landmark structure that may be located in a designated historic landmark district.

(3) *Public improvements.* The urban design commission shall recommend to the City Council acceptable architectural, landscape architectural and engineering design, for public street and street easement use, including street lighting, street furniture, signs, landscapes, utility facilities such as electric poles and wires, telephone lines, design textures of sidewalks and streets, such as brick, stone and tile, and such other elements as deemed necessary for enhancement and preservation of the district, before such elements are altered or installed. All city departments and public utilities shall work closely with the urban design commission in the integration of such designs by submitting plans of proposed alterations before any such work occurs.

(4) Procedure when building permit is required.

    a. When applying for a building permit for the exterior of a designated historic landmark, or nonhistoric landmark in a historical district, the applicant shall submit two (2) copies of all detailed plans, elevations, perspectives, specifications, photographs, renderings and other documents pertaining to the work to the building official, who shall forward such application to the urban design commission chairperson within five (5) days of receipt thereof. Any applicant may appear at a regular or special meeting of the urban design commission before submitting an application, and may consult with said commission during the review of the permit application.

    b. The urban design commission, upon ten (10) days written notice to the applicant, shall hold a hearing on the application. Upon review of the application, if the urban design commission finds that proposed work is of a nature which will not adversely affect any designated exterior architectural, historic or landscape architectural feature of the designated historic landmark or historic landmark district, and is appropriate and consistent with the spirit and purposes of this article, as submitted or with noted conditions, it shall notify the building official and forward a certificate of appropriateness to the applicant within ten (10) days after the public hearing.

    c. If the urban design commission finds that the proposed work will adversely affect or destroy any significant exterior architectural feature or landscape architectural feature of any historic landmark or historic landmark district, or is inappropriate or inconsistent with the spirit and purposes of this article, it shall notify the building official that the application has been disapproved and shall, within ten (10) days of the public hearing, notify the applicant in writing of the disapproval. Suggested changes in the application shall accompany the notice of disapproval.

    d. If no action has been taken by the urban design commission within sixty (60) days of original receipt by the urban design commission, a certificate of appropriateness shall be deemed issued by the urban design commission, and the building official shall so advise the applicant.

    e. No change shall be made in the application for any building permit after issuance of a certificate of appropriateness without resubmittal to the urban design commission and approval thereof in the same manner as provided above.

    f. After a decision is reached by the urban design commission denying an application for a certificate of appropriateness, a resubmittal of application will not be accepted for additional hearing within a twelve-month period from the date of final decision, except upon written request by the applicant indicating that there has been a change in conditions or that all changes in the application as recommended by the urban design commission have been met.

(5) Procedure when building permit is not required.

    a. Those proposed exterior changes and alterations not requiring a building permit shall be submitted in writing directly to the urban design commission for a certificate of appropriateness, which must be received before such work can be undertaken. Applicants shall submit a copy of all proposed alterations and changes to the commission. The application must describe the alteration or change proposed. Any applicant may appear at a regular or special meeting of the urban design commission before submitting an application, and may consult with said commission during the review of the application.

    b. The urban design commission, upon ten (10) days written notice to the applicant, shall hold a hearing on the application. Upon review of the application, if the urban design commission finds the proposed work of a nature which will not adversely affect any significant exterior architectural, historical or landscape architectural feature of a designated historic landmark or historic landmark district, and is appropriate and consistent with the spirit and purposes of this article, it shall forward a certificate of appropriateness to the applicant within ten (10) days of the hearing of said application.

    c. If the commission finds that the proposed work will adversely affect or destroy any exterior architectural or landscape architectural feature of the designated historic landmark or historic landmark district, or is inappropriate or inconsistent with the spirit and purposes of this article, the secretary shall notify the applicant in writing within ten (10) days of the hearing of said application that the application has been disapproved, and shall include in such notification the changes necessary for approval of the application.

    d. If no action has been taken by the urban design commission with [within] sixty (60) days of the receipt of the application, a certificate of appropriateness shall be deemed issued by the urban design commission.

    e. No change shall be made in the application for issuance of a certificate of appropriateness without resubmittal to the urban design commission and approval thereof in the same manner as provided above.

    f. After a decision is reached by the urban design commission denying an application for certificate of appropriateness, a resubmittal of an application will not be accepted for additional hearing within a twelve (12) month period from the date of final decision, except upon written request by the applicant indicating that there has been a change in conditions, or that all changes in the application as recommended by the urban design commission have been made.

(6) *Ordinary repair or maintenance.* Ordinary repair or maintenance which does not involve changes in architectural, landscape architectural or historical value, style or general design is exempt from the provisions of this section.

(7) *Appeal.* Any applicant or interested person aggrieved by a ruling of the urban design commission under the provisions of sections 22A.8 [29-25(i)] or 22A.9 [29-25(j)] may, within thirty (30) days after the ruling, appeal in writing to the City Council, via the planning and zoning commission which shall, after hearing thereon, forward its recommendation with the appeal to the City Council.

(k) *Historic landmarks; demolition or removal.*

(1) If an application is received for demolition or removal of a designated historic landmark, the building official shall immediately forward the application to the urban design commission. The urban design commission shall hold a public hearing on the application within thirty (30) days after the application is initially filed with the building official. The applicant shall be given ten (10) days written notice of the hearing. The urban design commission shall consider the state of repair of the historic landmark, the reasonableness of the cost of restoration or repair, the existing or potential usefulness, including economic usefulness, the purposes behind preserving the historic landmark, the character of the neighborhood, and all other factors it finds appropriate. If the urban design commission determines that in the interest of preserving historical values, and preserving an economically viable building or site, the historic landmark should not be demolished or removed, the secretary shall notify the building official that the application has been disapproved, and the building official shall so advise the applicant within ten (10) days therefrom.

If the urban design commission determines that the interest of preserving historical values will not be adversely affected by such demolition or removal, or that the interest of preserving historical values can best be served by the removal of a structure to another specified location, it shall issue its certificate of demolition or its certificate of removal, as may be appropriate, to the building official; and the building official shall so advise the applicant within ten (10) days therefrom.

In the event a historic landmark must be demolished and it is not the sole historic landmark in that historic landmark district, said site shall remain a part of that historic landmark district, but shall lose its historic landmark designation.

(2) If no action has been taken by the urban design commission within sixty (60) days of original receipt by the urban design commission of the application, a certificate of demolition or a certificate of removal shall be deemed issued by the urban design commission, and the building official shall so advise the applicant.

(3) After a decision is reached by the urban design commission denying an application for a certificate of demolition or a certificate of removal, a resubmittal of application for such a certificate will not be accepted for additional hearing within a twelve-month period from the date of final decision.

(4) Any person who is aggrieved by a ruling of the urban design commission concerning [an] historic landmark or historic landmark district under the provisions of [this] section may, within sixty (60) days after the ruling of the urban design commission, appeal to the City Council via the planning and zoning commission, which shall, after hearing thereon, forward its recommendation with the appeal to the City Council. Following a public hearing to be held within thirty (30) days of the filing of a notice of such appeal with the city secretary, the City Council may uphold or overturn any ruling of the urban design commission made pursuant to this section.

(l) *Procedure for obtaining building permit, removal permit, demolition permit and for altering the exterior of a building or structure, or altering a landscape architectural feature, during pendency of consideration of such building or structure as a historic landmark or as a part of a historic landmark district.*

(1) Subject to the following conditions, a moratorium shall be enforced during which time no person or entity with or without a building permit, shall construct, reconstruct, alter, change, restore, remove or demolish any exterior architectural feature of any certain building, structure or site or any certain landscape architectural feature. This moratorium shall be in effect whenever:

   a. The date on which the chairperson, vice-chairperson or executive secretary of the urban design commission by written order directs that said building, structure or site within the city be placed upon the agenda for any meeting of the urban design commission, or any committee thereof, for the purpose of considering or discussing whether or not the same should be designated as a historic landmark or historic landmark district; or

   b. The date whenever such item be placed on such agenda for such purpose, if dated; or

   c. If not dated, the date such agenda is posted in accordance with the provisions of V.A.C.S. article 6263-17, as amended.

   This moratorium shall continue in force and effect until the earliest of the following conditions are met:

   d. A final and binding certificate of appropriateness, removal or demolition, as may be appropriate, has been issued by the urban design commission;

   e. The urban design commission fails to recommend that some part or all of any such property be designated a historic landmark or be included within a historic landmark district within sixty (60) days following the earliest of the above described dates activating this section applicable under the circumstances; or,

   f. A final and binding decision has been made by the City Council that no part of any such property shall be designated a historic landmark or shall be included within any designated historic landmark district.

(2) It shall be the duty of the urban design commission and its officers to furnish the building official with a copy or written notice of each such written order or such agenda as promptly after the preparation thereof as is practicable. The failure to so furnish the building official with a copy or written notice thereof, however, shall not have the effect of validating any building permit, removal permit or demolition permit issued in ignorance of any such written order or agenda. In any instance in which any such permit may not be required, it shall be the duty of the urban design commission and its officers to give notice of any such written order or such agenda or such preservation plan or amendment thereof to the owner or owners of any

property included within the scope thereof, which notice shall be deemed complete when actually given, orally or in writing, to such owner or owners, or when written notice thereof is deposited in the United State[s] mail, postage prepaid, certified, with return receipt requested, addressed to such owner or owners, whichever event first occurs. No person or entity to whom any such permit is issued or who, if no such permit is required, commences to construct, reconstruct, alter, change, restore, remove, or demolish any exterior architectural feature of any such building or structure or of any such landscape architectural feature without actual or constructive notice of any such written order or such agenda or such preservation plan or amendment thereof, as the case may be, as required by the provisions of this subsection, may be found guilty of a misdemeanor as in this ordinance [chapter] provided; but each such person or entity shall be amenable to the civil sanctions provided in this [section].

(3) Any permit issued to any person or entity from or after the date of any such written order or such agenda shall be null, void and of no force or effect until the earliest of the events described in subparagraphs 22A.11-1-4, 22A.11-1-5, and 22A.11-1-6 of subsection 22A.11-1 [sections 29-25(l)(1)(d)—29.25(l)(1)(f)] occurs.

(m) *Historic landmarks; omission of necessary repairs.*

(1) A designated historic landmark shall be maintained to insure the structural soundness of such landmark.

(2) If the housing standards administrator or the urban design commission, or both, find there are reasonable grounds to believe that any structure which is a designated historic landmark is structurally unsound or in imminent danger of becoming structurally unsound, the housing standards administrator shall notify in writing the owner of record of the designated historic landmark of such fact, and shall otherwise proceed to enforce the minimum housing code of the City of Lubbock.

CHAPTER 4

Aesthetic Resources

THIS chapter includes several exemplary ordinances that establish various regulatory programs addressing aesthetic concerns.

Sign control ordinances from Lake Wales, Florida, and Lubbock, Texas, are included. The Lake Wales ordinance is especially useful for a small city or town looking for an uncomplicated but effective approach to sign regulation. This ordinance incorporates many of the concepts explained in Daniel R. Mandelker and William R. Ewald, *Street Graphics and the Law*, available from the American Planning Association.

The Lubbock, Texas, sign ordinance was enacted as part of a municipal beautification program, and requires individual review of proposed signs to ensure that signs are consistent with citywide sign standards. The ordinance also prohibits billboards from most sections of the city and establishes a six-and-one-half-year amortization period for nonconforming signs.

Two scenic highway district ordinances are included: from Charleston County, South Carolina, and Austin, Texas. The Charleston County program designates corridors in which outdoor advertising is prohibited, views of open landscapes must be protected, and vegetative buffers must be preserved.

Austin has enacted special restrictions for roadside land along designated scenic roadways. Land use restrictions depending upon the character of the roadway limit or prohibit signs, development density, heights, site design, landscaping, and road access.

A proven regulatory innovation enacted by Denver, Colorado, to protect scenic views—and applicable to smaller communities—has been included. The Denver ordinance protects views of the state capitol and views from designated parks of the mountain ranges west of the city by imposing building heights in a series of overlay zones that are designed to protect distinctive views.

Finally, the highly regarded appearance code enacted by Libertyville, Illinois, has been included. The Libertyville design code outlines a method used by communities to regulate the exterior design features of commercial, industrial, and multifamily development without excessively subjective decision-making criteria.

Lake Wales, Florida
Sign Ordinance

Sec. 3–1. Statement of Purpose

The objective of this chapter is to establish requirements which promote convenience, safety, property values and aesthetics while granting equal protection and fairness to all property owners.

(a) *Convenience.* The chapter is designed to encourage signs which help to visually organize the activities of the city, lend order and meaning to business identification and make it easier for the public and business delivery systems to locate and identify their destinations.

(b) *Safety.* The requirements with regard to placement, installation, maintenance, size and location of signs act to minimize unnecessary distractions to motorists, protect pedestrians and provide safe working conditions for those persons who are required to install, maintain, repair and remove the signs and their structures.

(c) *Property values and aesthetics.* An offensive sign is as detrimental to property values as an offensive odor or sound. Sight, sound and odor influence the value of property in the neighborhood and community. The city has the obligation to promote the general welfare. This includes enhancement of property values by enacting and enforcing ordinances which create a more attractive business climate and make Lake Wales a more desirable city in which to visit, trade, work, and live.

(d) *Equal protection and fairness.* The chapter is designed to be fair to each property owner in that each receives equal and adequate exposure to the public and no one is allowed to visually dominate his neighbor.

Sec. 3–2. Introduction to Chapter

The chapter is designed to be simple so that the average property owner will not require professional advice to understand and apply the provisions. At the same time, the chapter encourages the use of sophisticated signing which is permitted in complex and involved legislation existing in other communities. The chapter attempts to accomplish its objectives in a simple fashion by using three (3) approaches:

(a) *Basic rights and responsibilities.* These appear in the provisions which grant all property owners the right to have an adequate sign free of any discretion which may be imposed on the property owner by the community appearance board.

(b) *Community appearance board.* It is the intent of the chapter to encourage creative, unique and effective signs which are appropriate and symbolic of the business located on the premises. In the event such a sign conflicts with a provision of the chapter, the owner is encouraged to apply to the community appearance board for a special permit allowing the use of the sign. The applicant has the burden of showing that the sign contains aesthetic qualities which are an improvement over ordinary and typical signing practices and will enhance the aesthetics and property values of the neighborhood and community. In making its decision, the community appearance board will be guided by the principles expressed in Ewald, "Street Graphics," published by the American Society of Landscape Architects Foundation and, "Sign Sense: Arlington, Massachusetts," published by Vision, Inc., 2 Hubbard Park, Cambridge, Massachusetts.

Ground-mounted sign. Any sign which is supported by an upright, uprights, or braces in or upon the ground.

(c) *Recommended practices.* Occasionally, the chapter will, in addition to the basic rights and responsibilities, set forth recommended practices. These practices represent the preference of the city with regard to signs but do not carry the force of law. Amendments, including but not limited to the recommended practices, may be adopted by the city in the future as law. The recommended practices constitute notice to the public that a sign conflicting with a recommended practice runs the risk of being a nonconforming sign in the future.

Sec. 3–3. Definitions

Abandoned sign. A sign which no longer serves to advertise a bona fide business conducted, service performed or product sold.

Billboard. An off-premises sign usually placed on a free-standing structure which directs attention to a business, commodity, service, entertainment or attraction sold, offered or existing elsewhere than upon the same lot where such sign is displayed and includes signs which are made available to national and local advertisers for commercial, political and social messages. Since section 3–4(h) prohibits both off-premises and on-premises billboards, it is the intent of this definition to clearly distinguish between billboards and on-site business signs, which are allowed elsewhere in the chapter. On-site business signs advertise business, goods or services available on the property where the signs are located. They consist of either wall-mounted signs which are integrated within the normal lines of the building, or ground-mounted signs the size of which are determined by the speed of the traffic and the size of the road faced by the sign, the largest of which does not exceed one hundred eight (108) square feet.

Ground-mounted sign. Any sign which is supported by an upright, uprights, or braces in or upon the ground.

Recommended practice: The area at the foot of the ground-mounted sign should be landscaped and properly maintained. At minimum, the area should be mowed, free of weeds and should not present a fire hazard.

Nonconforming sign. A sign not in compliance with this chapter and which has not received a special permit pursuant to section 3–2(b) or extension of time pursuant to section 3–11.

Owner, or property owner. The owner of property, the tenant, agent, or person having the beneficial use of the building, structure, or property upon which a sign may be located.

Permanent window sign. Any sign mounted on or inside of a window for permanent display to the public passersby outside the window.

Portable sign. Any sign, whether on its own trailer, wheels or otherwise, which is designed to be transported from one place to another.

Right-angle sign. Any sign which is affixed to any building wall or structure and extends more than twelve (12) inches horizontally from the building wall.

Roofline. On a sloping roof, the roofline is the principal ridge line, or the highest line common to one or more principal slopes of the roof. On a flat roof, the roofline is the highest continuous line of the roof or parapet, whichever is higher.

Sign. Any letter, number, symbol, figure, character, mark, plane, design, pictorial, stroke, stripe, trademark or combination of these which shall be so constructed, placed, attached, painted, erected, fastened or manufactured in any manner whatsoever, so that the same shall be used for the attraction of the public to any place, subject, person, firm, corporation, public performance, article, machine or merchandise, whatsoever, which are displaced in any manner whatsoever, which can be seen from the right-of-way of a public street or highway including permanent window signs placed inside windows but intended to attract attention of those outside in the public right-of-way.

Sign area. The entire area within a continuous perimeter, and a single plane, composed of a square, circle or rectangle which encloses the extreme limits of the advertising message or announcement or wording together with any frame, background, trim or other integral part of the display excluding the necessary supports or uprights on which such sign is placed. The owner may not increase the allowed total area, but may use more than one square, circle or rectangle in order to calculate the area. Sign area of a ground-mounted sign is the entire area of one side of such sign so that two (2) sides which are back to back are counted only once.

Signable area of a building. A rectangular area on the facade of a building which is free of windows and doors or major architectural detail. Any portion of a roof less than twenty (20) feet from the ground is included. Illustrations of signable areas are on file with the city and should be consulted before applying for the required sign permit.

Wall-mounted sign. Signage mounted parallel to the face of the building and projecting not more than twelve (12) inches from the building wall. The area of individual letters, figures or signs shall be the area of the simple geometric form (rectangle, square, etc.) necessary to enclose same. (Ord. No. 78-5, § 2, 3-21-78; Ord. No. 80-9, § 2, 5-20-80; Ord. No. 82-4A, §§ 1, 2, 8-17-82)

Sec. 3–4. General Requirements

Unless otherwise provided in the chapter, the following requirements apply to all signs in the city:

(a) Permit required. To obtain city review and avoid expensive mistakes, all signs shall be required to have a permit indicating compliance with this chapter. No sign, except temporary window signs allowed by section 3–9 and real estate signs allowed by section 3–10, shall be constructed, altered or extended until such permit has been issued. Temporary permits may be issued for special events as provided by section 3–9 (f).

(b) Street address numbers are assigned by the city and are required for all buildings. The numbers shall be at least three (3) inches high and visible from the public thoroughfare. In the event a building does not contain such number within six (6) months from the effective date of this chapter, the post office will be requested to refuse delivery of mail.

(c) No sign shall be above the roofline.

(d) No sign, except those placed by an authorized governmental agency, shall be placed on the public right-of-way.

(e) No portable signs.

(f) No sign shall be designed with flashing lights or moving parts.

(g) No sign shall interfere with traffic or be confused with or obstruct the view or effectiveness of any official traffic sign, traffic signal, traffic marking or obstruct the sight distance of motorists or pedestrians.

(h) No sign shall be attached to a tree or utility pole. Billboards, whether off-premises or on-premises, are prohibited.

(i) The provisions of the chapter apply to on-premises signs only. Off-premises signs, except those specifically allowed by section 3–10 (d), are prohibited.

(j) Wind signs, including banners, pennants, spinners, streamers, and other wind actuated components, except pennants allowed by section 3–9 (g), are prohibited.

(k) This chapter shall not apply to vending machines, gasoline pumps, telephone booths, newspaper racks, "take-out" or "pick-up" windows and menus posted for reading in drive-in restaurant parking lots.
Recommended practice: Newspaper racks, vending machines and any facility dispensing merchandise or a service should be confined within a space which is part of or adjacent to a building so as to be an aesthetic asset to the building and the neighborhood.

(l) This chapter shall not apply to traffic-control signs, parking place designations and information signs located on off-street parking lots.
Recommended practice: Direction signs should be kept at a minimum in favor of direction markings on pavement.

(m) This chapter does not regulate the content of the message of the sign.
Recommended practice: A sign should identify the business rather than advertise its products. Product name or trade names should not be permitted within a sign unless the trade name is part of the occupant's name or the product identified constitutes over twenty-five (25) per cent of the total business done on the premises.

(n) Readerboards or price signs with removable copy may be allowed, providing the readerboard is included in the allowed sign area, does not constitute more than one-third ($1/3$) of the allowed sign area of any one side of the sign and is architecturally integrated into the sign.

(o) All signs must be legible, well painted, in good repair, properly maintained and sturdy enough to permit those persons working on the signs to do so in safety.
Recommended practice: Construction, installation, maintenance and repair of sign should be by a licensed sign maker only.

(p) Abandoned signs are prohibited. Removal may be by the owner or by the city pursuant to section 3–12. In making a determination as to abandonment, the enforcing official may consider, among other factors, the existence or absence of a current occupational license, utilities service deposit at that location, use of the premises and relocation of a business.
Recommended practice: All signs should be removable so as to minimize potential expense to the owner.

(q) Delivery signs. A sign identifying the business on the back wall of a building in a delivery area is allowed, provided the sign area does not exceed ten (10) square feet.

(r) Signs containing any statement, word, character or illustration of an obscene, indecent or immoral nature are prohibited.

(s) Lighted signs. White and yellow are the only colors of lights permitted for signs in areas classified residential or professional, except for Christmas or seasonal lighting. Colored lights are permitted in commercial and industrial areas provided they cannot be confused with traffic lights. Floodlights may not shine onto adjoining property or in the eyes of motorists or pedestrians.

(t) Community, civic and fraternal organizations sponsoring public service events shall be allowed a reasonable number of temporary signs designed to inform the public of such events.

(u) All signs not specifically allowed are prohibited.

Sec. 3–5. Area Classifications

Except for individually described land parcels designated as areas of special control by action of the city commission, all land parcels in the following zoning categories are classified as follows:

(a) *Commercial.* All land zoned C-1, C-2, C-3, C-4, and commercial uses within a C-2-R-3 zone are classified commercial.

(b) *Industrial.* All land zoned I-1, I-2, CIS-1, and CIS-2 is classified industrial.

(c) *Professional.* All land zoned P-1, P-2, and MSR-1 is classified professional.

(d) *Residential.* All land zoned R-1A, R-1B, R-1C, R-2, R-3 and the residential uses within a C-2-R-3 zone and a MSR-1 zone is classified residential.

Sec. 3–6. Residential Signs

Home-based occupations may have a sign not to exceed three (3) square feet, which shall be mounted flat against the residence.

Sec. 3–7. Professional Signs

(a) Each professional office is entitled to one sign per firm, not to exceed ten (10) square feet in area or ten (10) feet in height.

(b) In the event more than one firm occupies a building, then the building is entitled to one directory sign containing the names of the occupants. The dimensions of the directory sign shall be the same as the signs for the individual firm, except that the directory sign shall not exceed twenty (20) square feet.

Sec. 3–8. Industrial Signs

(a) *Wall-mounted sign.* Each business is entitled to signage on the front wall of its building or on any side wall which faces a public street or platted lot not containing another building. The sign on the front wall may occupy thirty (30) per cent of the signable area. A sign on a side wall shall be the same size as the sign on the front wall or thirty (30) per cent of the signable area of the side wall, whichever is less.

(b) *Ground-mounted sign.* If the nearest edge of a building wall is set back from the edge of the adjacent street by thirty-five (35) feet or more and the property otherwise complies with landscaping and off-street parking requirements, a business may also have a ground-mounted sign. The maximum allowable area for each of two faces (1) and height (2) depend on driving lanes and the controlling speed limit and are as follows:

Speed limit	2 Lanes	4 Lanes
35 mph or less	(1) 42 sq. ft. (2) 20 ft.	(1) 64 sq. ft. (2) 24 ft.
More than 35 mph	(1) 64 sq. ft. (2) 24 ft.	(1) 108 sq. ft. (2) 26 ft.

Spacing. Ground-mounted signs may be displayed only on a frontage of one hundred (100) feet or more and may not be closer than one hundred (100) feet to any other ground-mounted sign.

Sec. 3–9. Commercial Signs

(a) *Wall-mounted sign.* Each business is entitled to signage on the front wall of its building and on any side wall which faces a public street or platted lot not containing another building. The area on the front wall may occupy forty (40) per cent of the signable area. The area on a side wall may be the same size as the sign on the front wall or forty (40) percent of the signable area of the side wall, whichever is less.

Recommended practice: Instead of a grouping of separate signs within the allowed signable area, one sign painted or attached to a removable surface should be utilized. The wall-mounted sign on a side wall should not exceed fifty (50) per cent of the maximum possible area of the wall-mounted sign on the front wall.

(b) *Ground-mounted sign.* If the nearest edge of a building wall is set back from the edge of the adjacent street by thirty-five (35) feet or more and the property otherwise complies with landscaping and off-street parking requirements, a business may also have a ground-mounted sign. The maximum allowable area for each of two faces (1) and height (2) depend on driving lanes and the controlling speed limit and are as follows:

Speed limit	2 Lanes	4 Lanes
35 mph or less	(1) 42 sq. ft. (2) 20 ft.	(1) 64 sq. ft. (2) 24 ft.
More than 35 mph	(1) 64 sq. ft. (2) 24 ft.	(1) 108 sq. ft. (2) 26 ft.

Spacing. Ground-mounted signs may be displayed only on a frontage of seventy-five (75) feet or more and may not be closer than seventy-five (75) feet to any other ground-mounted sign.

(c) *Right-angle sign.* A business located on a street with a speed limit of no more than thirty-five (35) miles per hour and a public sidewalk may display one right-angle sign for each street faced. The sign must also:

(1) Clear the sidewalk by at least eight (8) feet and project no more than five (5) feet from the building or one half (½) the width of the sidewalk, whichever is less;
(2) Project from the wall at an angle of ninety (90) degrees;
(3) Not be higher than the windowsill of the second story;
(4) Not project at the corner of the building except at a building front;
(5) Not be displayed closer than thirty (30) feet from any other right angle sign; and
(6) Not be used if the business has a ground-mounted sign on the same frontage.

Recommended practice: Right-angle signs should be mounted away from the wall at least six (6) inches.

(d) *Pedestrian signs.* If any part of the building overhangs a public sidewalk, a business shall be entitled to an additional sign to be hung from the overhang which shall not be lower than eight (8) feet from the sidewalk.

(e) *Permanent window signs.* Permanent window signs may not occupy more than twenty-five (25) per cent of the total area of the window in which they are displayed. This area will be subtracted from the signable area of the wall-mounted sign on the same frontage.

(f) *Temporary window signs.* Temporary window signs may be displayed in addition to all other signs and should occupy no more than fifteen (15) per cent of the total area of the window in which they are displayed. A special permit is required if over fifteen (15) per cent of window area is used. A permit may not be issued for longer than sixty (60) days, and more than one permit shall not be issued in any given six-month period.

(g) Used car lots are allowed one string of pennants for each street faced.

(h) Ground-mounted signs for shopping centers and time and temperature signs must be approved by the community appearance board.

Sec. 3–10. Signs Allowed without Regard to Area Classification

These signs are utilized for activities which occur in all areas of the city.

Recommended practice: An owner should consider the character of the neighborhood so that the sign will be compatible with its surroundings. A sign adequate for commercial and industrial areas should be smaller when used in residential or professional areas.

Temporary signs for the sale or development of property.

(1) *Subdivision development sign.* These signs are permitted to identify subdivisions where an active building and development program is underway. Such signs shall be nonilluminated wall or ground-mounted and shall be permitted on a temporary basis for a maximum period of two (2) years or when seventy-five (75) per cent of the lots of the subdivision have been conveyed or after residences have been erected at seventy-five (75) per cent of the lots, whichever is the shorter time period.

   These signs shall not exceed thirty-two (32) square feet in area or exceed ten (10) feet in overall height and shall not be closer than fifteen (15) feet to any side property line. Where the subdivision abuts more than one street, additional signs must receive the approval of the community appearance board.

(2) *On-site development sign.* Those identifying the developer, architect, contractor, realtor, etc., on property where a building is actively under construction. Such signs shall be permitted on a temporary basis and shall not be erected more than sixty (60) days prior to the beginning of actual construction and shall be removed when construction is completed. One nonilluminated wall or ground-mounted sign not exceeding twenty (20) square feet in area or ten (10) feet in overall height may be erected no closer than fifteen (15) feet to any side property line.

(3) *Real estate signs.* Those signs indicating the owner's desire to sell or rent his property, either personally or through an agent. No sign permitted by this section shall be closer than fifteen (15) feet to any side property line. The sign shall be removed after the property has been sold and title has passed, or after an agreement to rent the property has been achieved.

   a. For sale of residences, there shall be permitted one on-site nonilluminated wall or ground-mounted sign not exceeding six (6) square feet in area and six (6) feet in height.

   b. For sale of acreage and commercial properties, one on-site nonilluminated wall or ground-mounted sign not exceeding twelve (12) square feet in area and not more than four (4) feet in overall height shall be permitted.

(b) *Apartments, condominiums and mobile home parks.* These signs may not advertise and can only identify the development and indicate availability of apartments or mobile home sites. One wall or ground-mounted sign not exceeding thirty-two (32) square feet in area or ten (10) feet in overall height may be erected for each street faced.

(c) *Church signs.* One wall or ground-mounted sign not exceeding ten (10) feet in overall height may be utilized per street faced. Sign area may not exceed fifty-four (54) square feet when facing a street with a speed limit of thirty-five miles per hour or less and may not exceed seventy-two (72) square feet when facing a street with a speed limit exceeding thirty-five (35) miles per hour.

(d) *Off premises signs.*

   (1) *Motels and restaurants.* The city recognizes that many motels and restaurants within the city limits have been deprived of exposure to traffic because of the relocation of two (2) major highways, thereby justifying an exemption to the city's prohibition against off-premises signs. Each motel or restaurant is allowed no more than three (3) off-premises signs not to exceed twenty (20) square feet in area or twelve (12) feet in height. These signs may not advertise and can only identify the motel or restaurant and provide directions as to its location.

   (2) *Directional signs.* Directional signs for visitor attractions, points of interest, churches, governmental services and other destinations which the city and other governmental agencies deemed to be of assistance to the motoring public shall be installed on the public right-of-way by such governmental agencies as

part of their traffic control responsibility. Such signs shall not be part of this chapter.

(3) *Reserved.*

(e) *Election signs.* Signs advocating a political candidate or other ballot issues are permitted; without the necessity of obtaining a permit, under the following restrictions:

(1) There shall be no more than one on-site nonilluminated wall or ground mounted sign not exceeding six (6) square feet in area and six (6) feet in height.

(2) The sign shall not be placed on the site more than thirty (30) days prior to the election in issue and shall be removed within five (5) days after the election in issue.

(3) No election sign shall be placed upon road right-of-way or upon any other location which may cause an obstruction of clear traffic visibility.

Sec. 3–11. Maintenance and Removal of Nonconforming Signs ⎯⎯⎯⎯⎯⎯

(a) Nonconforming signs shall maintain the same appearance and safe conditions as required by this chapter and the city's building code for conforming signs. Nonconforming signs that become damaged from any cause, and the cost to repair exceeds twenty-five (25) per cent of what it would cost the owner to conform with this chapter, the sign will lose its privilege to remain nonconforming and it shall be removed or made to conform within ninety (90) days.

(b) Alterations and modifications shall be permitted providing that the degree of nonconformity is not increased or the sign area increased. Changes in the name of the business or a change in the nature or character of the business shall cause the sign to lose its privilege to remain nonconforming and it shall be removed or made to conform within ninety (90) days.

(c) All nonconforming signs must be removed, changed, or altered to conform to the provisions of this chapter according to the following schedule:

(1) Portable signs representing no removal cost, and signs which have been placed on public property without permit, upon effective date of this chapter.

(2) Off-premises signs, April 15, 1980.

(3) On-premises signs, April 15, 1988.

(d) Extensions of time for removal may be granted by the community appearance board. The granting of extensions is discouraged. In considering extensions, the community appearance board shall balance the public gain against the private loss. In striking this balance, the board may consider relevant factors including original cost, date of installation, degree to which the sign is incompatible, remaining useful life, extent to which the sign has been depreciated for tax purposes, amount of unrecoverable cost involved, beneficial effect on the community of the eventual elimination of all nonconforming signs and the statement of purpose set forth at the beginning of this chapter.

Sec. 3–12. Enforcement; Rights and Duties of Enforcing Official ⎯⎯⎯⎯⎯⎯

The city manager or his designated agent shall be the enforcing official. The enforcing official is authorized and directed to lawfully enter all premises at reasonable times to determine whether a sign complies with the provisions of this chapter. If a violation exists, the enforcing official shall send written notice to the occupant and owner shown on the most recent tax roll and to the holder of the certificate of occupancy if different from both the occupant or owner. Service of the notice shall be deemed complete if mailed to the owner at the address appearing on the most recent tax roll. If this chapter is not complied within a reasonable time specified in the notice, the enforcing official is authorized to remove the sign at the owner's expense, utilize the provisions of section 1–8 of this Code and to revoke the certificate of occupancy for the premises.

Charleston County, South Carolina
Scenic Highway Districts

Authorization of Scenic Highway Districts —————————————————

SEC. 25.10.10. GENERALLY

The Planning Board and/or County Council may recommend and the County Council may adopt amendments to the zoning map and to the text of this ordinance establishing Scenic Highway Districts, after the conditions set forth in Sec. 25.10.40 have been met. Recommendation and adoption of such amendment shall be in accordance with Article 97.40.

A scenic highway zoning district, if approved, shall be superimposed over the existing zoning district classification(s) assigned to the area. All uses normally permitted for the existing zoning category as prescribed by this ordinance shall be permitted with the exception of the limitations prescribed in Article 97.40.

SEC. 25.10.20. PURPOSE OF A SCENIC HIGHWAY ZONING DISTRICT

The basic purpose of the Scenic Highway District is to conserve and enhance the natural beauty adjacent to and along our County highways in conjunction with the existing zoning classification(s). The program is established to prevent unsightly developments which may tend to mar or detract from the natural beauty and to exercise such reasonable control over the land within the restricted areas as may be necessary to accomplish this objective.

Secondly, a purpose of the scenic district is to eliminate, as much as possible, undue harshness to the eye and general chaos that could develop along the roadways in Charleston County and to insure a pleasant view free from clutter and/or visual blight.

Third, to protect and perpetuate our heritage.

SEC. 97.40.50. COUNTY PLANNING BOARD STUDY

1. The Planning Board shall review that application for a Scenic Highway zoning classification in the same manner as presented herein for other amendments to this ordinance.

2. The Planning Board shall determine a map designation for the district consisting of a designation of the district and a serial number, so that each district shall be individually identified.

SEC. 97.40.60. CRITERIA FOR SCENIC HIGHWAY ZONING DISTRICT

In addition to the regular criteria prescribed for a given zoning district by these or other lawful laws or regulations, the following basic criteria shall be imposed upon any district selected for a Scenic Highway classification, permitted uses stipulated elsewhere in these regulations notwithstanding.

1. The designated area shall be maintained free of outdoor advertising signs and authorized accessory signs may not be freestanding until a uniform design shall have been approved under Sec. 97.40.40.
2. Dumps established for the disposal or storage of fill, gravel, pipe, ashes, trash, rubbish, sawdust, garbage, offal, or any unsightly or offensive material shall not be permitted.
3. Salvage yards, used car lots, mobile home sales, or any other activity not visually attractive shall not be permitted.
4. Trees, six inches in diameter or over, or shrubs will not be destroyed, cut or removed except when cutting is necessary for the maintenance or enhancement of beautification of the district as defined under Sec. 97.40.40. The intention is to preserve the natural beauty of wooded areas as far as is reasonably possible.
5. General farming, including the addition or expansion of farm buildings, is normally permitted and encouraged. However, fur farming or farms operated for the disposal of garbage or related materials are prohibited.
6. New residential, commercial, and industrial uses shall be carefully planned in order to retain an open land appearance and present desirable views from becoming obstructed.
7. Nonconforming uses and structures shall be governed by Article 30.50.

SEC. 97.40.70. ACTIVITIES NOT NORMALLY PERMITTED WITHIN A SCENIC HIGHWAY DISTRICT

The following categories will not normally be permitted in a Scenic Highway District; however, with natural screening (trees, shrubs, etc.), they may be permitted by obtaining a Conditional Use Permit in accordance with Article 96.40:

2, 3.	Manufacturing Facilities
481.	Electric Generating Plants, Utility Substations, Transformer Banks, Overhead Transmission lines, and Above Ground Pipe Lines.
484.	Sewage Disposal
485.	Solid Waste Disposal
621.	Laundering, Dry Cleaning and Dyeing Plants
6241.	Crematories
815, 816.	Stockyards
6831.	Vocational and Trade Schools
7223.	Race tracks, or Courses for Autos, Motorcycles, Motorbikes, Horses, etc.
7312.	Amusement Parks
821.	Agricultural Processing
85.	Mining, including Burrow Pits

SEC. 97.40.75. REPORT TO COUNTY COUNCIL

The period within which the Planning Board's report shall be submitted to County Council will be 90 days from date application was submitted.

SEC. 97.40.80. ACTION BY COUNTY COUNCIL

1. The Scenic Highway zoning districts application to County Council shall consist of plans, agreements, inventories (trees) and other pertinent documents submitted with the application.

2. The County Council shall review the Scenic Highway District amendment in the same manner as provided for other amendments to this ordinance.

Austin, Texas
Hill Country Roadway Corridor Regulations

5180 Hill Country Roadway Corridors _____

5185 Title and Purposes _____

Sections 5180 through 5199 shall be known as the Hill Country Roadway Corridors regulations and are designed to achieve the following purposes:
a. To maintain the rugged natural beauty of the eastern edge of the Texas Hill Country as currently exists along Hill Country Roadways;
b. To encourage development which is compatible with and, wherever possible, enhances such natural beauty;
c. To allow people of the City of Austin to be able to live, work, and enjoy recreation within the area without reducing its natural beauty;
d. To encourage safe and efficient traffic flow along Hill Country Roadways;
e. To preserve the environment by providing clean air, clean water, and greenbelts of natural vegetation and wildlife;
f. To preserve the scenic character of the Hill Country Roadway Corridors and, where possible, scenic vistas from the roadways;
g. To encourage only orderly and sensitive development as appropriate in the City's environmentally-sensitive watersheds; and,
h. To accomplish the foregoing goals through thoughtful and cooperative planning in order to benefit all the people of Austin.

5186 Application _____

a. Unless otherwise provided by this Section, in a Hill Country Roadway Corridor, notwithstanding the zoning classification, no tract shall be developed and no building shall be erected or structurally altered in violation of this section. The provisions of this Section shall apply in addition to other ordinance requirements. In case of conflict therewith, the most restrictive provisions shall govern except as otherwise expressly provided in this Section.
b. The site plan submitted pursuant to this Section may, at the option of the applicant, include land not located within the Hill Country Roadway Corridor.

5187 Site Plan Required

No zoning change shall be approved and no structure shall be erected unless a site plan as approved for in this Section and in Section 5100 (Principal Roadway Area) has been approved by the City Council after recommendation of the Planning Commission. Site plans submitted under the provisions of this Section shall comply with all requirements set out by other provisions of this Code as well as the following:

a. The location of all improvements on the site plan shall be specific and no alteration or movement of proposed improvements in excess of twenty-five feet (25′) shall be permitted without the approval of the City Council.

b. The site plan shall include a tree survey. A construction line shall be delineated on each site plan submitted for City approval. This limit line shall include all building, parking, and vehicular use areas, and all areas of required cut and fill. Within this area, the requirements of Section 5189 (Landscaping) shall be shown. Outside this limit line, no tree survey shall be required and the project developer shall be required to leave undisturbed all areas of native vegetation including trees, shrubs, and understory vegetation to a reasonable and feasible extent.

c. The site plan shall illustrate the location of all trash receptacles, air conditioning and heating equipment, loading areas, parking areas, lighting and an indication of the methods to be used to screen all such areas from all public views. If air conditioning, heating units, penthouses, parapet walls, or water storage reservoirs for fire safety must be located on roofs of structures, they shall be screened from view, both horizontally and vertically.

d. The site plan shall illustrate the height calculation as provided for in Section 5188 by showing the cross sections required to demonstrate that each building complies with height limitations.

e. For projects requesting performance incentives for scenic vista protection as per Section 5192, the site plan shall illustrate the location and nature of any existing or potential scenic vistas from or in close proximity to public roadways or recreation areas, and shall show how such vistas would be impacted by the proposed development. For the purposes of this ordinance, a scenic vista shall be defined as a generally recognizable, noteworthy view of Lake Travis, Lake Austin, the valleys of the Colorado River, Barton Creek, Bull Creek, and West Bull Creek, or the downtown area of Austin. Protection of scenic vistas may be demonstrated through use of:

1. Photographs of all existing scenic vistas at the site.
2. Schematic plans and sections showing clearly the impact development will have on scenic vistas.
3. Elevations or perspective sketches showing the proposed development from the adjacent roadway.

The Office of Land Development Services shall develop a map indicating segments of Hill Country Roadways along which scenic vistas are prevalent.

5188 Site Development Regulations

All land and buildings within a Hill Country Roadway Corridor shall, unless otherwise specified, comply with all requirements of Section 5100 (Principal Roadway Areas) as well as the following: (861106-J)

a. <u>Intensity Zones.</u> Floor-to-Area Ratios and height shall be determined relative to low, moderate, and high intensity zones indicated below, consistent with the applicable comprehensive plan.

1. High Intensity—All land within one thousand feet (1000′) of the right-of-way of two intersecting State-maintained roadways, and with frontage on both highways or on one highway and an intersecting arterial or collector roadway, as well as all land along Loop 360 within three thousand five hundred feet (3500′) from its intersection with U.S. 290.

2. Moderate Intensity—All land not included in the High Intensity designation and with frontage on:
   (a) Loop 360 (excluding RR 2244–RR 2222 except as per (b)).
   (b) Loop 360 (1200 feet north and south of Westlake Drive).
   (c) RR 2222 (FM 620—2.1 miles east of RM 620).
   (d) FM 620 (Comanche Trail—Anderson Mill Road and Lohman's Crossing—Steward Road).
   (e) A Hill Country Roadway and an intersecting arterial or collector street, limited to land within five hundred feet (500′) of the right-of-way of the intersecting street, but excluding intersections along RM 2222 east of Loop 360.
   (f) A Low Intensity roadway segment where the sole access to such a tract is from an arterial or collector roadway other than the Hill Country roadway.

3. Low Intensity—All land not included in the Moderate or High Intensity designation.

b. <u>Nonresidential Floor to Area Ratio.</u> All nonresidential buildings shall be limited to a maximum Floor-to-Area Ratio computed by reference to slope gradients and intensity level as follows:

Slope Gradient of Land	Intensity Level		
	Low	Moderate	High
0–15%	.20	.25	.30
15–25%	.08	.10	.12
25–35%	.04	.05	.06

"Floor-to-Area Ratio" shall be defined as the ratio of gross floor area (exclusive of parking structures and atriums) to site area within the appropriate slope class within the Hill Country Roadway Corridor. For purposes of calculating allowable floor area and impervious cover (where applicable), the gross site area shall exclude additional dedicated right-of-way only to a maximum of sixty feet (60′) from the centerline of a Hill Country Roadway. In no event shall the Floor-to-Area Ratio on the 0-15% slopes exceed the following maximums including any additional credits added by Section 5192:

Intensity Level		
Low	Moderate	High
.25	.30	.35

Hill Country Floor-to-Area Ratio provisions shall not apply to Southwest Parkway. (861106-J)

c. <u>Construction on Steep Slopes.</u> No roadways or driveways shall be constructed on slopes in excess of fifteen percent (15%), except where necessary to provide access to areas of flatter slopes. Cuts and fills on roadways or driveways are to be restored as described herein. No building or parking areas shall be constructed on slopes in excess of fifteen percent (15%), provided, however, that buildings and parking structures may be located on slopes of 15%–25% when the following criteria are met:

1. Structures located upslope of slopes over fifteen percent (15%) area shall be constructed utilizing pier and beam techniques. Fill shall be placed to blend with the natural contour. No vertical walls shall extend beyond the lowest finished floor elevation, other than necessary to screen mechanical appurtenances, and shall be stepped, if appropriate. Terraced fill and walls shall be 1 to 1 grade limited to four feet (4') in height for each terrace. More than one level of terrace is permitted.

2. Structures located downslope of slopes over fifteen percent (15%) are encouraged to be terraced and consolidated into the hillside. Structural excavation shall not exceed a maximum of eight feet (8') in depth. Areas of cut not hidden from view shall be effectively screened by additional landscaping.

3. Hillside vegetation shall not be disturbed other than that necessary to locate the structure. All disturbed areas shall be restored with native vegetation as per Section 5189.

4. If terraces are not provided, cuts and fill are to be restored to 3 to 1 slopes and with vegetation. Naturally restored slopes are limited to eight feet (8') in length. Terraces are to be installed in between the slopes if more than a single eight foot (8') slope is required.

d. Height.

1. For all Hill Country Roadway Corridors, unless otherwise specified, the height of buildings shall be limited but the permitted height may increase as the distance from the right-of-way increases. Within two hundred feet (200') of the right-of-way of a Hill Country Roadway, no building shall exceed twenty-eight feet (28'). Beyond two hundred feet (200') from the right-of-way of a Hill Country Roadway, height may increase but shall not be permitted to exceed twenty-eight feet (28') in Low Intensity areas, forty feet (40') in Moderate Intensity areas, or fifty-three feet (53') in High Intensity areas, except as provided in Section 5192.

2. For the Southwest Parkway Corridor, height shall be limited to that permitted by the zoning or site plan approved by the City for the property; however, in no case shall a building exceed sixty feet (60') in height. (861106-J)

e. Underground Utilities. All on-site utilities shall be located underground unless required by the utility to be otherwise located.

f. Building Materials. Buildings shall be designed to utilize, to the greatest extent feasible, building materials such as rock, stone, brick, and wood, which are compatible with the Hill Country environment. No mirrored glass with a reflectance greater than twenty percent (20%) shall be permitted.

5189 Landscape Requirements

a. Tree Removal. For each tree removed with a trunk greater in diameter than six inches (6"), measured at a point four and one-half feet above ground level, or for each cluster of three (3) or more trees located within ten feet (10') of each other with trunk diameters greater than two inches (2"), of live oak, Spanish oak, cedar elm, shin oak, bald cypress, post oak, pecan, bur oak, or black walnut, and for small native trees such as Texas madrone, black cherry, Texas mountain laurel, evergreen sumac, Mexican buckeye, flameleaf sumac, or Texas persimmon, the developer must compensate by planting a sufficient amount of native species mentioned above within disturbed areas that will reasonably compensate for the loss of existing trees.

b. Highway Vegetative Buffer.

1. For all Hill Country Roadway Corridors, unless otherwise specified, except for clearing necessary to provide utilities and access to the site, no clearing of vegetation shall be permitted within one hundred feet (100') of the dedicated

right-of-way of a Hill Country Roadway; provided, however, that in no case shall such vegetative buffer exceed twenty percent (20%) of the acreage of the applicant's property. In cases where the buffer area has previously been substantially disturbed, it shall be revegetated with native trees, shrubs, and grasses and up to fifty percent (50%) of the buffer may be utilized for detention/sedimentation ponds and wastewater drain fields, subject to such restoration. (861106-J)

2. For the Southwest Parkway Corridor, except for clearing necessary to provide utilities and access to the site, no clearing shall be permitted within fifty feet (50') of the dedicated right-of-way or dedicated drainage easement of Southwest Parkway. Minimum required building setback shall be seventy-five feet (75') from the right-of-way or dedicated easement; however, in no case shall such vegetative buffer or building setback exceed twenty percent (20%) of the acreage of the applicant's property. In cases where the buffer area has previously been substantially disturbed, it shall be revegetated with native trees, shrubs, and grasses and up to fifty percent (50%) of the buffer may be utilized for detention/sedimentation ponds and wastewater drainfields, subject to such restoration. (870115-I)

   The City Council may, after a public hearing, waive the requirements of this paragraph 2 for properties where the dedicated right-of-way or dedicated drainage easement of Southwest Parkway has been granted to the public at no cost. (870115-I)

c. <u>Natural Area</u>. At least forty percent (40%) of the site, excluding dedicated right-of-way, shall be left in a natural state, except for sites on the Southwest Parkway, where this provision shall apply to forty percent (40%) of that part of the site which is within the Hill Country Corridor. Priority shall be given to protection of natural critical areas identified in the City's Comprehensive Plan in meeting this requirement. Natural areas located within parking medians and the required Highway Vegetative buffer may count toward such forty percent (40%) requirement. In the event that the natural area requirement conflicts with the requirements of another applicable ordinance, such conflict shall be resolved with the minimum departure from the terms hereof and approved by the City Council after recommendation of the Planning Commission. Up to twenty-five percent (25%) of the area required to be kept in a natural state may be used for sewage disposal fields; provided that such areas are appropriately revegetated. (861106-J)

d. <u>Landscaped Screening</u>. All parking areas and detention-sedimentation ponds shall use existing vegetation or installed landscaping to screen pavement, vehicles, and ponds from the roadway and from adjacent properties. This screening shall include dense massing of trees in addition to existing native understory vegetation or shrubs massing or berms. Topographic changes shall be considered in reviewing this provision. A median of not less than ten feet (10') in width containing existing native trees or dense massing of installed trees, shall be placed between each parking bay.

5190 Signs —————————————————————————————

In addition to applicable provisions of the City's sign ordinance, the following requirements shall apply to signs within a Hill Country Roadway Corridor:
a. <u>Permitted Signs</u>

1. One (1) freestanding berm or monument sign of up to sixty-four (64) square feet in area shall be permitted for each street frontage. Where street frontage exceeds six hundred feet (600'), two such signs shall be permitted. Such

signs shall not exceed twelve feet (12') in height or the square root of the distance from the sign to the right-of-way, whichever is less.

2. In multi-tenant projects, one (1) wall sign shall also be permitted for each individual business establishment, with lettering not to exceed twenty-four inches (24") in height.

b. Prohibited Signs. Internal lighting of signs, neon or flashing signs, building floodlighting, and freestanding pole or post signs shall not be permitted. All spotlights and exterior lighting shall be concealed from view and oriented away from adjacent properties and roadways.

5191 Traffic Requirements

a. Access. Access to a Hill Country Roadway may be prohibited from any tract having access to a street intersecting with a Hill Country Roadway or any tract with frontage on a Hill Country Roadway which has access through an existing joint-use access easement or driveway. Otherwise, access to a Hill Country Roadway shall be limited to one driveway except as follows:

1. the estimated daily traffic volume for the single driveway exceeds five thousand (5,000) vehicles per day;

2. the traffic using the single driveway would exceed the capacity of a stop sign controlled intersection during one peak street traffic hour or the peak site traffic hour; or

3. a competent traffic analysis demonstrates the need for an additional driveway due to traffic conditions and the Director of Office of Land Development Services agrees that an additional driveway is required.

No more than two access points shall be permitted from any one development onto a Hill Country Roadway.

b. Driveway Location. Maximum practical spacing between driveways shall be provided. Unless otherwise approved by the Director of Urban Transportation, no driveway accessing a Hill Country Roadway shall be located:

1. closer than three hundred feet (300') from the nearest adjacent driveway, unless no other access is available to a tract of land;

2. where the sight distance is less than five hundred fifty feet (550');

3. on the inside radius of a curve; or

4. where the roadway grade of the Hill Country Roadway exceeds eight percent (8%).

c. Joint Use Driveways. For purposes of this Section, a joint-use driveway means a driveway located entirely or partially on one tract of land which is available for use as access to and from a public street from an adjoining tract of land. Unless otherwise waived by the City Council and subject to the Highway Vegetative Buffer provisions hereof, each applicant may be required to provide a joint-use access easement across his or her tract from property line to property line generally parallel with the right-of-way of the Hill Country Roadway for the use of adjacent property owners when the adjacent lots have insufficient frontage, as determined under the provisions of this ordinance, by the Director of Land Development Services. No access to a Hill Country Roadway will be permitted for tracts which do not have frontage on a Hill Country Roadway, unless recommended by the Director of Land Development Services. The City Council may waive this requirement upon the recommendation of the Director of Urban Transportation or when the topography of the tract makes such joint-use impractical or undesirable. If the applicant is required by the City of Austin to construct improvements such as providing wider driveways or additional driveways

for use as a joint-use driveway, the landowner(s) of the adjoining tract(s) benefited by such joint-use driveway shall be required by the city of Austin to
participate in the cost of such improvements on a pro rata basis as follows:

1. If the owner of the tract benefiting from such joint-use driveway is not ready
   to participate in the cost of such improvements at the time of the construction
   of those improvements, the owner of the tract upon which the improvements
   are to be constructed may elect not to construct them to accommodate the adjacent tract but shall leave sufficient area for such construction.
2. If the applicant elects to construct such improvements to serve an adjoining
   tract, the City shall require the owner of a benefited tract to share in such cost
   at the time such adjoining tract is developed.

In computing the amount of impervious cover on the site, there shall be excluded from such computation: (i) one hundred-ten percent (110%) of
impervious cover required for the sole purpose of providing access from adjoining land to a joint-use driveway (excluding parking spaces and aisles serving
parking spaces) located entirely on the site; and (ii) fifty percent (50%) of the
impervious cover required for the sole purpose of providing a joint-use driveway
(excluding parking spaces and aisles serving parking spaces) where no portion
of such driveway is located on adjoining land.

d. Streets and Intersections. Minimum spacing between local streets shall be six
   hundred feet (600') and between collector streets shall be thirteen hundred and
   twenty feet (1320').

   Arterial streets must conform to the Austin Metropolitan Area Roadway Plan.
   Improvements to intersections with a Hill Country Roadway will be required
   when determined from a review of the Traffic Impact Analysis. The construction
   of grade separated interchanges which provide fifty percent (50%) of the access
   required for an individual project are discouraged unless the interchange is also
   located at the intersection of an arterial street, as shown in the Austin Metropolitan Area Roadway Plan, or is located based on appropriate spacing for
   weaving maneuvers at ramps and resulting capacity considerations.

e. Median Breaks. The number of median breaks on Hill Country Roadways should
   be minimized. Additional median breaks on Loop 360 are prohibited and future
   connecting streets should align with median breaks to the greatest extent practicable.

f. Driveway Permits. City of Austin permit applications for a Hill Country Roadway must be approved prior to consideration of site plan and zoning changes by
   the Planning Commission.

g. Procedure Where Applicant Requests Construction in Proposed Right-of-Way.
   Where the applicant requests site plan approval for construction of improvements in a proposed right-of-way in accordance with standards set forth in this
   Section, the Planning Commission shall notify the Director of Public Works that
   an application has been filed requesting construction of improvements in the
   proposed right-of-way and refer the request to the City Council, who shall determine whether construction of improvements in the proposed right-of-way
   should be permitted.

5192 Performance Incentives

a. The Planning Commission and City Council shall, as appropriate, approve any
   individual or combination of the following development bonuses in order to recognize innovative design beyond that required to comply with this and other
   City ordinances, and which is considered to better further the goals of the Hill
   Country Roadway Ordinance:

1. Floor-to-Area ratio increases of up to .05 to 1 for land of 0-15% slope.
2. Building height increases not to result in a maximum height exceeding forty feet (40') in Low Intensity areas, fifty-three feet (53') in Moderate Intensity areas, and sixty-three feet (63') in High Intensity areas.
3. Reduced setbacks of up to twenty-five feet (25') less than those required.

b. Performance criteria to be considered in recommending bonuses should relate reasonably to the bonuses being approved and may include the following:
    1. Preserving scenic vistas, including the provision of public observation points. This incentive is allowed only where a view can be preserved.
    2. Limiting access to roadways other than Hill Country Roadways where such roadways do not encourage traffic through residential areas.
    3. Reducing impervious cover by 15% or more beyond the minimum standards allowed by this or other ordinances.
    4. Increasing landscaping or setbacks by more than 50%, and increasing natural areas.
    5. Providing mixed-use development, particularly those that include residential uses and community facilities.
    6. Reducing building mass by breaking up buildings.
    7. Using "pervious pavers" when not receiving impervious cover credit.
    8. Consolidating small lots to create parcels with a minimum of three hundred feet (300') of frontage on a Hill Country Roadway.
    9. Using pitched roof design features.
    10. Constructing and/or dedicating public facilities such as parks, roadways and right-of-way, police, fire, or EMS sites, regional drainage facilities or other facilities in excess of that required by City ordinances.
    11. Maintaining the construction of all buildings and parking areas on 0-15% slopes.
    12. Using energy-conserving and/or water conserving devices which reduce consumption below what is required by City ordinances.

c. In order to qualify for bonuses under this section of the ordinance, a development should demonstrate compliance with at least fifty percent (50%) of the above criteria. The use of bonuses shall be limited to unusual circumstances which involve:
    1. An undue hardship imposed on a tract by the ordinance or the cumulative effect of several ordinances due to its peculiar configuration, topography, or location; or
    2. Demonstration of highly innovative architectural, site planning, and land use design of a caliber not previously utilized in the Austin area, and of such a quality as to set an excellent example for subsequent developments.

5193 Hill Country Roadway Corridor Master File

a. The Office of Land Development Services of the City of Austin shall compile and maintain a current Master File of the Hill Country Roadway Corridors consisting of the following:
    1. A master contour map of all of the Hill Country Roadway Corridors indicating all proposed and approved land uses.
    2. A master file of all site plans for the Hill Country Roadway Corridors including all submitted site plans whether ultimately approved, disapproved, or withdrawn.

3. A master map showing all specific existing or potential scenic vistas, scenic overlooks, etc., as identified by the Office of Land Development Services and by the scenic view analysis.

b. Immediately prior to the consideration of any project located within a Hill Country Roadway Corridor by the Planning Commission or City Council, the Office of Land Development Services shall present a summary of the current status of the Master File. In addition, at least ten (10) days prior to the Planning Commission public hearing on a proposed zoning change or site plan approval within the Hill Country Roadway Corridor, the Office of Land Development Services shall notify the two registered neighborhood groups that are closest to the proposed site of the date, time, and location of such public hearing.

5194 Waivers

An applicant presenting a site plan for approval as required by this Article may request in writing a waiver from one or more of the specific requirements upon a showing by the applicant that this ordinance imposes an undue hardship on the tract due to its peculiar configuration, topography or location or that the proposed project demonstrates the use of highly innovative architectural, site planning, or land use techniques. The City Council may approve any waiver to the minimum extent necessary to allow the project to be constructed. The applicant for any such waiver shall have the burden of showing that the proposed project, with such waiver granted, will be as good or better than a project developed under the standards of this Article in terms of environmental protection, aesthetic enhancement, land use compatibility, and traffic considerations.

5195 Exemptions

a. The provisions of this Section shall not apply to any site plan which has been approved by the City Council on or before the effective date of this ordinance. Modifications to such approved site plans which include moving a structure more than twenty-five feet (25') or increasing the height or square footage of a building are not exempted from this Section, unless a zoning change has been granted allowing such changes.

b. Site plans for which City of Austin site development permits have been issued on or before the effective date of this ordinance shall be exempted from the provisions of this Section; provided, however, that such development shall be required to comply with the requirements set forth in Section 5600 (Landscaping Requirements) and Chapter 9-12 (Trees) of the Austin City Code of 1981, as amended.

c. Site plans which were recommended for approval by the Planning Commission prior to November 6, 1985, and site plans which were submitted prior to May 23, 1985, shall be exempted from the provisions of this ordinance; provided, however, that such projects remain subject to applicable ordinances in effect at the time of submittal.

d. Single-family homes and duplexes on platted lots shall be exempt from the provisions of this Section.

e. Development on tracts abutting a Hill Country Roadway in segments designated in the Austin Metropolitan Area Roadway Plan as "Parkway" is exempt from Section 5189(b) (Highway Vegetative Buffer) of this ordinance. Provided, however, that on such tracts a minimum twenty-five foot (25') natural or landscaped buffer shall be provided with no buildings located closer than fifty feet (50') to the proposed right-of-way of the Hill Country Roadway, as specified in the Roadway Plan.

f. Any Planned Development Area (PDA) approved by the City Council prior to the effective date of this ordinance is exempt from provisions of this Article.

g. Notwithstanding any language to the contrary herein, this Article shall not apply to development located within one thousand feet (1000') of the dedicated public right-of-way of U.S. 183 or U.S. 290 West.

h. A landowner otherwise exempt from the provisions of this Ordinance may file a request with the Director of OLDS to come under the provisions hereof. The Director of OLDS shall make a recommendation to the Planning Commission and City Council with respect to the appropriate provisions that should be applied to the applicant's tract as well as any waivers that are appropriate taking into consideration the land use approvals that already exist for the applicant's tract, it being the intention of the City to attempt to bring such tracts into voluntary compliance as close as reasonably possible to the provisions of this Ordinance without creating an undue hardship on such applicant. The council shall approve waivers as may be appropriate to the minimum extent necessary based upon the recommendations of the Planning Commission and the Director of OLDS.

i. Zoning change applications which were filed prior to November 6, 1985, and which are recommended for approval by the Planning Commission prior to April 1, 1986, for properties located along the RM 620 corridor between RM 2222 and Anderson Mill Road may be processed without submission of a site plan. Notwithstanding the requirements of Section 5187, such properties may be zoned or rezoned without approval of a site plan if one or more of the following criteria are satisfied:

1. the property is subject to a traffic phasing agreement;
2. the property is not adjacent to a single-family neighborhood; or
3. the property is subject to specific design guidelines or restrictions on development density or maximum floor to area ratios.

No building permit shall be issued for construction on a property zoned or rezoned without concurrent approval of a site plan until a site plan has been approved, after public hearings, by the City Council after receiving the recommendation of the Planning Commission. No site plan shall be approved unless it complies with these Hill Country Roadway Corridors regulations and meets the criteria established by Section 13-2A-6245 (Review and Evaluation Criteria for Conditional Use Permit). Notice of the public hearings at the Planning Commission and the City Council shall be given in the same manner as notice of public hearings required by these Zoning Regulations to consider rezoning of property. (870115-H)

Denver, Colorado
Mountain View Ordinance

Article IV. Restrictions on Structures within Areas Necessary to Preserve Mountain Views

SECTION 10–56. PURPOSE

Upon consideration of a recommendation that an ordinance be enacted for the purpose of preserving and protecting the health, safety, and general welfare of the people of the city and their property therein situate, the council finds:

1. That the protection and perpetuation of certain panoramic mountain views from various parks and public places within the city is required in the interests of the prosperity, civic pride and general welfare of the people;
2. That it is desirable to designate, preserve, and perpetuate certain existing panoramic mountain views for the enjoyment and environmental enrichment of the citizens of the community and visitors hereto;
3. That the preservation of such views will strengthen and preserve the municipality's unique environmental heritage and attributes as a city of the plains at the foot of the Rocky Mountains;
4. That the preservation of such views will foster civic pride in the beauty of the city;
5. That the preservation of such views will stabilize and enhance the aesthetic and economic vitality and values of the surrounding areas within which such views are preserved;
6. That the preservation of such views will protect and enhance the city's attraction to tourists and visitors;
7. That the preservation of such views will promote good urban design;
8. That regular specified areas constituting panoramic views should be established by protecting such panoramic views from encroachment and physical obstruction.

(Code 1950, § 645.1)

SECTION 10–57. PROHIBITIONS

No land shall be used or occupied and no structure shall be designed, erected, altered, used, or occupied except in conformity with all regulations established in this article and upon performance of all conditions herein set forth.

(Code 1950, § 645.3-1)

SECTION 10—58. CRANMER PARK*

a. *Adoption of map.* The attached map shall be and hereby is approved and adopted and the portion thereon indicated by shading or crosshatching shall be and hereby is determined to be and is designated as an area necessary for the preservation of a certain panoramic view. The restrictive provisions of this article shall be in full force and effect as to the portion of the attached map indicated by shading or crosshatching.

b. *Limitations on construction.* No part of a structure within the area on the attached map indicated by shading or crosshatching shall exceed an elevation of five thousand four hundred thirty-four (5,434) feet above mean sea level plus one foot for each one hundred (100) feet that the part of a structure is horizontally distant from the reference point. Wherever a structure lies partially outside and partially inside of the area on the attached map indicated by shading or crosshatching, the provisions of this section shall apply only to that part of the structure that lies within the area indicated on the map by shading or crosshatching.

c. *Reference point.* Reference point is a point having an elevation of five thousand four hundred thirty-four (5,434) feet above mean sea level and established at the mountain view indicator in Cranmer Park, which point is identified on the attached map and which point is indicated in the aforesaid Cranmer Park by a cross set in the top step of the aforesaid mountain view indicator.

(Code 1950, § 645.4-1)

SECTION 10—63. ENFORCEMENT

a. This article shall be enforced by the director of building inspection. The director is hereby empowered to enter into and cause any building, other structure, or tract of land to be inspected and examined and to order in writing the remedy of any condition found to exist thereon or threat in violation of any provision of this article. Service of the order shall be by personal service upon the owner, authorized property management agent, agent, occupant, or lessee or, alternatively, service may be made upon such persons by certified mail. If such persons are not found, the order may be served by posting in a conspicuous place on the premises, in which event service shall be deemed complete as of the moment of posting.

b. No oversight or dereliction on the part of the director of building inspection or on the part of any official or employee of the city shall legalize, authorize, or excuse any violation of any provision of this article.

(Code 1950, § 645.2)

SECTION 10—64. VIOLATIONS

Any person or any officer, agent, member, servant, or employee thereof, or any lessee or occupant of premises who violates, disobeys, omits, neglects, or refuses to comply with the provisions of this article, shall be guilty of violation thereof; and every omission, neglect, or continuance of the thing commanded or prohibited for twenty-four (24) hours shall constitute a separate and distinct offense; provided, however, without affecting any penalty for a violation, no proceedings shall be instituted hereunder against an occupant who is not the owner, or against an agent, servant, employee, or lessee for any violations hereof until after the expiration of ten (10) days from the date of the service of a notice by the director of such building inspection to cease and desist such violation, such notice to be served as provided in Section 10-63.

(Code 1950, § 645.3-2)

* Note: There are eight sections similar to 10-58 covering about 14 square miles or 12.5 percent of the city. The map cited here and the one cited in Section 10-83 (below), but which are not included here, are two of the several maps that help illustrate the ordinance restrictions.

SECTION 10–65. REMEDIES

a. Any person violating any provision of this article shall be subject to the penalties provided by Section 1-13.
b. In addition to any penalty, the city or any person aggrieved by any violation of this article may maintain any appropriate action to prevent and restrain the violation including an action for injunctive relief and may apply for a temporary restraining order without posting bond.

(Code 1950, § 645.3-3)

Article V. Restrictions on Structures in the Civic Center Area

SECTION 10–81. PURPOSE

Upon consideration of a recommendation that an ordinance be enacted for the purpose of preserving and protecting the health, safety, and general welfare of the people of the city and their property therein situate, the council finds:

1. That the protection of the great governmental complex known as the civic center, which the state and the city share, is required in the interests of the prosperity, civic pride, and general welfare of the people;
2. That it is desirable to preserve the integrity of the civic center and to protect the openness of its unique public space as a relief from its intensely developed surroundings;
3. That it is desirable to protect the stature of its public buildings as the symbols of the city and the state and as important points of orientation for permanent residents and visitors;
4. That it is desirable to protect the substantial public investment that has been made in the civic center park, the state capitol building, the city and county building, and other public improvements;
5. That the protection of the civic center will stabilize and enhance the aesthetic values of the surrounding area;
6. That an act protecting the civic center emphasizes the national recognition given to this governmental complex;
7. That the protection of the civic center will promote good urban design.

(Code 1950, § 646.1)

SECTION 10–82. PROHIBITIONS

No land shall be used or occupied and no structure shall be designed, erected, altered, used, or occupied except in conformity with all regulations herein established and upon performance of all conditions set forth in this article.

(Code 1950, § 646.3-1)

SECTION 10–83. ADOPTION OF MAP

For the purposes of this article only, the attached map, which map in no way amends or repeals any other map contained in any other ordinance of the city, shall be and hereby is approved and adopted and the portion thereon indicated within the solid black boundary line shall be and hereby is determined to be and is designated as the area necessary for the protection and preservation of the governmental complex known as the civic center.

The restrictive provisions of this article shall be in full force and effect as to the portion of the attached map indicated within the solid black boundary line except that any area within the solid black boundary line that is also restricted by the restrictive provisions of Article IV of this chapter (restrictions on structures within areas necessary to preserve mountain views) shall be restricted by the restrictive provisions of such article and not by the restrictive provisions of this article.

(Code 1950, § 646.4-1)

SECTION 10–84. LIMITATIONS OF CONSTRUCTION

The restrictive provisions of this article are designed to create a pattern of height limitations in the form of three (3) stepped planes allowing greater height with increased distance from the civic center. Structures within the area on the attached map indicated within the solid black boundary line shall be limited in height as follows:

1. No part of a structure within the area on the attached map designated A and colored purple shall exceed an elevation of five thousand four hundred fifty-one (5,451) feet above sea level.
2. No part of a structure within the area on the attached map designated B and colored blue shall exceed an elevation of five thousand five hundred twenty-three (5,523) feet above sea level.
3. No part of a structure within the area on the attached map designated C and colored orange shall exceed an elevation of five thousand three hundred ninety-one (5,391) feet above sea level.
4. No part of a structure within the area on the attached map designated D and colored red shall exceed an elevation of five thousand four hundred fifty-one (5,451) feet above sea level.
5. No part of a structure within the area on the attached map designated E and colored green shall exceed an elevation of five thousand three hundred fifty-three (5,353) feet above sea level.
6. No part of a structure within the area on the attached map designated F and colored yellow shall exceed elevation of five thousand three hundred ninety-one (5,391) feet above sea level.

(Code 1950, § 646.4-2)

Lubbock, Texas
Sign Ordinance

Sec. 29–26. Signs

(a) *Purpose.* The purpose of this section is to provide uniform sign standards which promote a positive city image reflecting order, harmony and pride and thereby strengthening the economic stability of Lubbock's business, cultural and residential areas. Objectives to be pursued in applying specific standards are as follows:

(1) To identify individual business, residential, and public uses without creating confusion, unsightliness, or visual obscurity of adjacent businesses.

(2) To assure that all signs in terms of size, scale, height, and location are properly related to the overall adjacent land use character and development lot size.

(3) To assure that all signs, in terms of color, form, material and design are compatible with other structural forms on the development lots.

(4) To assure that off-premise advertising is compatible with adjacent land uses and does not obscure views of adjacent on-premise signs.

(5) To assure that all signs, sign supports and sign bases shall be so constructed and designed to provide for design compatibility with the development. Where possible, the materials used, the form, color, lighting and style should be similar to the materials used in the development.

(b) *General provisions.*

(1) All signs shall pertain to the identification of the primary uses and/or primary services provided or primary products sold on the premises, except for billboards, auxiliary, governmental or community service signs as provided.

(2) All signs[,] where applicable, shall meet the standards of the city building code.

(3) Except as herein provided, no person or business firm, acting either as principal or agent, shall alter the copy face or lettering of any sign, except for Section 2.14 [29-3(14)] signs and signs with temporary messages made from interchangeable characters attached to tracts or grooves on the sign board, either by changing the message or by renovating an existing message or shall erect any sign or sign structure until a sign permit for such work has been issued by the building official to a bonded contractor or the owner or occupant of the premises where the work is to be done. No permit shall be required for nonilluminated signs otherwise permitted in Sections 23.7-1, 23.7-2, 23.9-5-4, 23.10, 23.12, 23.13 or 23.14 [29-26(g)(1), 29-26(g)(2), 29-26(i)(5)(d), 29-26(j), 29-26(l), 29-26(m) or 29-26(n)].

(4) Not more than two (2) sides of a sign structure may be used for display.

(5) No sign, sign structure, or sign support shall project over any property line, except

that a sign placed flat against the wall of a building, which is on the property line may project eighteen (18) inches over the property line.

(6) Trees, rocks, bridges, fences, windmill towers and dilapidated buildings shall not be used as sign supports.

(7) All business locations shall be identified by a street address sign which is clearly visible from the street.

(8) [Reserved.]

(9) Signs with flashing, blinking or traveling lights shall have light bulbs which do not exceed thirty-five (35) watts each.

(10) Not more than twenty-five (25) percent of the area of any sign, except for Section 2.14 [29-3(14)] signs, provided by an off-premise business may be devoted to advertisement of products provided by that off-premise business.

(11) In the event that more than one sign-related definition applies to a nonprohibited proposed sign, resulting in conflicting regulations thereon, the sign applicant may choose the definition that is to apply, with the qualification that any regulations related to that definition must also be adopted. Where the proposed sign is of a type that is prohibited, it shall remain prohibited notwithstanding that it may also come within the definition of an approved type of sign.

(c) *Prohibited signs.* The following signs shall be prohibited in all districts:

(1) Any signs and supports, other than those signs and supports required by governmental authority, or for which a street use license has been issued, which are located on the public right-of-way, including on public street, alleys and parkways. This section shall not apply to signs on commercial vehicles or commercial trailers lawfully operated or parked in such areas, except that this exception shall not otherwise be used to legitimate the use of advertising vehicles and trailers prohibited in Section 23.5-1 [29-26(e)(1)] following or portable or wheeled signs prohibited in Section 23.3-8 [29-26(c)(8)] following.

(2) Signs with flashing, blinking, or traveling lights, regardless of wattage, which are located within forty-three (43) feet of any street right-of-way. Signs with flashing, blinking or traveling lights, regardless of wattage, and excepting time and temperature signs, which are located within one thousand (1,000) feet of any street intersection.

(3) Reserved.

(4) Banners, pennants, searchlights, twirling signs, sandwich or "A" frame signs, sidewalk or curb signs, balloons, or other gas filled objects. (Except banners, pennants, and searchlights may be permitted for a period not to exceed sixteen (16) days for grand openings. Permits for grand openings shall be obtained from the zoning administrator.)

(5) Flags, other than those of any nation, state, or political subdivision, or one flag which shows an emblem or logo of a firm or corporation, provided all other regulations of Section 23[29-26] are met.

(6) Any signs which resemble an official traffic sign or signal or which bears the words "Stop," "Go Slow," "Caution," "Danger," "Warning," or similar words.

(7) Signs which, by reason of their size, location, movement, content, coloring, or manner of illumination, may be confused with or constructed as a traffic-control sign, signal or device, or the light of an emergency or road equipment vehicle, or which hide from view any traffic or street sign or signal or device.

(8) Portable or wheeled signs.

(9) Any sign which emits sound, odor or visible matter, which serves as a distraction to persons within the public right-of-way.

(d) *Abandoned or damaged signs.*

(1) All abandoned signs and their supports shall be removed within ninety (90) days from the date of abandonment. All damaged signs shall be repaired or removed

within ninety (90) days. The administrator shall have the authority to grant a time extension not exceeding an additional ninety (90) days from an abandoned, non-damaged sign.

(2) Should the responsible party or parties, after due notice, fail to correct a violation of this section, the administrator shall cause such signs and their supports to be demolished and removed. If such sign cannot be demolished because it is painted on a building or other nonsign structure, such sign shall be painted over or removed by sandblasting. The administrator shall also file against the property a lien in the amount of the cost of all such work.

(e) *Parking of advertising vehicles.*

(1) No person shall park an advertising vehicle or trailer on a public right-of-way or on public property. Any such vehicle parked on private property, visible from the public right-of-way, shall be used on a regular basis within each business week as a means of transportation for the business that is advertised.

(f) *Nonconforming sign abatement.*

(1) The following signs and/or advertising items shall become nonconforming on the effective date of this ordinance [chapter] and shall be brought into compliance or removed within six (6) months of the effective date of this ordinance [chapter].

a. Signs with flashing, blinking, or traveling lights, regardless of wattage, which are located within forty-three (43) feet of any street right-of-way. Signs with flashing, blinking, or traveling lights, regardless of wattage, and excepting time and temperature signs which are located within one thousand (1,000) feet of any street intersection.

b. Any sign which is affixed to sign supports prohibited in section 23.2-6 [29-26(b)(6)].

c. Banners, pennants, searchlights, twirling signs, sandwich, or "A" frame signs, sidewalk or curb signs, balloons, or other gas-filled objects, except as provided in section 23.3-4 [29-26(c)(4)].

d. Flags, other than those of any nation, state or political subdivision, or one flag which shows an emblem or logo of a firm or corporation.

e. Any signs which resemble an official traffic sign or signal or which bears the words "Stop," "Go Slow," "Caution," "Danger," "Warning," or similar words.

f. Signs which, by reason of their size, location, movement, content, coloring or manner of illumination may be confused with or construed as a traffic-control sign, signal or device, or the light of an emergency or road equipment vehicle, or which hide from view any traffic or street sign or signal or device.

g. Portable or wheeled signs.

h. Any sign which emits sound, odor or visible matter, which serve[s] as a distraction to persons within the public right-of-way.

i. Any signs and their supports in violation of section 23.3-1 [29-26(c)(1)] are hereby deemed to be in trespass on public property and shall be immediately removed by the administrator or his agent. This removal shall be done in a manner, if reasonably possible, to preserve the value of such signs and supports. If the administrator directs an independent contractor to remove said signs and supports, the cost of such work shall be minimized by the administrator to whatever extent is reasonably possible.

The owners of any removed signs and supports, except signs made of paper or cardboard or their supports, shall be notified. The first attempt at notice shall be within three (3) days of the removal of the sign and supports. The manner of notice shall be that which will best achieve notice under the circumstances, including the use of certified mail, hand delivery or publication. Refusal of certified mail which has been properly addressed and posted shall not void the notice. Hand delivery may be employed where the addressee is within the city limits and when his whereabouts are specifically known. Publication may be used when the addressee or his whereabouts are unknown and said publication shall be done in the same manner as prescribed in Vernon's Annotated Civil Statutes for service of process by publication. Notice by publication shall be deemed sufficient regardless of its effect as actual notice.

Said notice shall inform the recipient that the City of Lubbock is in possession of that certain sign and supports, why they were removed, and where they may be reclaimed, as well as the information contained in the remainder of this section.

With the exception of signs made of paper or cardboard and their supports which may be disposed of immediately, removed signs and supports shall be stored a period not to exceed fourteen (14) days beginning the first day of effective notice, whether actual or constructive. A storage charge of five dollars ($5.00) per day will be levied beginning the fourth day of that fourteen (14) day period. Before the expiration of the storage period, the owner of the sign and supports may reclaim his property upon payment of any storage charges and the cost of removal, if such removal was done by an independent contractor. If said sign and support have not been reclaimed by the expiration of the storage period, they may be disposed of in whatever manner the administrator shall choose. If in his opinion the sign and supports are not capable of being sold they may be discarded, but if sold, the proceeds therefrom shall be first applied to the storage charge and removal charge if any, and the remaining balance shall be mailed to the past owner of the sign and supports, if reasonably possible, or if not, then to the general fund of the city.

(2) All signs not covered by Section 23.6-1 [29-26(f)(1)] which are in violation of other provisions of Section 23 [29-26] shall become nonconforming. Said signs shall be brought into compliance by alteration or removal, by January 1, 1982, unless the height, area, location or supports of an existing sign are altered, in which case the sign shall be brought into compliance at the time of alteration. Nothing in this section shall prevent the removal of damaged or abandoned signs under Section 23.4 [29-26(d)] or the termination of nonconforming uses under Section 24 [29-27].

(3) The abatement periods provided in subsections (f)(1) and (f)(2), immediately above, commenced on the effective date of Ordinance No. 7084, which was July 19, 1975, and were effective as to all such defined nonconforming signs within the corporate limits on such effective date. The abatement periods for the defined nonconforming signs located in areas annexed into the corporate limits on or after the _____ day of _____, 1985, shall commence to run on the effective date of annexation of the area in which such nonconforming signs are located. For such purpose the effective date of annexation shall be either the date of final passage of the annexation ordinance involved, or, the date upon which such annexation is approved under the provisions of the Voting Rights Act, whichever action is the last to occur. The abatement periods for the defined nonconforming signs located in areas annexed between July 19, 1975, and _____, 1985, shall commence to run on the _____ day of _____, 1985, or, the date upon the effective date of annexation of the area in which the nonconforming sign is located, whichever action is the last to occur.

(g) [*Signs permitted in "R-1" and "R-2" Districts.*] The following signs shall be permitted in the "R-1" and "R-2" Districts:

(1) One sign not exceeding one and one-half (1½) square feet in area, indicating only the name and address of the occupant, for each residential unit.

(2) One (1) unlighted sign, not exceeding four (4) square feet in area, on each development lot pertaining to the prospective sale or rental of the property on which it is located. On each development lot where newly constructed residences are being advertised for sale or rent, one (1) additional unlighted sign not exceeding four (4) square feet in area indicating builder, contractor or other construction/development information may be displayed.

(3) Specific use district. Signs shall be specifically described and indicated on the site plan. The sign requirement for each use shall not be less restrictive than those of the respective district in which the use is otherwise permitted.

(4) Conditional uses. Sign requirements for all conditional uses shall be set by the zoning board of adjustment, and in no case shall the requirements exceed the requirements for that use or similar type uses in the district in which the use is ordinarily permitted.

(h) [*Signs permitted in "A-1," "A-2," "AM" and "GO" Districts.*] The following signs shall be permitted in the "A-1," "A-2," "AM" and "GO" Districts:

(1) Signs for R-1 and R-2 uses shall meet the requirements of their respective R-1 and R-2 Districts.

(2) Permitted uses.

a. Primary identification signs, each having an area not exceeding ten (10) percent of the area of one (1) wall or five (5) percent of the area of two (2) walls, where applicable, or fifty (50) square feet, whichever is less.

b. Informational-type signs not exceeding ten (10) square feet in area per building.

c. All signs shall be placed flat against the wall of a building and shall not project above the parapet wall or side wall of the building.

d. All signs, except for the information signs, shall identify the development by name and address only. Signs may be back lighted, indirect lighted, internal lighted, or lighted by spots.

(3) Specific use district. Signs shall be specifically described and indicated on the site plan. The sign requirement for each use shall not be less restrictive than those of the respective district in which the use is otherwise first permitted.

(4) Conditional uses. Sign requirements shall be set by the zoning board of adjustment, and in no case shall the requirements exceed the requirements for that use or similar type uses in the district in which the use is ordinarily permitted.

(5) Freestanding signs in the "GO" District. In the GO District freestanding signs shall be permitted subject to the following regulations:

a. One (1) freestanding sign for each freestanding building, not to exceed one (1) freestanding sign per development lot (except as provided in section 29-26(h)(5)(b.1)), shall be permitted only as indicated below:

1. "GO" District that has frontage on a thoroughfare.

(i) Area: The area of a freestanding sign shall not exceed an amount equal to 0.40 square feet per front foot of lot and in no case shall this sign area exceed two hundred fifty (250) square feet.

(ii) Height: For lots with frontage of zero feet [to] ninety-nine (99) feet, sign height shall not exceed five (5) feet. For lots exceeding ninety-nine (99) feet of lot frontage, the sign heights shall not exceed five (5) feet, plus one (1) foot of sign height for each twenty (20) feet of lot frontage. In no case shall sign height exceed thirty (30) feet.

(iii) Setback: Setbacks shall be a minimum of ten (10) feet or one and forty-three one-hundredths (1.43) feet for each foot of sign height, whichever is greater.

(iv) Spacing: Freestanding signs shall not be placed closer to a side lot line than a distance equal to one-fourth of the lot frontage.

2. "GO" District that has frontage on expressway right-of-way.

(i) Area: The area of a freestanding sign shall not exceed an amount equal to 0.40 square feet per front foot of lot and in no case shall this sign area exceed two hundred fifty (250) square feet.

(ii) Height: For lots with frontage of zero feet [to] ninety-nine (99) feet, sign height shall not exceed twenty (20) feet. For lots exceeding ninety-nine (99) feet of lot frontage or more, the sign height shall not exceed twenty

(20) feet, plus one (1) foot of sign height for each forty (40) feet of lot frontage. In no case shall sign height exceed thirty-five (35) feet.

      (iii) Setback: Setbacks shall be a minimum of one and twenty-two one-hundredths (1.22) feet for each foot of sign height.

      (iv) Spacing: Freestanding signs shall not be placed closer to a side lot line than a distance equal to one-fourth of the lot frontage.

  3. "GO" District that does not have frontage on a thoroughfare or an expressway street.

      (i) One (1) freestanding sign shall be permitted on a development lot.

      (ii) Freestanding signs shall be of a pedestal or monument type with the entire structure built as one (1) unit. Construction materials shall be compatible with other structural forms on the development lot. Elevation drawings shall be submitted for staff review prior to issuance of a building permit, showing construction materials and detail.

      (iii) The area, height and setback shall be as determined by the standards of section 29-26(i)(7)a.1.(i), (ii), (iii). The maximum height of any freestanding sign shall be ten (10) feet.

      (iv) The sign shall be at least twenty-five (25) feet from any driveway curb cut, alley return, or driveway-alley combination; or on corner lots the permitted freestanding sign may be placed on the corner provided it is not within the visibility triangle.

 b. All freestanding signs permitted shall comply with the following:

  1. On corner lots, that frontage on the major or primary street shall be construed to be the development lot frontage, and no more than one (1) sign shall be permitted, except that on a development lot located at the intersection of two (2) major thoroughfares or two (2) expressways or a major thoroughfare and an expressway, a freestanding sign shall be permitted on each such thoroughfare or expressway or one (1) sign, of the same size, height, and setbacks, may be placed on the corner, provided it is not within the visibility triangle.

  2. No sign shall be placed within the visibility triangle as defined in this chapter.

  3. To compute the allowable square footage of sign area, only one (1) side of a double face sign shall be considered.

  4. Development lot frontage shall be defined as that frontage under one (1) development at the time of application for sign permit.

  5. Freestanding signs may rotate not more than six (6) revolutions per minute.

  6. Freestanding signs may be placed on the roof of a building provided the height, setback, square footage and location requirements of this section are met.

(i) *Regulations applicable in "C," "C-1," "C-2A," "C-3," "C-4," "M-1," "M-2," "IHO," "IHC," and "IHI" Districts.* The following regulations shall apply in the "CA," "C-1," "C-2A," "C-2," "C-3," "C-4," "M-1," "M-2," "IHO," "IHC," and "IHI" Districts:

(1) Specific use district. Freestanding sign locations shall be specifically indicated on the site plan. The sign requirements for each use shall not be less restrictive than those of the respective district in which the use is otherwise first permitted.

(2) Conditional uses. A conditional use shall have the sign requirements for the zone district in which it is to be allowed unless the signs are described on a site plan approved by the zoning board of adjustment in which case the sign requirements for each use shall not be less restrictive than those of the respective district in which the use is otherwise first permitted.

(3) The combined area of all signs excluding Section 2.14 [29-3(14)] signs shall not exceed one and one-half (1½) square feet of area for each lineal foot of lot frontage on the principal or fronting street, except as provided in Section 23.9-7-2-1 [29-6(i)(7)(b)(1)].

(4) Wall signs. Wall signs shall project no more than two (2) feet perpendicular from the wall and not more than three (3) feet vertically above the wall of a building. Not more than ten (10) percent of any wall shall be devoted to wall signs, except when freestanding signs are allowed but not used, this may be increased to not more than fifteen (15) percent.

(5) Canopy signs. Canopy signs shall be counted as a part of, and limited to the percentage allowable for wall signs.

   a. Signs on front side of building canopy, excluding detached accessory island canopy with or without enclosed booth. Signs placed on the front side of a building canopy shall not project beyond the width of that canopy, more than six (6) feet above the top of the canopy, or more than three (3) feet above the building roof line. For the purposes of Section 23.9-5 [29-26(i)(5)] the front side of a canopy shall be any side parallel to, or more nearly parallel to than perpendicular to, the building wall on which the canopy is attached.

   b. Signs on lateral side of building canopy excluding detached accessory island canopy with or without enclosed booth. Signs placed on the lateral side of a building canopy shall project neither beyond the width of that canopy side nor more than two (2) feet above the canopy roof line, except that the vertical dimension of said signs shall not exceed three (3) feet. For the purposes of section 23.9-5 [29-26(i)(5)] the lateral side of a canopy shall be any side perpendicular to, or more perpendicular than parallel to, the building wall on which the canopy is attached.

   c. Signs on roof of building canopy excluding detached accessory island canopy with or without enclosed booth. Signs placed on the roof of a building canopy and which are parallel to, or more nearly parallel to than perpendicular to, the front side of the canopy shall be regulated in Section 23.9-5-1 [29-26(i)(5)(a)] above. Signs placed on the roof of a building canopy and which are parallel to, or more nearly parallel to than perpendicular to, a lateral side of the canopy shall be regulated in Section 23.9-5-2 [29-26(i)(5)(6)] above.

   d. Signs under building canopy excluding detached accessory island canopy with or without enclosed booth. Signs may be attached to and suspended from the underside of building canopies with the following restrictions:

     1. Not more than one such sign is permitted per business.
     2. Such sign must identify only the store's name.
     3. Such sign must have an area not exceeding four and one-half (4½) square feet.
     4. The bottom edge of such sign must not be more than one (1) foot below the bottom edge of the canopy.
     5. Such a sign may be placed perpendicular to the front wall of the building except that nothing in this Section 23.9-5-4 [29-26(i)(5)(d)] shall supersede Section 23.2-5 [29-26(b)(5)] herein.

   e. Signs placed on freestanding canopy or detached accessory island canopy. Signs may be located any place on a canopy that is not attached to a building (except for gasoline pump islands which may have a booth) except that such signs shall not project beyond the width of that canopy, more than two (2) feet above that canopy or more than one (1) foot below that canopy.

(6) Sloping roof signs. Sloping roof signs shall not project horizontally or vertically beyond the roof line. Not more than ten (10) percent of any sloping roof area shall be devoted to these signs.

(7) Freestanding signs.

   a. One (1) free-standing sign for each freestanding building, not to exceed one (1) freestanding sign per development lot (except as provided in section 23.9-7-2-1 [29-26(i)(7)(b)(1)]), shall be permitted only as indicated below.

     1. "CA", "C-1", "C-2A", "C-2", "C-3", "C-4", "IDP", "M-1", "M-2", "IHO", "IHC", and "IHI" Districts with frontage on a thoroughfare.

      (i) *Area:* The area of a freestanding sign shall not exceed an amount equal to 0.40 square feet per front foot of lot and in no case shall this sign area exceed two hundred and fifty (250) square feet.

     (ii) *Height:* For lots with frontage of zero feet—ninety-nine (99) feet, sign height shall not exceed five (5) feet. For lots exceeding ninety-nine (99) feet of lot frontage, the sign heights shall not exceed five (5) feet, plus one (1) foot of sign height for each twenty (20) feet of lot frontage. In no case shall sign height exceed thirty (30) feet.

   (iii) *Setback:* Setbacks shall be a minimum of ten (10) feet or one and forty-three one-hundredths (1.43) feet for each foot of sign height, whichever is greater.

   (iv) *Spacing:* Freestanding signs shall not be placed closer to a side lot line than distance equal to one-fourth of the lot frontage.

2. "CA", "C-1", "C-2A", "C-2", "C-3", "C-4", "IDP", "M-1", "M-2", "IHO", "IHC", and "IHI" Districts with frontage on expressway right-of-way.

      (i) *Area:* The area of a freestanding sign shall not exceed an amount equal to 0.40 square feet per front foot of lot and in no case shall this sign area exceed two hundred and fifty (250) square feet.

     (ii) *Height:* For lots with frontage of zero feet—ninety-nine (99) feet, sign height shall not exceed twenty (20) feet. For lots exceeding ninety-nine (99) feet of lot frontage or more, the sign height shall not exceed twenty (20) feet, plus one (1) foot of sign height for each forty (40) feet of lot frontage. In no case shall sign height exceed thirty-five (35) feet.

   (iii) *Setback:* Setbacks shall be a minimum of one and twenty-two-one-hundredths (1.22) feet for each foot of sign height.

   (iv) *Spacing:* freestanding signs shall not be placed closer to a side lot line than a distance equal to one-fourth of the lot frontage.

b. All freestanding signs permitted shall comply with the following:

1. On corner lots, that frontage on the major or primary street shall be construed to be the development lot frontage, and no more than one (1) sign shall be permitted, except that on a development lot located at the intersection of two (2) major thoroughfares or two (2) expressways or a major thoroughfare and an expressway, a freestanding sign shall be permitted on each such thoroughfare or expressway or one (1) sign, of the same size, height, and setbacks, may be placed on the corner, provided it is not within the visibility triangle.

2. No sign shall be placed within the visibility triangle as defined in this ordinance [chapter].

3. To compute the allowable square footage of sign area, only one (1) side of a double face sign shall be considered.

4. Development lot frontage shall be defined as that frontage under one development at the time of application for sign permit.

5. Freestanding signs may rotate not more than six (6) revolutions per minute.

6. Freestanding signs may be placed on the roof of a building provided the height, setback, square footage, and location requirements of this section are met.

3. "C-A", "C-1", "C-2A", "C-2", "C-3", "C-4", "IDP", "M-1", "M-2", "IHO", "IHC", and "IHI" Districts that do not have frontage on a thoroughfare or an expressway street.

      (i) One (1) freestanding sign shall be permitted on a development lot.

     (ii) Freestanding signs shall be of a pedestal or monument type with the entire structure built as one (1) unit. Construction materials shall be compatible with other structural forms on the development lot. Elevation drawings shall be submitted for staff review prior to issuance of a building permit, showing construction materials and details.

(iii) The area, height and setback shall be as determined by the standards of section 29-26(i)(7)a.1.(i), (ii), (iii). The maximum height of any free-standing sign shall be ten (10) feet.

(iv) The sign shall be at least twenty-five (25) feet from any driveway curb cut, alley return, or driveway-alley combination; or on corner lots the permitted freestanding sign may be placed on the corner provided it is not within the visibility triangle.

(8) Roof signs. Roof signs on a building which is eight (8) stories or more in height shall not be limited by section 23.9-7-2-6 [29-26(i)(7)(b)(6)] except for its allowable square footage requirement. No roof signs, regardless of height, may rotate more than six (6) revolutions per minute.

(j) [*Auxiliary signs.*] Auxiliary signs not exceeding ten (10) square feet in total area per building may be placed in a window or flat against the wall of a building. Freestanding auxiliary signs of not more than two and one-half (2½) feet in height and three (3) square feet in area are permitted on private property if limited to traffic direction or parking direction. Auxiliary sign area shall not be counted against total permitted sign area.

(k) *Temporary construction site and for-sale and rental signs.*

(1) For-sale signs, rental signs or temporary construction site signs not exceeding one hundred (100) square feet in area and ten (10) feet in height may be placed at a development site, on property of one (1) acre or more during construction.

(2) One (1) for-sale or rental sign, not exceeding thirty-two (32) square feet in area and ten (10) feet in height, may be placed on a commercial tract. Any such sign must be maintained and kept in good repair, or it must be removed. The sign must be removed when the property is no longer for sale or rent.

(l) *Governmental signs.* Governmental signs not exceeding thirty-two (32) square feet in area and not exceeding ten (10) feet in height, shall be permitted. Such standards shall not apply where state or federal regulations are in conflict with these standards.

(m) *Temporary business promotional signs.* Any temporary business promotional signs shall only be placed in or on windows and shall have a combined area not exceeding ten (10) percent of the area of all windows on that same wall. Said sign area shall not be counted against permitted wall sign area.

(n) *Community service signs.* Any community service signs for seasonal celebration shall have no size limitation if placed in or on windows. Any community service signs, not of a seasonal celebration nature, shall be placed in or on windows and shall have a combined area not exceeding ten (10) percent of the area of all the windows on that same wall. Such sign area shall not be counted against permitted wall sign area.

(o) *Billboards (poster panels or bulletins, multi-prism signs, or painted or printed bulletins).* Outdoor advertising signs of this type shall be permitted in the "C-4," "M-1," and "M-2" Districts, subject to the following conditions.

(1) Billboards shall be constructed to meet the construction standards as established in the City of Lubbock Building Code.

(2) Billboards located in a "C-4" District shall be a minimum of eighty (80) feet from any residentially zoned property line.

(3) The maximum area of any billboard located in a "C-4" District shall be three hundred (300) square feet.

(4) The maximum area of any billboard located in the "M-1," "M-2" Districts shall be seven hundred and fifty (750) square feet.

(5) There shall be a minimum separation of two hundred (200) feet between all billboards on the same side of the street, provided however, this shall be increased to five hundred (500) feet on expressways.

(6) Billboards shall have a front setback of not less than the greater of (1) forty-three (43) feet, or (2) the greatest setback of all the front buildings on the lot on which the

billboard is located, or if none, then that of the lots contiguous to the lot upon which the billboard is located.

(7) Billboards shall have a maximum height of thirty-five (35) feet.

(8) All lighting of billboards shall be so shielded as not to produce intensive or excessive light or glare on adjacent property.

(9) Billboards shall be prohibited from being placed within the Canyon Lakes Policy Zone and Memorial Civic Center area.

Definitions

(105) *Sign:* Any words, numbers, figures, devices, designs, trademarks or other symbols, which attract attention to or make known such things as an individual, firm, profession, business, commodity or service, and which is [sic] visible from any public street. This definition of "sign" shall include any structure designed to be used for said display. For the purpose of removal, "sign" shall also include sign supports.

(105a) *Sign, abandoned:* Any sign, including off-premise signs unless owned and operated by a bona fide billboard company, which no longer correctly directs or exhorts any person or advertises a bona fide business lessor, owner, product, service, or activity.

(105b) *Sign, advertising vehicle or trailer:* Any vehicle or trailer, which has as its basic purpose the advertisement of products or direction of people to a business or activity, whether located on or off-premise.

(105c) *Sign area:* The area of any freestanding sign or billboard shall be the sum of the areas enclosed by the minimum imaginary rectangles, triangles, or circles which fully contain all extremities of the sign, including the frame but excluding any supports. Sign area for all other signs shall be the sum of the areas of the minimum imaginary rectangles, triangles, or circles which fully contain all words, numbers, figures, devices, designs or trademarks by which anything is made known.

(105d) *Sign, auxiliary:* Any sign indicating general information, such as pricing, trading stamps, credit cards, official notices or services required by law, trade associations, and signs giving directions to offices, rest rooms, exits and like facilities.

(105e) *Sign, billboard:* (See section 2.14 [29-3(14)].)

(105f) *Sign, canopy:* Any sign affixed to a canopy.

(105g) *Sign, community service:* Any sign which solicits support for or advertises non-profit community use, public use, or social institution. Such signs may include, but shall not be limited to[,] seasonal holidays, such as Christmas, Easter, school activities, charitable programs, or religious activities.

(105h) *Sign, damaged:* Any sign which has become so deteriorated or dilapidated as to require more than minimal reconditioning to restore it to an average, normal state of repair.

(105i) *Sign, free standing:* Any sign permanently affixed to the ground and which is not affixed to a building and which is not used for off-premises advertising.

(105j) *Sign, governmental:* Any sign indicating public works projects, public services or other programs or activities conducted or required by any governmental subdivision.

(105k) *Sign height:* Sign height shall be the vertical distance between the highest part of the sign or its supporting structure, whichever is higher, and the average established ground level beneath the sign.

(105l) *Sign, portable:* Any sign not permanently affixed to the ground or to a building and which is designed to permit removal and reuse.

(105l.1) *Sign, primary identification:* Any sign identifying the name of a shopping center or group of commercial buildings. Such signs shall commit a minimum of fifty (50) per cent of the allowable area to the primary identification while the remainder may identify businesses within the shopping center or group of commercial buildings.

(105m) *Sign, realty:* Any sign used to advertise a real estate development site or to advertise that real estate is for sale or lease.

(105n) *Sign, roof:* Any signs which are affixed to building roofs, excepting mansard or sloping roofs.

(105o) *Sign setback:* Sign setback shall be the horizontal distance between a sign and the front lot line, as measured from that part of the sign, including its extremities and supports, nearest to any point on an imaginary vertical plane projecting from the front lot line.

(105p) *Sign, sloping or mansard roof:* Any sign affixed to a sloping or mansard roof.

(105q) *Sign, temporary business promotion:* Any sign which is designed to produce revenue by advertising services, sales, or other temporary promotional programs and which have a limited duration.

(105r) *Sign, wall:* Any sign affixed flat against and parallel to a building wall. For the purposes of this definition, wall shall include window areas.

Libertyville, Illinois
Appearance Code

30.2.1 Intent and Purposes

The purpose of the criteria in the Appearance Code is to provide overt and professionally appropriate standards for the evaluation of external design features in the Village. The criteria are not intended to restrict imagination, innovation or variety, but rather to assist in focusing on design principles which can result in creative solutions that will develop a satisfactory visual appearance within the Village, preserve taxable values, and promote the public health, safety and welfare.

30.2.2 Definitions

Because many of the words or terms used in the Appearance Plan are not in common usage, or they could be misconstrued as to meaning, the following definitions are to be used in the context of the use of the Plan.

1. *Appearance.* The outward aspect visible to the public.
2. *Appropriate.* Sympathetic, or fitting, to the context of the site and the whole community.
3. *Appurtenances.* The visible, functional objects accessory to and part of buildings.
4. *Architectural concept.* The basic aesthetic idea of a building, or group of buildings or structures, including the site and landscape development, which produces the architectural character.
5. *Architectural feature.* A prominent or significant part or element of a building, structure, or site.
6. *Architectural style.* The characteristic form and detail, as of buildings of a particular historic period.
7. *Attractive.* Having qualities that arouse interest and pleasure in the observer.
8. *Berm.* A raised form of earth to provide screening or to improve the aesthetic character.
9. *Code.* The Libertyville Municipal Code (Ordinance No. 77-0-61).
10. *Cohesiveness.* Unity of composition between design elements of a building or a group of buildings, and the landscape development.

119

11. *Compatibility.* Harmony in the appearance of two or more external design features in the same vicinity.

12. *Conservation.* The protection and care which prevent destruction or deterioration of historical or otherwise significant structures, buildings, or natural resources.

13. *Exterior building component.* An essential and visible part of the exterior of a building.

14. *External design feature.* The general arrangement of any portion of a building, sign, landscaping or structure and including the kind, color, and texture of the materials of such portion and the types of roof, windows, doors, lights, attached or ground signs or other fixtures appurtenant to such portions, as will be open to public view from any street, place or way.

15. *Graphic element.* A letter, illustration, symbol, figure, insignia, or other device employed to express and illustrate a message or part thereof.

16. *Harmony.* A quality which represents an appropriate and congruent arrangement of parts, as in an arrangement of varied architectural and landscape elements.

17. *Landscape.* Plant materials, topography, and other natural physical elements combined in relation to one another and to man-made structures.

18. *Light cut-off angle.* An angle from verticle extending downward from a luminaire which defines the maximum range of incident illumination outward at the ground plane.

19. *Logic of design.* Accepted principles and criteria of validity in the solution of the problem of design.

20. *Mechanical equipment.* Equipment, devices, and accessories, the use of which relates to water supply, drainage, heating, ventilating, air conditioning, and similar purposes.

21. *Miscellaneous structures.* Structures, other than buildings, visible from public ways. Examples are: memorials, stagings, antennas, water tanks and towers, sheds, shelters, fences and walls, kennels, transformers, drive-up facilities.

22. *Plant materials.* Trees, shrubs, vines, ground covers, grass, perennials, annuals, and bulbs.

23. *Proportion.* Balanced relationship of parts of a building, landscape, structures, or buildings to each other and to the whole.

24. *Scale.* Proportional relationship of the size of parts to one another and to the human figure.

25. *Screening.* Structure of planting which conceals from view from public ways the area behind such structure or planting.

26. *Shrub.* A multi-stemmed woody plant other than a tree.

27. *Site break.* A structural or landscape device to interrupt long vistas and create visual interest in a site development.

28. *Street hardware.* Man-made objects other than buildings which are part of the streetscape. Examples are: lamp posts, utility poles, traffic lights, traffic signs, benches, litter containers, planting containers, letter boxes, fire hydrants.

29. *Streetscape.* The scene as may be observed along a public street or way composed of natural and man-made components, including buildings, paving, planting, street hardware, and miscellaneous structures.

30. *Structure.* Anything constructed or erected, the use of which requires permanent or temporary location on or in the ground.

31. *Utilitarian structure.* A structure or enclosure relating to mechanical or electrical services to a building or development.

32. *Utility hardware.* Devices such as poles, crossarms, transformers and vaults, gas pressure regulating assemblies, hydrants, and buffalo boxes that are used for water, gas, oil, sewer, and electrical services to a building or a project.

33. *Utility service.* Any device, including wire, pipe, and conduit which carries gas, water, electricity, oil, and communications into a building or development.

34. *Village.* The Village of Libertyville, Illinois.

30.2.3 Criteria for Appearance

1. BUILDING DESIGN

(a) Architectural style is not restricted, however, extremes of style not indigenous to the Village are not encouraged. Evaluation of appearance of a project shall be based on quality of its design and relationship to surroundings.

(b) Buildings shall be in scale and harmonious with permanent neighboring developments.

(c) Materials shall be in harmony with adjoining structures.

(d) A minimum of different types of exterior wall materials should be used. Materials shall be selected for suitability to the type of building and design in which they are used.

(e) Materials shall be of durable quality.

(f) There should be definite transitions between changes of material and plane while maintaining an overall simple geometry for the building mass.

(g) In any design in which the structural frame is exposed to view, the structural materials shall be compatible within themselves and harmonious to their surroundings.

(h) Exterior building components such as windows, doors, eaves, and parapets shall have balanced proportions.

(i) All sides of a structure should receive design consideration. A facade unrelated to the rest of the building is not in keeping with acceptable design.

(j) Colors shall be harmonious, and accents, if used, shall be compatible.

(k) All projections and mechanical details such as louvers, exposed flashing, flues, vents, gutters and downspouts are to be recognized as architectural features and are to be treated to match the color of the adjacent surface or an approved complementary color.

(l) Mechanical equipment or other utility hardware on the roof, ground, or elevations shall, wherever possible, be located so as not to be visible from any public ways or adjacent residential areas. Where such limitation on location is not possible, the facilities shall be screened from public view with materials harmonious with the building.

(m) Refuse and waste removal areas, service yards, storage yards, and exterior work areas shall be screened from view from public ways with materials harmonious with the building.

(n) Monotony of design in single or multiple building projects shall be avoided. Variation of detail, form and siting shall be used to provide visual interest. In multiple building projects, variable siting of individual buildings may be used to prevent a monotonous appearance.

2. RELATIONSHIP OF BUILDINGS TO SITE

(a) Projects shall reflect the character of the site upon which they are located. Compatibility to grade conditions, degree of exposure from passers-by, the context of adjacent structures, exceptional views, tree masses, and size of the lot are some of the factors to be considered.

(b) The site shall be planned to accomplish a desirable transition with the streetscape, and to provide for adequate planting, safe pedestrian movement, and parking areas.

(c) Consideration of the appropriateness of providing setbacks and yards in excess of zoning restrictions is encouraged to enhance compatible relationships between buildings, and between buildings and adjacent streets.

(d) All plans shall demonstrate a concern for the conservation of energy by their sensitivity to factors such as the orientation of a building, the use and location of glass, and the use of landscape materials on the site.

(e) Parking areas shall be treated with decorative elements, building wall extensions, plantings, berms or other means so as to minimize the impact of parked vehicles on the view from public ways and adjacent residential areas.

(f) Fencing plans must be a part of the submittal at the earliest stages and should be consistent with the general plan for the site.

(g) The design of fences and screening walls shall give specific consideration to the relief of monotony, such as breaking up major lengths by complementary landscaping.

(h) Newly installed utility services, and service revisions necessitated by exterior alterations, shall be underground.

(i) Grades of walks, parking spaces, terraces, and other paved areas shall provide an inviting and stable appearance for walking and, if seating is provided, for sitting.

3. RELATIONSHIP OF PROJECT TO ADJOINING AREA

(a) Designers shall demonstrate a harmony in texture, lines, and masses between all adjacent buildings. Monotony shall be avoided.

(b) Without restricting the permissible limits of the applicable zoning district, the height and scale of each building shall be compatible with its site and existing (or anticipated) adjoining buildings.

(c) Adjacent buildings of different architectural styles shall be made compatible by such means as screens, sight breaks and materials.

(d) Attractive landscape transition to adjoining properties or compatible use characteristics shall be provided.

(e) Project features which may have negative impacts upon adjacent properties, such as parking lots, service entrances, loading zones, mechanical equipment, etc., shall be buffered from the adjacent properties.

4. LANDSCAPE AND SITE TREATMENT

(a) Where natural or existing topographic patterns contribute to beauty and utility of a development, they shall be preserved and enhanced. Modification to topography will be permitted where it contributes to good appearance.

(b) Each landscape plan shall address the functional aspects of landscaping such as drainage, erosion prevention, wind barriers, provisions for shade, energy conservation, sound absorption, dust abatement and reduction of glare.

(c) Landscape treatment shall be provided to enhance architectural features, strengthen vistas and important axes, and to provide shade.

(d) Unity of design shall be achieved by repetition of certain plant varieties and other materials, and by correlation with adjacent developments.

(e) Plant material shall be selected for interest in its structure, texture, and color and for its ultimate growth. Plants that are indigenous to the area and others that will be hardy, harmonious to the design, and of attractive appearance shall be used.

(f) Parking areas and related trafficways shall be enhanced with landscaped areas, including trees or tree groupings.

(g) In locations where plants will be susceptible to injury by pedestrian or motor traffic, they shall be protected by appropriate curbs, tree guards, or other devices.

(h) Where building sites limit planting, the placement of approved trees in parkways is encouraged.

(i) Where landscaping is used as screening, it shall be equally effective in winter and summer.

(j) In areas where general planting will not prosper, other materials shall be used, such as: fences, walls, and pavings of wood, brick, stone, gravel, and cobbles. Suitable plants shall be combined with such materials where possible.

(k) Landscape screening shall be of a height and density so that it provides the full desired effect within three years growing time.

5. SIGNS

(a) Every sign shall have appropriate scale in its design and in its visual relationship to buildings and surroundings.

(b) Every sign shall be designed as an integral architectural element of the building and site to which it principally relates.

(c) The height of a sign shall not exceed the predominant height of the principal building to which it relates, or the maximum height permitted by the Village's sign regulations, whichever is lower.

(d) The colors, materials and lighting of every sign shall be restrained and harmonious with the building and site to which it principally relates.

(e) The number of colors and graphic elements on a sign shall be held to the minimum needed to convey the sign's major message, and shall be composed in proportion to the area of the sign face. The listing of individual services rendered or items offered for sale, and the use of telephone numbers, street addresses, arrows, and multiple logos on a sign are generally unacceptable.

(f) Identification signs of a prototype design and corporation logos shall conform to the criteria for all other signs.

(g) Each sign shall be compatible with signs on adjoining premises, and shall not compete for attention.

6. LIGHTING

(a) All exterior lighting should balance the need for energy conservation with needs for safety, security and decoration.

(b) Where decorative exterior floodlighting is used, it shall consist of an appropriate composition of brightness relationships, textures, and restrained colors to dramatize a setting and extend the hours of the setting's usefulness. Floodlighting fixtures shall be located or shielded so that their presence is minimized.

(c) All exterior lighting shall be part of the architectural and landscape design concept. Fixtures, standards and all exposed accessories shall be concealed or harmonious with other project design materials.

(d) In general, the height of exterior lighting fixtures shall not exceed the predominant height of the principal building to which it relates.

(e) Exterior lighting shall not be designed to permit an adverse effect upon neighboring properties. Designers shall specify appropriate light cut-off angles for all sources of strong illumination.

(f) All free-standing parking lot and internal access route lighting shall be high pressure sodium vapor luminaires, color corrected where necessary for compatibility.

7. MISCELLANEOUS STRUCTURES AND STREET HARDWARE

(a) Miscellaneous structures and street hardware shall be designed to be part of the architectural and landscape design concept. The materials shall be compatible, the scale shall be appropriate, and the colors shall be in harmony with buildings and surroundings.

8. MAINTENANCE DESIGN FACTORS

(a) Continued quality of appearance depends upon the extent of quality of maintenance. The choice of materials and their use, together with the types of finishes and other protective measures, must be conducive to easy maintenance and upkeep.

(b) Materials and finishes shall be selected for their durability and wear as well as for their beauty. Proper measures and devices shall be incorporated for protection against the elements, neglect, damage and abuse.

(c) Provisions for washing and cleaning of buildings and structures, and control of dirt and refuse, shall be included in the design. Configurations that tend to catch and accumulate debris, leaves, trash, dirt and rubbish shall be avoided.

30.2.4 Additional Criteria for the Libertyville Heritage Area

The following criteria are unique to the Libertyville Heritage Area as defined by the *Heritage Development Plan* published in February, 1980. Applicants whose projects lie within the boundaries of the Heritage Area are subject to review based upon both the previous criteria listed in the Appearance Code and the additional criteria listed below.

The intent of the criteria for the Heritage Area is to create a recognition and enhancement of the significant 19th and early 20th century architecture that characterizes the area. However, the intent is not to encourage fake history or the proliferation of pseudo-period stylistic details. Designers should respect the scale, rhythm, materials, palette, and attention to detail that the traditional architecture conveys.

1. CRITERIA

(a) False and "add-on" building facades should be removed where possible to expose original architectural detail.

(b) Building facades shall respect the architectural heritage of the individual building and adjacent structures.

(c) The color of paint used on trim shall complement the color of brick, character of the building and adjacent structures. The range of colors shall be kept to a minimum.

(d) The original scale, proportions, lines and textures of the surrounding environment shall be respected and enhanced.

(e) The introduction of "colonial" or other foreign stylistic detailing on original 19th and early 20th century structures should be avoided.

(f) Elements that must be replaced should be of the same size, proportion and material as the original.

(g) Shutters, if utilized, shall be sized to appear as though they could work. It should be noted that shutters were seldom used on 19th and early 20th century buildings.

(h) Storm windows shall reflect the appearance and detail of the inner window as closely as possible.

(i) Preference should be given to building at the front setback line where a feeling of enclosure is desirable to define the urban space.

(j) The relationship of width to height of new structures shall be consistent with the ratio of the adjacent structures. If the site is large, the mass of the resulting facade can be broken into a number of smaller bays.

(k) The relationship of width to height of windows and doors shall relate to adjacent buildings.

(l) The rhythm of structural mass to voids (windows, doors, etc.) of a front facade shall relate to rhythms established in adjacent buildings.

(m) The rhythm of building mass to open spaces shall be reflected during new construction.

(n) New structures shall use materials that are predominant in the Heritage District to complement the existing buildings.

(o) The color of new structures shall relate to and complement the adjacent buildings.

(p) Detailing on new structures should relate to adjacent buildings.

(q) The roof design of new structures should reflect the predominant style of neighboring buildings.

(r) The scale of new construction shall contain appropriate elements which are oriented to the pedestrian.

(s) The materials selected for signs shall reflect the style, texture, and color of the related building facade.

(t) Accent lighting to highlight objects for aesthetic and safety reasons is encouraged.

(u) The orientation of buildings to provide access through rear entrances is encouraged. Such items as signage, paving, and landscape treatment are key items to such orientation.

(v) No new construction shall add any obstacles to a barrier-free exterior pedestrian system.

30.2.5 Continuing Maintenance

Even the best initial designs can be compromised by improper and inadequate maintenance. Such maintenance problems decrease property values and provide a negative impact on the whole community. Therefore, it is a necessary function for the Appearance Review Commission to be concerned about continuing maintenance.

1. BUILDINGS AND APPURTENANCES

(a) Buildings and appurtenances, including signs, shall be cleaned and painted or repaired as required to present a neat appearance.

(b) Deteriorated, worn, or damaged portions shall be rebuilt or replaced.

(c) Illuminated elements of buildings and signs shall be replaced as required to maintain the effect for which designed.

(d) No color, texture, shape, or other exterior design feature approved by the Appearance Review Commission shall be modified as a result of maintenance procedures, unless approved by the Commission.

2. SITE

(a) Landscape materials, other than plantings, which have deteriorated or have been damaged or defaced, shall be properly repaired or replaced.

(b) Plantings should be kept watered, fed, cultivated, and pruned as required to give a healthy and well groomed appearance during all seasons. Plant materials which have deteriorated or died shall be replaced with healthy plantings.

(c) Parking areas should be kept in good repair, properly marked, and clear of litter and debris.

(d) Vacant property shall be kept free of refuse and debris, and shall have the vegetation cut periodically during the growing season.

(e) No landscape design, plant materials, or other exterior design feature characteristic of the site approved by the Appearance Review Commission shall be modified as a result of maintenance procedures, unless approved by the Commission.

30.2.6 Relationship to Other Ordinances

Nothing herein contained shall be deemed or construed to modify or alter the provisions of any other chapter of the Municipal Code. In the event of a conflict between the requirements of this chapter and those of any other chapter of the Code, the latter shall prevail and control.

CHAPTER 5

Open Space and Land Use Planning

THIS section includes a pioneering hillside protection ordinance and hillside development guidelines enacted in San Diego, California. The ordinance applies as an overlay zone to areas with a natural gradient in excess of 25 percent and a minimum elevation differential of 50 feet. Within these areas, development must comply with several qualitative development guidelines and criteria designed to minimize disturbance of the natural terrain and to conserve the aesthetic quality of the hillside. This ordinance includes guidelines for both urban and urbanizing areas.

Also included is a zoning provision enacted in Falmouth, Massachusetts, to protect wildlife habitat corridors. This bylaw contains several standards to mitigate the impact of development on wildlife habitat and movements. It demonstrates how simple and inexpensive development standards can be incorporated into subdivisions and other development to reduce the impact on wildlife.

Finally, this chapter includes two ordinances that implement techniques described in the glossary. These ordinances have widespread application in protecting all types of key local resources and assets.

The first of these is an impact fee ordinance enacted by Martin County, Florida. This impact fee is designed to ensure that new development funds its share of beach land acquisition to fulfill the recreational demands of new residents. The standards and methodology used to assess a fair and defensible beach impact fee are relevant to a variety of local circumstances.

Also included is a moratorium ordinance (interim growth management regulations) enacted by the city of Dover, New Hampshire. This interim ordinance was enacted to provide the planning department with time to undertake a comprehensive revision of the city's comprehensive plan and zoning regulations. It demonstrates the factual circumstances under which a development moratorium is appropriate and likely to be upheld, and includes several provisions (an administrative appeal process, exemptions for minor developments, and exemptions for downtown, where development is encouraged) designed to fulfill the objectives of the moratorium while reducing the potential for litigation and minimizing the impact of the moratorium on property owners to that which is necessary.

San Diego, California
Hillside Review Overlay Zone and Hillside
Design and Development Guidelines*

Sec. 101.0454
A. Purpose and Intent _____

It is the purpose of the Hillside Review Overlay Zone to provide supplementary development regulations to underlying zones to assure that development occurs in such a manner as to protect the natural and topographic character and identity of these areas, environmental resources, the aesthetic qualities and restorative value of lands, and the public health, safety and general welfare by insuring that development does not create soil erosion, silting of lower slopes, slide damage, flooding problems, and severe cutting or scarring. It is the intent of this zone to encourage a sensitive form of development and to allow for a reasonable use which complements the natural and visual character of the City. Reference will made to the community plan recommendations and the hillside design guidelines when making the required findings of fact. In the case of conflict between the community plan and the guidelines, the plan shall apply.

B. Application of the Hillside Review Overlay Zone _____

After public hearing conducted pursuant to Chapter X, Article 1, Division 2 of the Municipal Code, and upon finding that the public health, safety, general welfare and good zoning practice will be served thereby, the Hillside Review Overlay Zone may be applied to property having slopes with a natural gradient in excess of 25 percent (25 feet of vertical distance for each 100 feet of horizontal distance) and a minimum elevation differential of 50 feet. If at such hearing it is determined that land located adjacent to the slope, either above or below, must be included in the Hillside Review Overlay Zone in order to promote the purpose and intent of this zone, such rim or bottom land may be included in the Hillside Review Overlay Zone provided that such area is within 300 feet of the nearest point of the slope to which the Hillside Review Overlay

* Every effort has been made to reproduce the presented material in an accurate form. Illustrations have been omitted due to difficulty in reproduction. For a copy of the original document, write to: San Diego City Hall, Office of the Clerk, 202 "C" Street, San Diego, CA 92101.

Zone is to be applied. The overall average slope will be used for property with varying slope gradients when determining the application of this overlay zone.

C. Permitted Uses

Permitted uses shall be those permitted by the underlying zone subject to the regulations and restrictions of the underlying zone in addition to the regulations and restrictions of this overlay zone.

D. Development Regulations

Within a Hillside Overlay Zone no building, improvement or portion thereof shall be erected, constructed, converted, established, altered or enlarged or used, or demolished, nor shall any lot or premises be excavated or graded until a Hillside Review Permit is obtained in accordance with the procedure set forth in this section, or a Conditional Use Permit is obtained in accordance with the procedure set forth in Chapter X, Article 1, Division 5, or a Planned Development Permit is obtained in accordance with the procedure set forth in Chapter X, Article 1, Division 9; provided, however, that a Hillside Review Permit will not be required in those cases where said building, improvement or portion thereof does not in any way alter the ground coverage of an existing building or structure. The granting of a Hillside Review Permit does not relieve the applicant for such permit of the responsibility for obtaining other applicable permits from the City and other governmental agencies, including a Land Development Permit from The City of San Diego, if such permit is required by the Municipal Code.

E. Hillside Review Permit

1. Upon the filing of an application with the Planning Director for a Hillside Review Permit, which application shall be accompanied by appropriate site plans, grading plans, sections and elevations, the Planning Director shall either: (1) approve the application; or, (2) deny the application. The plans, sections and elevations required to be submitted with a request for a Hillside Review Permit shall be only those required to inform the City as to the facts listed in paragraph "E.5." of this section.
2. The Planning Director shall examine the environmental document, plans, sections and elevations submitted with the application for a permit and determine whether or not a Hillside Review Permit should be issued. The Planning Director shall not issue a Hillside Review Permit unless the available information supports the findings of fact set forth in paragraph "E.5." of this section. In issuing a Hillside Review Permit, the Planning Director or Planning Commission may impose such conditions, including modification of the property development, parking and other regulations of the underlying land use zone, as deemed necessary and desirable to protect the public health, safety and general welfare in respect to the facts listed in paragraph "E.5." of this section and to protect the environment in keeping with the provisions of the California Environmental Quality Act and Chapter VI, Article 9 of the Municipal Code.

   Prior to approving or denying an application the Planning Director shall solicit the recommendations and comments of other public agencies, City Departments and interested groups. Where a tentative map or tentative parcel map is required, the decision of the Planning Director in regard to the Hillside Review Permit shall be made at the time action is taken on the map.
3. The Planning Director shall not approve any Hillside Review Permit unless the proposed development was publicly noticed in accordance with SEC. 101.0220.

4. Any decision of the Planning Director regarding a Hillside Review Permit may be appealed to the Planning Commission within 10 days of that action. The appeal shall be noticed in accordance with SEC. 101.0220 and filed in accordance with SEC. 101.0230.

5. In reviewing an application for a Hillside Review Permit, the Planning Director and/or the Planning Commission shall make the following findings of fact in the review process:

   a. The site is physically suitable for the design and siting of the proposed development. The proposed development will result in minimum disturbance of sensitive areas.

   b. The grading and excavation proposed in connection with the development will not result in soil erosion, silting of lower slopes, slide damage, flooding, severe scarring or any other geological instability or fire hazard which would affect health, safety and general welfare as determined by the City Engineer. Disturbed slopes are planted with native and self sufficient vegetation.

   c. The proposed development retains the visual quality of the site, the aesthetic qualities of the area and the neighborhood characteristics by utilizing proper structural scale and character, varied architectural treatments, and appropriate plant material.

   d. The proposed development is in conformance with the Open Space Element of the General Plan, the Open Space and Sensitive Land Element of the community plan, any other adopted applicable plan, and the zone. An open space easement or dedication is taken on portions of the development site, as appropriate, after consultation with the Park and Recreation Department.

   e. The proposed development is in conformance with the qualitative development guidelines and criteria as set forth in Document No. RR-26219 "Hillside Design and Development Guidelines."

6. The Planning Director, or the Planning Commission after the public hearing referred to in paragraph "E.3." of this section, may grant a Hillside Review Permit if, after considering the information presented in the application and after reviewing the plans, sections and elevations submitted with the application and after considering the testimony presented at the hearing, concludes that the available information supports the findings of fact set forth in paragraph "E.5." of this section.

7. In granting a Hillside Review Permit, the Planning Director or Planning Commission may impose such conditions as may be deemed necessary and desirable to protect the public health, safety and general welfare in respect to the facts listed in paragraph "E.5." of this section.

8. If the Planning Director or Commission, after considering the available information is unable to reach the findings of fact set forth in paragraph "E.5." of this section, the application shall be denied.

9. The decision of approving or denying the application shall include the findings of fact relied upon by the Planning Director or Planning Commission. The decision shall be filed with the City Clerk, the Zoning Administrator, Engineering and Development Department and the Building Inspection Department and a copy shall be mailed to the applicant.

10. The decision of the Planning Commission shall be final on the eighth day from the date of the Commission's decision except when an appeal is taken to the City Council as provided in SEC. 101.0240.

F. Assignment of Public Hearing Responsibility

Applications for a Hillside Review Permit requested or required in conjunction with other permits or variances requiring discretionary action by more than one decision-making authority or body, shall be heard by the senior granting authority or body.

The order of seniority from most senior to least senior is as follows:

1. City Council
2. Planning Commission
3. Planning Director or Subdivision Board
4. Zoning Administrator

G. Failure to Utilize Hillside Review Permit or Failure to Conform to or Comply with Conditions

1. Any Hillside Review Permit granted by the City as herein provided shall be conditioned upon the privileges granted being utilized within 36 months after the effective date thereof, except as otherwise provided within a phasing program, contained in: 1) a development agreement entered into between the City and owners of land located within the Hillside Review Permit area, 2) a specific plan applicable to the subject property, or 3) as otherwise provided by resolution approved by the City Council upon recommendation of the Planning Commission. Failure to utilize such permit within such period will automatically void the same, unless an extension of time has been granted by the Planning Director as set forth in paragraph "H" herein. Construction must actually be commenced within the stated period and must be diligently pursued to completion.
2. During the 36-month period referred to in this paragraph, the property covered by the Hillside Review Permit shall not be used for any purpose or use other than that authorized by the Permit.
3. The Planning Director shall determine whether the conditions and requirements of the Permit and the environmental report have been met by the permittee. The determination by the Planning Director shall be final and conclusive on all affected parties.

H. Extension of Time to a Hillside Review Permit

1. The Planning Director may, by resolution, grant an extension of time up to 36 months on the time limit contained in a currently valid Hillside Review Permit. To initiate a request for an extension of time, the property owner or owners shall file a written application with the Planning Director in the office of the Planning Department, prior to the expiration of the Hillside Review Permit. The Planning Director may grant the extension of time if it is found from the evidence submitted that there has been no material change of circumstances since the permit was originally granted.
2. The decision of the Planning Director may be appealed to the Planning Commission within 10 days of that action. The appeal shall be noticed in accordance with SEC. 101. 0220 and filed in accordance with SEC. 101.0230. The decision of the Planning Commission shall be final on the eighth day from the date of the Commission's decision except when an appeal is taken to the City Council as provided in SEC. 101.0240.

I. Cancellation of a Hillside Review Permit

A valid Hillside Review Permit granted by the Planning Director, or by the Planning Commission on appeal, or by the City Council on appeal, may be cancelled at any time during the 36-month period referred to in paragraph "G" herein. Cancellation may be initiated by the owner of the property covered by the permit by means of a communication directed to the Planning Director in the office of the Planning Department. The permit becomes void 120 days after receipt of the communication in the office of the Planning Department.

J. Annual Review

The City Council shall review this ordinance and the hillside design and development guidelines annually in accordance with the Permanent Rules of the Council.

Hillside Design and Development Guidelines: Purpose and Intent

It is the purpose of these guidelines to be used in conjunction with the Hillside Review Overlay Zone. The guidelines serve as a tool for a designer of hillside projects to be used during the design stage. The guidelines will also be used by City personnel in enhancing a project for a Hillside Review Permit.

It is the intent of these guidelines to provide direction for proposed development on hillsides: The guidelines are divided into urbanized and urbanizing communities and it is recognized that development needs of the two types of communities are different. It is also recognized that commercial and industrial lands have different property development regulations than residential lands. Lot sizes and structures are larger, pads need to be flat, and more parking and landscaping is needed. For this reason the designer of commercial and industrial property using these guidelines should consult the community plan and zoning requirements as well as these guidelines before final design preparation.

Urbanized Communities

FINDING: THE SITE IS PHYSICALLY SUITABLE FOR THE DESIGN AND SITING OF THE PROPOSED DEVELOPMENT. THE PROPOSED DEVELOPMENT WILL RESULT IN MINIMUM DISTURBANCE OF SENSITIVE AREAS.

Guideline 1: Design structures to fit into the hillside rather than altering the hillside to fit the structure.

    a. Standard prepared pads resulting in grading outside of the building footprint and driveway area shall be discouraged.

    b. Use retaining structures as an alternative to banks of cut and fill, and design and site such structures to avoid adverse visual impact.

    c. Consider "unconventional structures" which will fit into the hillside. This would include:

        1) stilt houses;

        2) reduced footprint design;

        3) multiple "step-up" or "step-down" structures; or

        4) structures with open foundations, if landscaping screens the underside area of the building.

    d. Use a foundation type that is compatible with existing hillside conditions.

Guideline 2: Development shall be sited on the least sensitive portion of the site to preserve the natural landforms, geological features and vegetation.

a. Design and locate structures so they fit into the contour of the hillside and relate to the form of the terrain.

b. Locate development to minimize disturbance of the sensitive area.

c. Minimize coverage by using multi-level structures.

d. Cluster development away from open space canyons as close to existing development as possible.

e. Avoid disturbance of major rock outcroppings, major trees, waterways, ridge lines, natural plant formations, and known archaeological sites.

f. Development should not overwhelm hillside vegetation to where the natural character of the hillside is destroyed.

g. When appropriate, place structure as close to the street as possible to preserve the natural terrain. In some cases this would require development on the steep portions to preserve the canyons; or development on the flat portions to preserve the hillsides.

h. Avoid, whenever possible, development encroachment into slope areas of 25 percent or more.

Guideline 3: A geological reconnaissance report shall be required for all proposed projects located within a "moderate" (C), "high" (D), or "variable" (BC or AC) Risk Zone, as identified on the geo-technical land use capability maps referenced by the Seismic Safety Element of the General Plan, with only the following criteria allowed: (as approved by the City Engineer)

a. Only low density or open space uses should be allowed.

b. Only allow grading which implements the required stabilization devices needed in highly erodable and unstable areas.

FINDING: THE GRADING AND EXCAVATION PROPOSED IN CONNECTION WITH THE DEVELOPMENT WILL NOT RESULT IN SOIL EROSION, SILTING OF LOWER SLOPES, SLIDE DAMAGE, FLOODING, SEVERE SCARRING OR ANY OTHER GEOLOGICAL INSTABILITY WHICH WOULD AFFECT HEALTH, SAFETY AND GENERAL WELFARE. DISTURBED SLOPES ARE PLANTED WITH NATIVE OR SELF-SUFFICIENT VEGETATION.

Guideline 4: Limit the amount of impervious surfaces. Design and site such surfaces to support the natural system of drainage.

a. Design drainage systems away from neighboring properties and into the existing water flow pattern.

b. Use wooden decks instead of concrete slabs for patios and parking.

c. Reduce width of street improvements, reduce sidewalk requirements, use common driveways and cluster units, if open space will thereby be preserved.

Guideline 5: The site should be replanted with self-sufficient trees, shrubs and ground-cover that is compatible with existing surrounding vegetation.

a. All manufactured slopes shall be planted with erosion control, fire resistant, and self-sufficient plantings.

b. Transitional slopes should be planted to enhance the blending between manufactured and natural slopes.

c. Landscaping plans should not require excessive irrigation needs.

Guideline 6: Utilize the structural quality of the soil as a determinant of the type of construction.

Assure hillside stability both during and after construction by recognizing soil characteristics, hydrology, and the steepness of the terrain. (For further guidance refer to "Technological Guidelines for Soil and Geology Reports," Engineering and Development Department, City of San Diego).

Guideline 7: In cases where cut and fill grading are required, the slopes shall avoid straight and unnatural slope faces.

a. All manufactured slopes shall be planted with erosion control, fire resistant, and self-sufficient plantings.
b. Transitional slopes should be planted to enhance the blending between manufactured and natural slopes.

FINDING: THE PROPOSED DEVELOPMENT RETAINS THE VISUAL QUALITY OF THE SITE, THE AESTHETIC QUALITIES OF THE AREA, AND THE NEIGHBORHOOD CHARACTERISTICS BY UTILIZING PROPER STRUCTURAL SCALE AND CHARACTER, VARIED ARCHITECTURAL TREATMENTS, AND APPROPRIATE PLANT MATERIAL.

Guideline 8: Employ a variation in architectural design.
   a. Design the garage space to be either under or over the structure depending on whether the lot is uphill or downhill from the street.
   b. Use deck areas, either on the roof of the garage, or the house, or extending from the house to reduce the amount of grading.
   c. Employ zero-lot line developments where permitted by zoning if visual or open space qualities can be gained.
   d. Vary the treatment of rooftops to avoid the monotony of materials, forms and colors. Rooftop utilities should be avoided except for solar-type improvements. Such improvements, however, should be an integral part of roof design.

Guideline 9: Consider existing vegetation when landscaping the site.
   a. Protect existing resources from being trampled or destroyed.
   b. Keep new landscaping compatible with existing vegetation and the scenic character of the area.
   c. Preserve the natural landscaping on slopes adjacent to natural canyon areas.

Guideline 10: Match scale and character of buildings with scale and character of terrain and the surrounding neighborhood.
   a. Keep the scale (height and bulk) of the structure compatible with the site and the neighborhood.
   b. Do not create development patterns which form visually protruding horizontal bands or vertical bulk. A mixture of shapes subordinate and compatible with the site and area should be achieved.
   c. Irregular architectural edges should be used to interlock structures with hillside contours and vegetation.
   d. Avoid visible construction cuts and permanent scarring.

Guideline 11: Provide pedestrian walkways to visual overlook areas.
   a. Pathways should provide public access to natural and recreational open spaces and vistas.

Urbanizing Communities: Tentative Maps and Planned Developments _____

FINDING: THE SITE IS PHYSICALLY SUITABLE FOR THE DESIGN AND SITING OF THE PROPOSED DEVELOPMENT. THE PROPOSED DEVELOPMENT WILL RESULT IN MINIMUM DISTURBANCE OF SENSITIVE AREAS.

Guideline 1: Roadways should not be parallel to one another to avoid a shelving effect. Roadways should follow the natural contours to avoid excessive cut and fill and emphasize the existing hillside topography, existing significant trees, major rock outcroppings, and other significant physical constraints.
   a. Roadways should follow the natural contours.
   b. Reduce roadway width if the design minimizes cut and fill. City policy allows deviations from standard requirements in areas of difficult terrain where flexibility is required.

c. When feasible, sidewalks should be on one side of the street only.

d. Encourage cul-de-sacs, loop streets and common driveways. Cul-de-sacs should contain sufficient turning radius to accommodate fire trucks.

e. Route streets around trees and major rock outcroppings.

Guideline 2: Parking should be unobtrusive and not cause additional grading.

Guideline 3: Place all utilities underground.

Guideline 4: Design the development to adapt to the natural hillside topography, terrain, and vistas.

a. Keep development close to the street to minimize the need for long driveways.

b. When feasible orient lots toward views and vistas, at right angles to contour lines.

c. Allow for different lot shapes and sizes, with the prime determinant being the natural terrain. Encourage split pads in large development projects.

d. Allow for flag lots in areas where the available building area is limited by topography. Flag lots should be used if the end result is the preservation of topography by minimizing grading. Twenty-five percent grade driveways should be discouraged.

Guideline 5: Significant hillsides in the urbanizing areas are defined as those areas unique to the particular site that deserve special attention and design consideration. These significant areas which shall be given priority for preservation include: 1) unique finger canyons, especially ones which are highly visible from public areas outside the project, 2) native tree stands or man-made groves which have matured into unique visual characteristics or environments, 3) rock outcroppings of unique character, 4) ridgelines where they are highly visable from adjacent public areas or neighborhoods, and 5) areas which are a part of or adjacent to an open space linkage system. While these areas may vary from site to site, project designs should give priority to their preservation. The intent is not to stop development, but to direct it toward the least sensitive areas of the site.

a. The project design should strive to preserve significant hillsides. Isolated pockets of 25 percent sloping land would not be classified as significant.

b. A tentative map should strive toward a design that does not create lots which are in their entirety in significant HR areas. Where creation of such lots cannot be avoided, such lots shall not be conventionally padded but shall be left in a natural slope. However, in certain cases where grading of the lots will result in a natural appearance, an overall grading plan will be considered on a case-by-case basis.

c. Encourage development on areas of the site and lot with less than a 25 percent natural grade.

Guideline 6: Cluster development to emphasize the existing topography and conserve existing resources.

a. Minimize coverage by using multi-story structures.

b. Identify all designated open space areas for preservation.

Guideline 7: A geologic reconnaissance report shall be required for all proposed projects. If a geological problem is suspected a more detailed geological report will be required.

FINDING: THE GRADING AND EXCAVATION PROPOSED IN CONNECTION WITH THE DEVELOPMENT WILL NOT RESULT IN SOIL EROSION, SILTING OF LOWER SLOPES, SLIDE DAMAGE, FLOODING, SEVERE SCARRING OR ANY OTHER GEOLOGICAL INSTABILITY WHICH WOULD AFFECT HEALTH, SAFETY AND GENERAL WELFARE. DISTURBED SLOPES ARE PLANTED WITH NATIVE OR SELF-SUFFICIENT VEGETATION.

Guideline 8: Identify on grading plan which slopes shall be landform graded and which slopes shall be conventionally graded. "Landform Grading" shall mean a contour grading method which creates artificial slopes with curves and varying slope ratios in the horizontal plane designed to simulate the appearance of surrounding natural terrain. The concept of Landform Grading incorporates the created ravine and ridge shapes with protective drainage control systems and integrated landscaping design.

   a. Slopes which shall be landform graded include slopes adjacent to scenic corridors, major and secondary highways; slopes subject to public view; slopes adjacent to open space areas, and slopes internal to the project which may be significant to public view.

   b. Slopes internal to the project may be conventionally graded, if deemed compatible with "a" above.

Guideline 9: On slopes where landform grading has been deemed appropriate, the required grading plans shall be designed to accomplish the following:

   a. Curved slopes. Linear slopes are to be avoided. Instead, cut and fill slopes shall have curved configurations which reflect as closely as possible the forms and shapes of surrounding topography. The toe and the top of the slope shall be curved in a concave and convex manner, respectively.

   b. Transition with Natural Slopes. At the intersections of manufactured and natural slopes, abrupt angular intersections should be avoided, contours should be curved to blend with the natural slope.

Guideline 10: "Step" development on existing slopes to maximize views. Utilize rooftops for private outdoor spaces.

Guideline 11: Use retaining structures when it significantly reduces grading or can eliminate long sliver cuts or fills.

Guideline 12: Design project to maximize public access to canyons, overlooks, or open space areas.

   a. Provide an easement between lots or near the end of streets or cul-de-sacs.

   b. Designate public pathways to scenic vistas.

Falmouth, Massachusetts
Wildlife Corridor Protection Bylaw

4600 Wildlife Corridor ————————————————————————

SECTION 4610 PURPOSE

Given that an enumerated purpose of zoning is the conservation of natural resources and that wildlife is a valued natural resource in Falmouth and finding that the Commonwealth of Massachusetts has established the importance of protecting wildlife through numerous laws, and finding that Falmouth has a significant stock of wildlife which moves through a large, defined area of town, and further finding that development under zoning can be designed to co-exist with the wildlife and important habitat areas, the purpose of this bylaw is to establish and protect permanent and contiguous corridors and special areas for the feeding, breeding and normal home range movement of wildlife through the defined habitat areas.

SECTION 4620 APPLICABILITY

All uses of land within the Wildlife Overlay District as shown on the Official Zoning Map shall be subject to the requirements of these sections. This includes: A. All sub-divisions and divisions of land. B. All special permits. C. All site plan reviews. D. As-of-right construction if it involves an area of disturbance greater than one-quarter ($1/4$) acre or movement of material equaling more than 2,000 cubic yards.

SECTION 4630 PROCEDURE

1. Upon submittal to the normal reviewing agency of plans for development, all plans subject to this section shall be referred to the Natural Resources Department.

2. Within thirty-five (35) days of such referral, the Natural Resources Department shall file a recommendation with the reviewing agency. This time may be extended at the request of the applicant. These recommendations shall be considered prior to the final decision of the agency, and all restrictions to the property added as a result must be shown on the final approved plan.

3. All areas on the plan set aside for protection of wildlife habitat shall be permanently conveyed in accordance with Section 6127, Ownership of Open Spaces, or shall be subject to a permanent conservation easement, and/or restriction.

SECTION **4640** STANDARDS

1. For those sites within Area 1, Deer Migration Areas, the following standards shall apply:

a. Subdivisions including "approval not required" subdivisions submitted in accordance with Sections 81-P of Ch. 41 M.G.L., which total more than 10 acres in the AGA, AGB, RA, PU and RB zones and more than 20 acres in the AGAA and RAA zones must submit to the Planning Board for a Special Permit under this Section and Section 7300. The Planning Board may require a cluster-type subdivision in accordance with Section 6100 of these bylaws if it facilitates the purposes of this bylaw.

b. The applicant shall establish contiguous corridors with a minimum three hundred foot width across the subject site and to adjacent parcels and corridors. Corridors less than 300 feet in width may only be allowed upon a finding by the Natural Resources Department that the purpose of this bylaw is not compromised and that proper mitigating measures are provided.

c. Fencing or any structural barrier to wildlife movement within corridors shall be prohibited.

d. The applicant shall ensure drainage from roadways be diverted away from depressed areas that may be used as shelter for wildlife.

e. Natural, indigenous vegetation shall be encouraged or enhanced by the project. Disturbed areas shall be re-vegetated as rapidly as possible or within a time required by the reviewing agency.

f. Dramatic changes in topography shall be discouraged and the footprint of disturbed areas shall be limited.

g. Speed limits shall be posted on all roads in the subdivision to lessen the probability of wildlife vs. vehicle accidents.

2. For those sites within Area 2, Dispersal Areas, the standards shall be the same as 4640.1, above, with the exception of 1.A, which shall not apply.

SECTION **4650** ANNUAL REVIEW

1. Annual reports from the Natural Resources Department shall be filed with the reviewing agency and the owner or owners of the subject property. These reports shall re-evaluate the corridors and open space and make recommendations for any adjustments in vegetative plantings.

SECTION **4660** REDUCTION IN LOT SIZE

1. Subdivisions of land with less area than the acreage specified in Section 4640 may vary lot size from that required by the applicable zoning district by up to 25% less than that required by Section 3441, Dimension Requirements, so long as the total number of lots is no more than the zoning district would allow under a conventional grid subdivision, and upon a finding by the Natural Resource Department that this variance is necessary to effect the purpose of this bylaw, or do or take any other action in this matter. On request of the Planning Board.

Martin County, Florida
Beach Impact Fee Ordinance

Resolution No. 83-1 _____

WHEREAS, Martin County's beaches are one of its finest recreational assets, providing the opportunity for enjoyment of various outdoor recreational activities in a healthful and natural environment; and

WHEREAS, the Martin County Comprehensive Plan Park, Recreation and Open Space Element provides that the county shall assure the acquisition and development of sufficient lands to meet recreational needs of Martin County citizens, and that beach acquisition shall be the top recreation priority; and

WHEREAS, Martin County has the authority to charge a beach impact fee to new Martin County residents in order to acquire the beach lands necessary to meet the new resident demand for recreational beach land; and

WHEREAS, Martin County has conducted or caused to be conducted the necessary and expert studies to develop an accurate and equitable formula by which to determine the appropriate fee per dwelling unit to charge new development to pay for the cost of acquiring recreational beach land; and

WHEREAS, the Beach Acquisition Committee of Martin County is charged with the responsibility of reviewing and adopting an accurate and equitable beach impact fee formula;

NOW, THEREFORE, be it resolved that the following beach impact fee formula is hereby adopted:

The beach impact fee formula herein provides a systematic method by which to determine an appropriate fee to be assessed against new residents to pay for the recreational beach lands needed as a result of new resident demand. The formula is based upon each new resident's average expected frequency of usage, and standard amount of beach needed per person. This is calculated as the "beach land acquired per new resident" and is derived from State of Florida Recreational Planning Standards. The "cost per linear foot of beach land" is based on the existing market value in Martin County for a linear foot of beach land. Using these two factors, the formula establishes the beach acquisition cost per person. The cost per person is then converted to an impact fee per dwelling unit, based upon average household sizes per dwelling unit as provided for in the Martin County Comprehensive Plan. The formula for the beach impact fee is set forth below. Additionally, a credit will be computed, and a refund given to the developer as the dwelling unit is placed on the County tax roll, based on the property tax estimated to be paid per dwelling unit for the Martin County beach acquisition bond over the remaining life of the bond. A computational procedure for the fee credit is included on page 142.

Beach Impact Fee Formula

The formula for determining the appropriate beach impact fee for each dwelling unit type is:

$$\text{Beach land required per new resident} \times \text{Cost per Linear foot of beachland} \times \text{Average household size for dwelling unit type}$$

The formula is based on the following standards:

1. Beach land required per new resident = .0211 linear feet. This demand factor is based upon established recreational standard of 2.5 linear feet of beach land per person, per day, and assuming that the same beach land will be used twice during the same day. It is also based upon the standard of new resident beach land usage of 3.42 times per year. Finally, the factor is modified by a "peaking factor" representing the fact that beach use occurs more often at various peak times during the year, specifically, 55% of the total attendance will occur on 111 days of the year.

The demand factor is thus derived from the following calculations:

a) $\dfrac{2.5 \text{ linear feet}}{2 \text{ uses per day}} = 1.25$ linear feet per user occasion

b) $\dfrac{3.42 \times .55}{111} = 0.0171$ uses per resident per peak day

c) $1.25 \times .0171 = .0211$ linear feet per new resident

2. Cost of linear foot of beach land = $3,000.00. Each linear foot also includes a minimum depth from the mean high water line of 80 feet. The cost does not include that of site improvements.

3. Average household size for dwelling unit type follows the schedule below:

Dwelling Unit Type	Average Household Size
Single family/duplex	2.9 persons
Mobile home	2.3
Multi-family/ Condominium	2.0

Fee Schedule

Using the formula above, the following fee schedule is established:

Dwelling Type	Per Capita Requirement (3000 = .0211)	Average Household Size Per Dwelling Unit	Beach Impact Fee
Single family	$63.30	2.9	$183.57
Mobile home	$63.30	2.3	$145.59
Multi-family/ Condominium	$63.30	2.0	$126.60

Application of the Formula

All new Residential Planned Unit Developments in Martin County and those Residential Planned Unit Developments having agreed to a beach impact fee shall be assessed a beach impact fee according to the formula. However, in the case in which a new Residential Planned Unit Development will be located west of the Florida Turnpike, the fee payor shall be granted the option of paying the fee as determined by the formula, or providing an independent calculation of a beach impact fee based on documented evidence that the development impact is less than that determined by the formula. The documentation must include evidence in regard to the factors set out in the beach impact fee formula.

After a certificate of occupancy is issued for a dwelling unit, and after the taxes for the following year have been paid for that dwelling unit, the developer shall be entitled to a rebate of the estimated share of the property taxes which that dwelling unit will contribute to the retirement of the 1982 beach bond issue. The method of calculating this credit is shown on page 142.

In the event that a Residential Planned Unit Development shall be located on the beach and thus provides beach land for use by new residents of that development, a credit shall be given to the development for the beach lands provided. The amount of the credit shall be determined by the Board of County Commissioners after recommendation by the Community Development Department.

Future Refinements

The fee formula and resulting fee schedule shall be subject to future refinements based on new information or further studies. For example, should present beach acquisition costs change, the cost factor of the formula will be modified to reflect that change.

Similarly, should future County studies indicate that beach usage varies according to the particular locations within the County, the application of the fee may also change to reflect any such geographical differential.

DULY PASSED AND ADOPTED by the Beach Acquisition Committee this 21 day of July, 1983.

COMPUTATION OF REFUND CREDIT FOR BEACH BOND ISSUE

After a Certificate of Occupancy is issued for each dwelling unit and the taxes for the following year have been paid, the developer shall be entitled to a rebate representing the present value of the stream of future ad valorem tax payments which that dwelling unit can be expected to pay toward the remaining debt service on the 1982 beach bond issue.

The procedure for computing present value of each year's ad valorem tax payment is illustrated below. This procedure must be replicated for each year of remaining bond issue payments. The rebate will be the sum of computations for each year.

Computational Procedure

$$\frac{\text{Bond issue debt service payment}}{\text{Countrywide total taxable valuation}} = \text{Countrywide millage necessary to meet bond issue debt service payment}[1]$$

$$\text{Countrywide millage necessary to meet beach bond issue debt service payment} \times \text{Taxable value of dwelling unit}[2] = \text{Ad valorem tax payment for beach bond issue}$$

$$\text{Ad valorem tax payment for beach bond issue} \times \text{Present value factor based on discount rate \&}[3] \text{ number of years}[4] = \text{Present value of Ad valorem tax payment}$$

[1] The millage rates used to calculate the stream of tax payments over the remaining life of the bond issue will be those rates which, when applied to the County's total taxable valuation (existing valuation for the first year and estimated valuation for subsequent years), yield the debt service payment required by the bond issue as recited on Page Three of the bond issue prospectus dated December 1, 1982.

[2] The assessed value of the dwelling unit used to calculate the stream of tax payments over the remaining life of the bond issue will be the taxable value of the dwelling unit (existing for the first year and estimated for subsequent years) taking into account the exemptions for which the unit may become eligible.

[3] The discount rate employed in this present value calculation shall be the Average Municipal Bond Yield published in the most recent issue of the Weekly Bond Buyer.

[4] The period over which this present value shall be calculated will begin on the date on which the dwelling unit is entered on the tax roll and will end with the 1992 tax year, the last year of the bond issue debt service.

Dover, New Hampshire
Interim Growth Management Regulations

Section I. Findings of Fact _____

1. Growth rates in Dover since 1983 are unprecedented. Previously, development pressures were low for several years. The city did not anticipate this recent level of development and could not reasonably be expected to have done so.

2. Current growth in Dover threatens to exceed the design capacity of the existing wastewater treatment plant. At the current rate of growth, sewage demand of new development may exceed the capacity of the facility before a new facility, currently in the design and engineering phase, is operational.

3. The substandard character of many rural roads is not suited for the traffic generated by increasing residential development in outlying areas of Dover. Existing development regulations fail to ensure that these roads can adequately and safely serve traffic generated by new residential development.

4. Dover's current growth imminently threatens to exceed the capacity of the school system's capital facilities. The City Council is actively investigating options for expanding the capacity of the elementary schools. The School Committee has requested the Council to expand the system. Current growth may cause the city to fall into non-compliance with state Board of Education standards until new facilities are operational. Existing regulations fail to ensure that the school system's capital facilities will be adequate to meet demands caused by increased rates of residential development.

5. The City of Dover relies in part on subsurface aquifers for its water supply needs. Aquifer recharge areas have been identified within the city, but have not yet been mapped in detail. Mapping and analysis of these areas are under way. To protect the integrity of aquifer recharge areas, development which will be incompatible with aquifer protection should be constrained until these areas are definitively mapped, and regulations enacted to protect their integrity.

6. The City of Dover has experienced a disproportionate percentage of residential, and specifically multi-family, development. The existing zoning regulations do not ensure that types of development in Dover will be properly balanced to promote the welfare of the community.

7. The last comprehensive revision of the Master Plan for the City of Dover was in 1971, with minor revisions made in 1979. The Planning Department has commenced, and is diligently pursuing, comprehensive revisions to the Master Plan. The current Master Plan is outdated because of its age and because conditions in Dover have significantly changed due to recent growth.

8. The existing zoning regulations for the City of Dover inadequately address the city's current level and scope of development pressure. The Zoning Code fails to ensure the city the ability to provide essential municipal services at levels required by recent growth. In particular, the regulations for multi-family housing fail to ensure that multi-family housing will be serviced adequately by essential municipal services.

Section II. Purpose

This interim regulation is adopted to promote and ensure the orderly development of land within the City of Dover; to promote the public health, safety and welfare of its residents; and for the following specific purposes:

1. To manage growth to ensure its compatibility with the Master Plan for the City of Dover.
2. To prevent premature approval of new development which will be incompatible with the Master Plan currently being revised, and with the growth management process.
3. To provide the city adequate time to revise the Master Plan and the Zoning Code so that the City of Dover can effectively manage its growth.
4. To permit the opportunity for reasoned public debate on desired Master Plan and Zoning Code revisions.
5. To ensure, for the existing and future population of the City of Dover, that essential municipal services, such as transportation, surface drainage, water supply, sewage disposal, schools, recreation and other services, are available and will have sufficient capacity and quality to accommodate new development.

Section III. Authority

This interim regulation is enacted pursuant to the authority granted in RSA 674:23.

Section IV. Enactment

The City of Dover Planning Board, City Council, or Zoning Board of Adjustment shall not formally accept, consider or act upon any applications for multi-family housing, mobile home parks as defined in Chapter 170-6 of the Code of the City of Dover, or condominiums proposed pursuant to the New Hampshire Condominium Act, RSA Sections 356-B:1 to 356-B:69, which would result in the creation of three or more dwelling units, or for the subdivision of land for residential purposes until the expiration of this interim regulation unless specifically excepted in this regulation. For the purpose of this interim regulation, multi-family housing is defined as: "a building designed for, or used as, three or more dwelling units." This interim regulation shall apply to any application for multi-family housing, mobile home parks or condominiums, or for any subdivision of land for residential purposes on any land located within the City of Dover formally accepted by the Planning Commission after the effective date of this interim regulation, unless specifically excepted in this regulation.

Section V. Expiration

This interim regulation shall remain in effect for a period of one year from the date of enactment. The City Council may repeal this interim regulation sooner than the expiration date if, in its judgment, the unusual circumstances requiring its enactment no longer apply and its repeal is justified.

Section VI. Zoning District Exemptions

A. Purpose

The downtown districts are exempted from this interim regulation for the following reasons:

1. Commercial growth in Dover has been moderate. Interim growth controls are therefore unnecessary to control commercial growth.
2. There is a pressing public need for downtown revitalization, and for rehabilitation and reuse of vacant downtown buildings.
3. Downtown businesses and the entire city benefits from the promotion of pedestrian traffic emanating from residential development in the downtown districts.
4. An appropriate mix of uses, including residential uses, is necessary for an effective and successful downtown reuse project.
5. A newly enacted element of the Master Plan for the City of Dover addresses downtown development, and accurately guides development and land use within the downtown districts.
6. Downtown development will not appreciably increase impervious surfaces and will therefore not affect aquifer recharge areas.
7. Reuse of vacant downtown buildings is likely to increase the diversity of regional housing types, provide affordable housing, and produce fewer school children per unit.
8. The UMUD and CWD zoning districts were established in 1983 and provide effective control over downtown development.

B. Enactment

Notwithstanding anything herein to the contrary, this interim regulation shall not apply to applications for multi-family housing regardless of the form of ownership, within the UMUD, CWD or B-2 zoning districts, as those zoning districts appeared on the zoning map on May 1, 1987.

Section VII. Development Proposals Exemptions

A. Purpose

Minor subdivisions are exempted from this interim regulation for the following reasons:

1. The Planning Board and City Council wish to address the pressing growth related concerns stated in Section I while interfering with the expectations of property owners as little as possible.
2. The Planning Board and City Council find that the regulation of minor subdivisions under the interim regulation is unnecessary to meet the purposes of this interim regulation.

B. Enactment

Notwithstanding anything herein to the contrary, this interim regulation shall not apply to: 1) applications for minor subdivisions as defined in Chapter 155-60 of the Code of the City of Dover; 2) applications for single-family or two-family residences proposed for lots of record existing on the effective date of this regulation; or 3) developments which have received Planning Board approval prior to the effective date.

Section VIII. Pending Applications

The provisions of this interim regulation shall not apply to any plat or application which has been formally accepted by the Planning Board prior to the first legal notice of the first public hearing on this proposed interim regulation.

Section IX. Administrative Appeals

An administrative appeals procedure shall be created to provide administrative review of decisions under this interim regulation. Any person aggrieved by any decision of an administrative official or the Planning Board denying any application due to this interim regulation may appeal to the Zoning Board of Adjustment. The Zoning Board of Adjustment shall have the following authority: To hear appeals where it is alleged there is an error in an order, requirement, decision or determination of an administrative official in the enforcement of the interim regulation; and to authorize a variance from the terms of this interim regulation in cases where unusual difficulty or special hardship would be imposed by the literal application and rigorous enforcement of the interim regulation. The provisions of §170-52 of the Dover City Code shall govern appeals under this interim regulation.

Section X. Conflicts

Where any provision of this interim regulation imposes restrictions different from those imposed by any other provision of the Code of the City of Dover, or any other rule or regulation or other provision of law, whichever provision is more restrictive or imposes higher standards shall control.

Section XI. Separability

If any part of provision of this interim regulation, or the application thereof to any person or circumstances is adjudged invalid by a court of competent jurisdiction, such judgment shall not affect or impair the validity of the remainder of this interim regulation or the application thereof to other persons or circumstances.

Section XII. Amendments

This interim regulation may be amended by the City Council after a public hearing on said amendment(s).

Section XIII. Construction

Unless the context clearly indicates to the contrary, words used in the present tense include the future tense; words used in the future tense include the present tense; words used in the plural number include the singular; words used in the singular include the plural; and a "building" includes any part thereof.

CHAPTER 6

Articles of Incorporation

THIS chapter includes the articles of incorporation and bylaws for two land trusts—the Triangle Land Conservancy in North Carolina and the Brandywine Conservancy, which is active in Pennsylvania and Delaware.

The Triangle Land Conservancy represents a conventional land conservancy that principally acquires and preserves land.

The Brandywine Conservancy is a "full-service" land use group that acquires land for preservation,

acquires lands and undertakes development projects that reconcile conservation objectives with the financial need for limited development, conducts land use planning studies, assists landowners with land conservation plans, operates a museum, and undertakes historic preservation and rehabilitation efforts.

Both samples contain provisions that have proven helpful for the efficient management and administration of land conservation organizations.

Articles of Incorporation and Bylaws
of
Triangle Land Conservancy

We, the undersigned natural persons of the age of eighteen (18) years or more, acting as incorporators for the purpose of creating a non-profit corporation under the laws of the State of North Carolina, as contained in Chapter 55A of the General Statutes of North Carolina, entitled "Non-Profit Corporation Act," and the several Amendments thereto do hereby set forth:

I.
The name of the corporation is TRIANGLE LAND CONSERVANCY

II.
The period of duration of the corporation shall be perpetual.

III.
The purposes for which the corporation is organized are:

(a) To identify and characterize lands and properties which have a unique public value and which would be of greatest benefit to the area if held in public trust.

(b) To educate the people and their elected officials of our region about the connection between land use decisions and the health, prosperity, and stability of present and future generations.

(c) To acquire rights to property, including scenic and conservation easements, development rights and fee simple ownership, and to hold or assign these rights as the trust deems appropriate.

(d) To manage certain important lands and properties for the public benefits that derive from natural diversity and productivity and to encourage public access to and the use of land in order to provide enjoyment and education consistent with good stewardship.

(e) To provide a flexible, efficient means for operation within the real estate market to preserve important lands for the public benefit.

(f) To supplement, complement, and aid private and public efforts to achieve conservation purposes.

(g) To encourage scientific evaluation and reporting on lands of importance to the region.

(h) To obtain funds which would be available for the above purposes of the trust.

IV.
The corporation shall have members. The qualifications, rights, and classes, if any, of the members shall be established in the By-Laws of the corporation.

V.
The initial directors of the corporation shall be elected by the Board of Delegates of Triangle J Council of Governments. Thereafter, the Directors shall be elected by the members of the corporation. The number of Directors, their term of office and the election procedures shall be as established in the By-Laws of the corporation.

VI.

The address of the initial registered office of the corporation is _____ Street, City of Raleigh, North Carolina, 27602, County of Wake. The name of the initial registered agent of the corporation at the above address is: David H. Permar.

VII.

The number of directors constituting the initial Board of Directors shall be three (3), and the names and addresses (including street and number, if any) of the persons who are to serve as directors until the first meeting of the corporation or until their successors are elected and qualified are:

NAME	STREET ADDRESS	CITY OR TOWN
1. _____	_____	_____
2. _____	_____	_____
3. _____	_____	_____

VIII.

The names and addresses (including street and number, if any) of all the incorporators are:

NAME	STREET ADDRESS	CITY OR TOWN
1. _____	_____	_____
2. _____	_____	_____
3. _____	_____	_____

IX.

The corporation shall have all the powers granted to non-profit corporations under Chapter 55A of the General Statutes, and in particular, but not limited to, under N.C.G.S. Sections 55A-15.

X.

In general, and subject to such limitations and conditions as are or may be prescribed by law, the corporation will exercise such other powers which may be necessary or incidental to the attainment of the purposes under the corporation and as may be exercised by an organization exempt under Section 501(C)(3) of the Internal Revenue Code of 1954 and its Regulations, as they now exist or may hereafter be amended, and by an organization, contributions to which are deductible under Section 170(C)(2) of such Code and Regulations.

XI.

Notwithstanding any other provision of this certificate, the corporation shall not conduct or carry on any activities not permitted to be conducted or carried on by an organization exempt under Section 501(C)(3) of the Internal Revenue Code of 1954 and its Regulations, as they now exist or they may hereafter be amended or by an organization, contributions to which are deductible under Section 170(C)(2) of such Code and Regulations.

XII.

In the event of the dissolution of the corporation, all of the assets of the corporation shall be distributed exclusively to be used and dedicated as nearly as practicable in accordance with the purposes of this corporation as set forth herein, provided that no such assets shall be distributed other than to or for the benefit of organizations qualifying at the time of such distributions under the provisions of Section 501(C)(3) of the Internal Revenue Code of 1954 and its Regulations as they may now exist or may hereafter be amended.

IN TESTIMONY WHEREOF, we have hereunto set our hands this the 11 day of February, 1989.

Bylaws
of
Triangle Land Conservancy

ARTICLE I
Name, Seal and Address

1. Name.—The name of this corporation is:
   TRIANGLE LAND CONSERVANCY

2. Seal.—The seal of the corporation shall be:

3. Address.—The address of the corporation shall be:
   100 Park Drive
   Research Triangle Park, NC 27709

ARTICLE II
Purposes

The purposes of the corporation shall be those set forth in the Articles of Incorporation.

ARTICLE III
Membership

1. Eligibility.—Public and private organizations and individuals interested in the objectives and purposes of the corporation and willing to uphold its policies and subscribe to its By-Laws shall be eligible for membership upon payment of dues as hereinafter provided.

2. Classes.—There shall be five classes of membership: individual, family, fixed income, organizational and corporate.

3. Individuals.—Any individual the age of eighteen years or over desiring to become a member of the corporation in an individual membership category may do so by application for such membership, the payment of dues specified for that class of membership, and the approval of the Board of Directors. An individual membership shall be entitled to one vote on all matters submitted to a vote of the membership.

4. Families.—Any family unit desiring to become a member of the corporation in a family membership category may do so by application for such membership, the payment of dues specified for that class of membership, and the approval of the Board of Directors. A family membership shall be entitled to one vote on all matters submitted to a vote of the membership.

5. Individuals with fixed incomes.—Any individual, either students or elderly or those on limited incomes, desiring to become a member of the corporation may do so by application for such membership, the payment of dues specified for that class of membership, and the approval of the Board of Directors. Members in this category will be entitled to one vote on all matters submitted to a vote of the membership.

6. Organizations.—Any organization desiring to become a member of the corporation in an organizational membership category may do so by submitting to the Board of Directors a statement by its president and secretary that the organization has voted to apply for membership, by payment of dues specified for that class of membership, and the approval of the Board of Directors. An organizational membership shall be entitled to one vote on all matters submitted to a vote of the membership.

7. Corporations.—Any corporation desiring to become a member of the corporation in a corporate membership category may do so by submitting to the Board of Directors a statement by its president and/or representative to the community that the corporation is

interested in membership, and has paid dues specified for that class of membership. A corporate membership shall be entitled to one vote on all matters submitted to a vote of the membership.

8. Ineligibility.—No individual shall hold membership in more than one membership category.

9. Duration.—Memberships shall run for one year. Administration of membership, recruitment, and enrollment will be according to the policy of the Board.

10. Termination.—Membership shall be terminated by resignation or by non-payment of dues.

ARTICLE IV
Officers

1. Officers.—The officers of the corporation shall be a President, Vice-President, Treasurer and Secretary, each of whom shall be a member and shall be elected at an annual meeting of the membership for the term of one year or until his successor is duly elected and qualified. The President can be elected to no more than two consecutive terms.

2. Absence.—Except as otherwise provided herein, in case of the absence of an officer or, for any reason, the inability of an officer to act, the Board of Directors may appoint a member to perform the duties of such officer during the period of his absence or inability to act.

3. Vacancy.—In case of a vacancy in an office, the Board of Directors may appoint a member by an affirmative vote of $2/3$ of the Board to fill such vacancy until the next annual meeting.

4. Removal.—Any officer may be removed, upon recommendation of a majority of the Board of Directors, by a two-thirds ($2/3$) vote of the members present and voting at a meeting of the corporation.

5. President.—The President shall be the chief executive officer of the corporation. The President shall preside at all meetings of the members and of the Board of Directors at which he is present. The President shall have a prepared statement of the affairs of the corporation to be submitted at the annual meeting. The President shall have the general powers and duties usually vested in the office of president of a corporation, including the appointment of committees as may be deemed appropriate or as the Board of Directors may authorize or as may be otherwise required. The following shall be considered standing committees: Finance, Land Acquisition, Properties and Maintenance, Community Relations, Education, and Membership. In addition, an advisory board shall be appointed by the President. The President is an ex-officio member of all committees, with voting power. Chairmen of all standing committees shall be appointed by the President (see Section 9).

6. Vice-President.—The Vice-President shall work and cooperate with the President in the exercise of the powers and duties of the President as the President may request from time to time and shall act in place of and for the President in event of the latter's absence.

7. Secretary.—The Secretary shall attend the meetings of the members and directors and shall record in the record book of the corporation the proceedings of the members and directors at their respective meetings. The Secretary shall maintain membership records, shall notify the members and directors of their respective meetings in accordance with these By-Laws and shall perform such other duties as are usually incident of the office or as the Board of Directors shall from time to time prescribe.

8. Treasurer.—The Treasurer shall have the custody of all funds of the corporation and shall deposit the same in the name of the corporation in such bank or financial institutions as the Directors may choose; the Treasurer shall collect all dues and other income; shall sign all checks, drafts, notes and orders for the payment of money, and shall pay out and dispose of the same under the direction of the Board of Directors; the Treasurer shall at all reasonable times keep books and accounts open to any director or member of the corporation and shall be prepared to give financial reports as the Board of Directors may require (see Section 9).

9. Limitations of Authority.—

a) President—The President will not act in matters relating to the acceptance or transfer of land or interests in land, or in executing papers including deeds, mortgages, leases, transfers, contracts, bonds, notes, powers of authority and other obligations made, without approval of a majority of the Board.

b) Treasurer—The Treasurer will not execute checks, drafts, notes, and other orders for the payment of money for land transactions without approval of the majority of the Board.

ARTICLE V
Board of Directors

1. Election, composition.—The Board of Directors shall consist of the President, the Vice-President, the Secretary, the Treasurer and no more than nine and no less than five other members. The President shall be Chairman of the Board of Directors. Each member of the Board other than the President, the Vice-President, the Treasurer and the Secretary shall serve for terms of three years or until a successor is qualified. Terms shall be staggered. Successors to Directors whose terms are expiring shall be elected at each annual meeting.

2. Honorary Board Members.—The Board shall elect, by a ⅔ majority of members present, Honorary Board Members who shall serve for up to 3 years. They may perform such duties as may be prescribed in these By-Laws or assigned by the Board of Directors.

3. Meetings.—The Board of Directors shall meet as often as it considers necessary to transact the business of the corporation. Meetings shall be called by the President or by any two Directors. The Secretary shall notify the members of the Board of Directors at least seventy-two (72) hours before the meeting, to each such member at his usual place of business or abode. The 72 hours notice may be waived at the discretion of the President in the event of an emergency. Unless otherwise specified in the notice any and all business may be transacted at any meeting of the Board. A majority of the Board of Directors shall constitute a quorum. The President, and in his absence the Vice-President, shall preside at all meetings of the Board of Directors. In the event of the absence of both, any other Director designated by the President may preside at said meeting.

3. Powers.—The Board of Directors shall have the control and management of the affairs, business and property of the corporation. In addition to exercising all the powers conferred upon it as set forth in these By-Laws and the Articles of Incorporation, and do all such lawful acts and things as are not by statute or by these By-Laws divested or required to be exercised or done by the members.

4. Vacancies.—In case of any vacancy in the Board of Directors, another member shall be appointed by the Board to serve for the remainder of the term of the vacated seat.

5. Removal.—Any Director may be removed upon recommendation of a majority of the Board of Directors by an affirmative vote of ⅔ of the Board of Directors present and voting at a meeting of the corporation.

ARTICLE VI
Meetings of the Corporation

1. Annual Meeting.—The annual meeting of the members of the corporation shall be held at the principal office of the corporation, or at such other place in the Triangle J Region as the Board of Directors may fix in each year to elect officers or directors, hear reports of officers and transact other business. An annual meeting of the Board of Directors shall be held immediately after, and at the same place, as the annual meeting of members.

2. Special Meetings.—Special meetings of the members of the corporation may be fixed by a majority of the Board of Directors, or, upon the written application of ten or more members in good standing, stating the time, place, and purpose of the special meeting and directed to the Secretary. Special meetings of the Board of Directors may be called by or at the request of the President or any four Directors by stating the time, place, and purpose of the special meeting at least 2 days in advance of such meeting.

3. <u>Quorum</u>.—At any meeting of the members of the corporation a quorum for the transaction of business shall consist of not less than ten (10) members.

4. <u>Notice</u>.—Notice of all meetings of members of the corporation shall be given in the following manner: A written notice stating the place, day and hour of the meeting shall be given by the Secretary, by mail, to each member at least ten (10) days before the date fixed for such meeting. For special meetings the notice shall also contain a brief statement of the purpose of such meeting.

ARTICLE VII
Elections and Voting

1. <u>Ballots</u>.—A majority of the ballots cast by all voting members shall be necessary for election as an officer or director. In the event no candidate receives a majority on the first ballot, there shall be a second ballot between the two candidates receiving the greatest number of votes on the first ballot.

3. <u>Nominations</u>.—The President shall, prior to the annual meeting, appoint a nominating committee which shall report to the annual meeting and nominate members for election as officers and directors of the corporation. Nominations may also be made at the annual meeting by any member entitled to vote.

3. <u>Majority</u>.—Except as herein provided all votes shall be determined by a simple majority of those members present and voting.

ARTICLE VIII
Nominating Committee

1. There shall be a nominating committee composed of four members selected by the Board of Directors from the membership. The chairman shall be selected by the members of the nominating committee.

2. The nominating committee shall nominate one eligible person for each office and directorship to be filled and report its nominees at the annual meeting at which time additional nominations may be made from the floor.

3. Only these persons who have signified their consent to serve if elected shall be nominated for or elected to such offices or directorship.

ARTICLE IX
Publications

Publications and public statements bearing the corporation's name shall be issued under the supervision of the Board of Directors. Any material concerning the activities or public positions of the corporation or of any of its committees, which is prepared by any member for publication or public statement shall be approved by majority vote of the Board of Directors prior to release of publication.

ARTICLE X
Execution of Papers

All deeds, mortgages, leases, transfers, contracts, bonds, notes, powers of attorney and other obligations made, executed or endorsed by the corporation, except checks, notes, drafts and other instruments for the payment of money, shall be signed by the President. Checks, notes, drafts and other instruments for the payment of money drawn or endorsed in the name of the corporation may be signed by the President or the Treasurer. The Board of Directors may authorize and empower one of said officers or other agent of the corporation to execute and deliver any and all papers or documents or to do any other acts or things on behalf of the corporation, including any required by or convenient in dealings with governmental authority.

ARTICLE XI
Fiscal Year

The fiscal year of the corporation shall end on the June 30th day of each year.

ARTICLE XII
Prohibition Against Sharing in Corporate Earnings

No member, officer, director or any other private individual shall receive at any time any of the net earnings or pecuniary profit from the operations of the corporation, provided that this shall not prevent the payment of any such person of reasonable compensation for services rendered to or for the corporation in carrying out any of its tax exempt purposes; and no such person or persons shall be entitled to share in the distribution of any of the corporate assets upon the dissolution of the corporation.

ARTICLE XIII
Prohibited Activities

Notwithstanding any other provision of these By-Laws, no member, officer, employee, director or representative of this corporation shall take any action or carry on any activity by or on behalf of the corporation not permitted to be taken or carried on by an organization exempt under Section 501(c)(3) of the Internal Revenue Code and its Regulations, as they now exist or may hereafter be amended, or by an organization contributions to which are deductible under Section 170(c)(2) of such Code and Regulations, as they now exist or as they may hereafter be amended.

ARTICLE XIV

These By-Laws may be amended at a meeting of the corporation by a majority of the Board members present or represented by written proxy, provided that notice of the proposed amendment shall have been given to each member at least ten days prior to said meeting.

ARTICLE XV
Parliamentary Authority

Robert's Rules of Order Revised shall govern the association in all cases in which they are applicable and in which they are not in conflict with By-Laws or the Articles of Incorporation.

Certificate of Incorporation and Bylaws
of
Brandywine Conservancy

FIRST: The name of the corporation is Brandywine Conservancy, Inc.

SECOND: Its registered office in the State of Delaware is to be located at 3801 Kennett Pike, Greenville, county of New Castle Wilmington, Delaware, 19807, and its registered agent at such address is American Guaranty & Trust Company.

THIRD: The nature of the business or objects or purposes to be transacted, promoted or carried on in any part of the world by the corporation are:

(a) to preserve or to aid in the preservation of areas and objects of scenic, natural, geological, biological, historical, artistic or recreational importance in the Brandywine valley and elsewhere;

(b) to establish or aid in the establishment of nature reserves or other protected areas for scientific, educational or aesthetic purposes;

(c) to conduct land use planning studies;

(d) to establish, operate and maintain a museum to be known as the Brandywine River Museum for the exhibition and preservation of the artistic heritage of the Brandywine valley and elsewhere;

(e) to further natural history, conservation, artistic and cultural education, to the end that this corporation shall serve the people as an agency for popular enlightenment, for cultural improvement and for scientific progress, recognizing through its programs the essential relationship among the natural, artistic and historic elements of the Brandywine valley and elsewhere;

(f) to buy, exchange, contract for, lease and in any and all other ways, acquire, take, hold and own, and to deal in, sell, mortgage, lease or otherwise dispose of real property, and rights and interests in and to real property, and to manage, operate, maintain, improve and develop the same;

(g) to borrow or raise money for any of the purposes of the corporation and, from time to time, without limit as to the amount, to draw, make, accept, endorse, execute and issue promissory notes, drafts, bills of exchange, bonds, debentures and other negotiable or non-negotiable instruments and evidences of indebtedness, and to secure the payment of any thereof and of the interest thereon by mortgage upon or pledge, conveyance, or assignment in trust of the whole or any part of the property of the corporation, whether at the time owned or thereafter acquired or by the assignment of any moneys owing or to be owing to the corporation or otherwise;

(h) in general, to carry on any other business in connection with the foregoing and to have exercise all the powers conferred by the laws of Delaware upon corporations, and to do any and all of the things hereinbefore set forth to the same extent as natural persons might or could do; provided, however, that nothing herein contained shall be deemed to

155

authorize this corporation to carry on any activities such as are now or hereafter may be impermissible for organizations exempt under §501(c)(3) of the United States Internal Revenue Code of 1954, as amended (or the corresponding provision of any future United States Internal Revenue Law).

FOURTH: The corporation shall be a membership corporation and shall have no authority to issue capital stock. The corporation is not organized and shall not be conducted for profit and no profits shall be distributed to the members, trustees, officers or other private persons, except that the corporation shall be authorized and empowered to pay reasonable compensation for services rendered and to make payments and distributions in furtherance of the purposes set forth above in Article THIRD. The conditions of membership in the corporation shall be stated in the By-Laws.

FIFTH: The affairs and business of the corporation shall be managed and conducted by the Board of Trustees. The Trustees shall be elected to office in such manner and for such term and shall have such powers and duties as are specified in the By-Laws. Vacancies on the Board of Trustees caused by death, resignation, removal or otherwise shall be filled in the manner provided for in the By-Laws. A quorum of the Board of Trustees for the transaction of business shall consist of three trustees unless the By-Laws otherwise specify.

SIXTH: The corporation is to have perpetual existence.

SEVENTH: The private property of the members shall not be subject to the payment of the corporate debts to any extent whatever.

EIGHTH: In furtherance and not in limitation of the powers conferred upon the Board of Trustees by law, the Board of Trustees shall have power to make, alter, adopt, amend and repeal, from time to time, the By-Laws of the corporation.

NINTH: In the event of the liquidation, dissolution or winding up of the corporation, whether voluntary, involuntary or by operation of law, except as may otherwise be provided by law, any assets remaining after payment of or reasonable provisions for its then existing liabilities and commitments, shall be distributed, exclusively for the purposes of the corporation in such manner, or to such organization as shall then qualify as an exempt organization under §501(c)(3) of the United States Internal Revenue Code of 1954, as amended (or the corresponding provision of any future United States Internal Revenue Law).

TENTH: The corporation reserves the right to amend, alter or repeal any provision contained in this Restated Certificate of Incorporation in the manner now or hereafter provided by statute, and all rights conferred on members herein are granted subject to this reservation, except that no such amendment shall be made which would cause the objects or purposes of the corporation to include any object or purpose which would be deemed to authorize this corporation to carry on any activities which would not be exclusively charitable, scientific or educational or which would permit part of the principal of or net earnings of the corporation to inure to the benefit of any of its members, trustees or officers or of any private individual.

Bylaws
of
Brandywine Conservancy, Inc.

ARTICLE I
Name
Section 1.1. The name of this Corporation is BRANDYWINE CONSERVANCY, INC.

ARTICLE II
Corporate Seal
Section 2.1. The corporate seal shall have inscribed thereon the name of the Corporation, the year of its incorporation and the words "Corporate Seal, Delaware."

ARTICLE III
Powers of Corporation

Section 3.1. The Board of Trustees shall have and may exercise all the powers of the Corporation, except such as are conferred upon the members by law. The purposes of the Corporation shall be accomplished by the Board of Trustees, which shall constitute the governing body of the Corporation.

ARTICLE IV
Members

Section 4.1. Qualifications; Term; Resignation. The Corporation shall have as many members as there are Trustees. The election of a person as a Trustee shall automatically make him a member of the Corporation. A person shall remain a member so long as he remains a Trustee. If the person ceases to be a Trustee, he shall automatically thereby cease to be a member. All members shall file their address with the Secretary of the Corporation. A member may resign by written resignation to the Secretary of the Corporation but only if he simultaneously therewith resigns as a Trustee; such resignation shall be effective upon receipt thereof.

Section 4.2. Meetings. Meetings of the members may be held within or without the State of Delaware upon call of any member or Trustee. A written notice of the time, place, and purpose of every meeting of the membership shall be given to each member by the Chairman of the Board or the Secretary of the Corporation or in the case of the death, absence, incapacity or refusal of either of them, by some other officer or by any member, at least 10 days before such meeting, either personally or by mailing a copy, postage prepaid, to his address as it appears on the books of the Corporation, provided, however, that any meeting held without formal call and/or notice shall be valid if all the members are present in person or represented by proxy or if the members sign a written waiver of notice, whether before or after the time stated therein. Each member shall be entitled to one vote which may be exercised by him in person or by proxy. One-third of the members at the time of the meeting shall constitute a quorum at any meeting. No action shall be taken at a meeting at which less than a quorum is present or represented by proxy, except to adjourn, and an adjourned meeting may be held as adjourned without further notice. Action may be taken at any meeting at which a quorum is present in person or represented by proxy by majority vote of the members present.

ARTICLE V
Board of Trustees

Section 5.1. Composition; Term. The Board of Trustees shall consist of not less than 15 nor more than 21 persons elected by the members, the exact number thereof to be determined from time to time by resolution of the Board of Trustees. The term of office of one-third of the members of the Board of Trustees (to be determined at the discretion of the President) serving on April 15, 1975, shall terminate on April 15, 1976; the term of one-third of the remaining Trustees shall terminate on April 15, 1977, and the term of the remaining Trustees shall terminate April 15, 1978, or in respect of each Trustee, until his successor is elected and qualified or until his earlier resignation or removal. Thereafter each Trustee shall hold office for a term of three years or until his successor is elected and qualified or until his earlier resignation. No person shall be eligible for election as a Trustee of the Conservancy if such person has not served as a trustee for the full year preceding such election or unless the Board specifically finds that it is imperative to the continuing successful operation of the Conservancy for a person who is completing two consecutive full terms to be renominated. Any vacancy in the Board occurring for any cause between annual meetings of the members may be filled by a vote of a majority of the members of the Board of Trustees present at a meeting of the Board at which there is a quorum. Each Trustee so elected shall hold office for the whole or balance of the term to which he was so elected or until his successor is elected and qualified or until his earlier resignation. Whenever the Board increases its own size, it shall designate the term of any added member of the Board.

Section 5.2. <u>Honorary Trustees.</u> The Board of Trustees may choose other persons to serve as Honorary Trustees. An Honorary Trustee shall serve for life or for so long as he or she is willing to serve. Such persons may participate in the deliberations of the Board but shall not be Trustees for the purposes of quorum or notice and shall not be entitled to vote.

ARTICLE VI
Organization of Board of Trustees

Section 6.1. <u>Regular Meetings.</u> Regular meetings of the Board of Trustees may be held at such places within or without the State of Delaware and at such times as the Board of Trustees may from time to time determine, and if so determined notices thereof need not be given.

Section 6.2. <u>Special Meetings.</u> Special meetings of the Board of Trustees may be held at any time or place within or without the State of Delaware whenever called by the Chairman of the Board, if any, by the Vice Chairman of the Board, if any, by the President or by one-third of the members of the Board of Trustees. Reasonable notice thereof shall be given by the person or persons calling the meeting.

Section 6.3. <u>Telephonic Meetings Permitted.</u> Members of the Board of Trustees, or any committee designated by the Board, may participate in a meeting of such Board or committee by means of conference telephone or similar communications equipment by means of which all persons participating in the meeting can hear each other, and participation in a meeting pursuant to this By-Law shall constitute presence in person at such meeting.

Section 6.4. <u>Quorum.</u> At all meetings of the Board of Trustees, one-third of the Trustees then in office shall constitute a quorum for the transaction of business. Except in cases in which the Certificate of Incorporation or these By-Laws otherwise provide, the vote of a majority of the Trustees present at a meeting at which a quorum is present shall be the act of the Board of Trustees.

Section 6.5. <u>Organization.</u> Meetings of the Board of Trustees shall be presided over by the Chairman of the Board, if any, or in his absence by the Vice Chairman of the Board, if any, or in his absence by the President, or in their absence by a chairman chosen at the meeting. The Secretary shall act as secretary of the meeting, but in his absence the chairman of the meeting may appoint any person to act as secretary of the meeting.

Section 6.6. <u>Informal Action by Trustees.</u> Unless otherwise restricted by the Certificate of Incorporation or these By-Laws, any action required or permitted to be taken at any meeting of the Board of Trustees, or of any committee thereof, may be taken without a meeting if all members of the Board or of such committee, as the case may be, consent thereto in writing, and the writing or writings are filed with the minutes of proceedings of the Board or committee.

Section 6.7. <u>Committees.</u> The Board of trustees may, by resolution passed by a majority of the whole Board, designate one or more committees, each committee to consist of one or more of the Trustees of the Corporation and any other persons designated by the Board, except that the Executive Committee shall consist only of members of the Board of Trustees. One-third of the members of any committee shall constitute a quorum at any meeting of that committee. Any such committee, to the extent provided in the resolution of the Board of Trustees, shall have and may exercise all the powers and authority of the Board of Trustees in the management of the business and affairs of the corporation, and may authorize the seal of the corporation to be affixed to all papers which may require it but no such committee shall have power or authority in reference to amending the Certificate of Incorporation of the corporation, adopting an agreement of merger or consolidation, recommending to the members a dissolution, or amending these By-Laws.

Section 6.8. <u>Committee Rules.</u> Unless the Board of Trustees otherwise provides, such committee designated by the Board may make, alter and repeal rules for the conduct of its business. In the absence of such rules each committee shall conduct its business in the same manner as the Board of Trustees conducts its business.

ARTICLE VIII
Officers

Section 7.1. <u>Executive Officers; Election; Qualification; Term of Office; Resignation; Removal; Vacancies.</u> The Board of Trustees shall choose a President and a Secretary, and it may, if it so determines, choose a Chairman of the Board and a Vice Chairman of the Board from among its members. The Board of Trustees may also choose an Executive Director, one or more Vice Presidents, one or more Assistant Treasurers. Each such officer shall hold office until the April 15 after the annual meeting of members following his election or until his successor is elected and qualified or until his earlier resignation or removal. Any officer may resign at any time upon written notice to the Corporation. The Board of Trustees may remove any officer with or without cause at any time, but such removal shall be without prejudice to the contractual rights of such officer, if any, with the Corporation. Any number of offices may be held by the same person. Any vacancy occurring in any office of the Corporation by death, resignation, removal or otherwise may be filled for the unexpired portion of the term by the Board of Trustees at any regular or special meeting.

Section 7.2. <u>Powers and Duties of Executive Officers.</u> The officers of the Corporation shall have such powers and duties in the management of the Corporation as may be prescribed by the Board of Trustees and, to the extent not so provided, as generally pertain to their respective offices, subject to the control of the Board of Trustees. The Board of Trustees may require any officer, agent or employee to give security for the faithful performance of his duties.

ARTICLE VIII
Fiscal Policies

Section 8.1. <u>Fiscal Year.</u> The fiscal year for all business transactions shall be the calendar year.

Section 8.2. <u>Depositories.</u> The Board of Trustees may establish such accounts with banks, trust companies, and other financial institutions as it deems appropriate.

Section 8.3. <u>Disbursements.</u> Disbursements shall be made only in accordance with a specific authorization by the Board of Trustees or within a general budget approved by the Board, except that in the absence of an approved budget the Treasurer may pay bills for normal running expenses as authorized by the President, Vice President or Secretary.

Section 8.4. <u>Audit.</u> There shall be an annual audit of accounts by an independent public accountant.

Section 8.5. <u>Endowment Funds.</u> An endowment fund may be maintained and shall consist of all monies allocated to it by the Board of Trustees. No part of the endowment may be expended in violation of stipulations by the donor accepted by the Conservancy at the time of gift.

ARTICLE IX
Amendments

Section 9.1. These By-Laws may be amended at any meeting of the Trustees or any meeting of the members by a majority vote of the Trustees or members present at such meeting, provided that a quorum be present.

CHAPTER 7
Easements and Conservation Restrictions

THIS chapter includes several noteworthy samples of land and historic resource protection deed restrictions. These deeds represent approaches for local governments or citizen groups to protect key resources by acquiring land or buildings and reselling the property subject to restrictions to ensure that the property will not be developed in a manner inconsistent with the objectives of the community or citizen group.

The first instrument is the Deed of Agreement Relating to Development Rights used by King County, Washington, in its agricultural protection program. The deed restricts the use of property to agricultural and open space uses. The county does not acquire the right to develop the property; rather, the deed simply extinguishes the development rights.

The second instrument is the agricultural land preservation easement used by Lancaster County, Pennsylvania in its highly successful farmland preservation program. This easement is similar in effect to the deed restrictions used in King County, Washington. In both cases, the county extinguishes in perpetuity the landowner's right to develop the property for nonagricultural uses.

Finally, the historic preservation deed restrictions and covenants developed by the Galveston Historical Foundation are included. The first of these is a warranty deed that the Foundation uses to regulate the use, maintenance, and rehabilitation of residential historical structures. The second instrument contains covenants entered into between the Foundation and recipients of funds from the Foundation's revolving loan fund.

King County, Washington
Agreement Relating to Development Rights

THIS DEED AND AGREEMENT is made this _____ day of _____, 198__, BY AND BETWEEN _____ hereinafter referred to as "Grantors," AND KING COUNTY By and Through THE KING COUNTY REAL PROPERTY DIVISION, having its principal offices at the King County Administration Building, Seattle, Washington 98104, hereinafter referred to as "Grantee."

WHEREAS:

The Grantors are the present owners of the lands described in Exhibit A which is attached hereto and incorporated herein by reference (the "Land").

The Grantors recognize that the Land is Farmland or Open Space Land as defined in King County Ordinance No. 4341, and they desire to cooperate with the Grantee in preserving land devoted to agricultural and open space uses.

The Grantors are willing to grant and convey to the Grantee the Development Rights in the Land as such rights are defined in King County Ordinance No. 4341 (said rights being the interest in and the right to use and subdivide land for any and all residential, commercial, and industrial purposes and activities which are not incident to agricultural and open space uses), on the terms and conditions and for the purposes hereinafter set forth. The Grantee is willing to purchase the Development Rights in the Land and accept this instrument of conveyance.

The Grantee has determined that the acquisition by the Grantee of Development Rights in Farmland and Open Space Land will benefit the public through the preservation of property devoted to agricultural and open space uses.

The grant and conveyance of Development Rights by the Grantors to the Grantee will preserve the Land for activities consistent with agricultural and open space uses in perpetuity in accordance with the specific terms and conditions hereinafter set forth.

NOW THEREFORE WITNESSETH, that the Grantors, for and in consideration of _____ _____ DOLLARS ($_____) lawful money of the United States of America, paid to the Grantors by the Grantee, the receipt whereof is hereby acknowledged, and the Grantors being therewith fully satisfied, do by these presents grant, bargain, sell, transfer and convey unto the Grantee forever all Development Rights in respect to the Land, hereby perpetually binding the Land to the restrictions limiting permitted activities to agricultural and open space uses as specifically delineated in the covenants, terms, and conditions contained herein, and do also grant such interests, rights and easements, make such covenants and subject the land to such servitudes as are necessary to bind the Land in perpetuity to such restrictions.

162

The Grantors and Grantee hereby agree that the Land shall be bound by and permanently subject to the following restrictive covenants, terms, and conditions. None of these covenants, terms, and conditions shall be construed as allowing a use that is not otherwise permitted by applicable state and local laws, codes, standards, and ordinances.

Restrictions on Use of the Land

I. Uses Restricted to Agricultural and Open Space Uses; Agricultural and Open Space Uses Defined. Use of the Land is permanently restricted to solely agricultural and open space uses.
   A. "Agricultural uses," as used herein, means:
      (1) The growing, raising, and production of horticultural and agricultural crops, including, but not limited to, vegetables, berries, other fruits, cereal grains, herbs, hay, and silage, and the processing and the marketing for off-premises consumption of such crops grown, raised, or produced on the Land;
      (2) All forms of animal husbandry, including the processing and marketing for off-premises consumption of the animals raised on the Land or the products of the same;
      (3) The lying fallow or disuse of the Land. Agricultural uses do not include the construction, habitation, or other use of a dwelling unit, except to the extent such use is specifically reserved in this instrument.
   B. "Open space uses," as used herein, means:
      (1) Agricultural uses as defined above;
      (2) Non-agricultural uses that conserve and enhance natural, scenic, or designated historic resources and that do not permanently compact, remove, sterilize, pollute, or otherwise impair the use of the soil on the Land for the raising of horticultural or agricultural crops.
   Neither open space nor agricultural uses include the following: The construction, habitation, or other use of a dwelling unit, except to the extent such use is specifically reserved in this instrument; construction or expansion of buildings or structures for non-agricultural uses; the construction or use of golf courses, parking lots unassociated with agricultural uses, athletic fields, campgrounds, or vehicle raceways or animal raceways other than those principally used for the exercise of animals grown, raised, or produced on the Land. Open space may include trails for non-motorized use by the public that are maintained and owned by or for the benefit of a government agency or are maintained and owned by a non-profit conservation agency.
II. Reservation of Dwelling Unit(s). The Grantors reserve the right to the use of _____ single-family dwelling unit(s) on the Land for the sole purpose of accommodating the Grantors and their successors in interest to the Land, the farm operator, or the families of such persons, or for accommodating agricultural employees of the owner or operator and their families. No more than _____ dwelling unit(s) in total will be permitted regardless of whether the Land is subdivided by the Grantors or by any successor in interest of the Grantors. If the Land is subdivided, the number of dwelling units allocated to each subdivided parcel out of the total number of dwelling units specified above shall be indicated in the deed to each such parcel and on the face of any plat or other instrument creating the subdivision or conveying an interest in the Land; however, failure to indicate the number of such dwelling units thereon shall not invalidate or otherwise affect the restriction of the total number of dwelling units on the Land. The dwelling unit(s) shall be (a) permanent or mobile structure(s) designed and used for single-family residential occupancy.
III. Further Restriction on Use of the Land. Potential uses of the Land are limited in that the Grantors, their heirs, successors, and assigns shall only be entitled to use, lease, maintain, or improve the Land for agricultural and open space uses, and they shall comply with the following terms, conditions, restrictions, and covenants, which are permanently binding on the Land:

A. No subdivision of the Land that reduces any parcel to less than 10 acres shall be permitted. All restrictions imposed by this instrument shall survive any subdivision.

B. No more than 5 percent of the Land, or of any parcel thereof resulting from a subdivision of the Land, shall be covered by structures and/or non-tillable surfaces. "Structures" shall include but are not limited to residences, barns, machine sheds, permanent greenhouses, associated structures, retail and processing facilities, surfaced parking areas, surfaced driveways, surfaced roadways, and surfaced pads. Temporary shelter for soil-dependent cultivation of horticultural or viticultural crops is not considered a structure. "Non-tillable surfaces" shall include but are not limited to asphalt, concrete, gravel, and any other cover material not normally associated with cultivation of the soil.

C. No mining, drilling, or extracting of oil, gas, gravel, or minerals on or under the Land shall be permitted that causes disruption of the surface of the Land to any extent inconsistent with agricultural uses, and no part of the surface of the Land shall be used for storage or processing of gas, oil, or minerals taken from the Land, other than storage for the private use of the occupants of the Land.

D. No subsurface activities, including excavation for underground utilities, pipelines, or other underground installations, shall be permitted that cause permanent disruption of the surface of the Land. Temporarily disrupted soil surfaces shall be restored in a manner consistent with agricultural uses, including restoration of the original soil horizon sequence within a reasonable period of time after such installation.

E. No dumping or storage of non-agricultural solid or liquid waste, or of trash, rubbish, or noxious materials shall be permitted.

F. No activities that violate sound agricultural soil and water conservation management practices shall be permitted.

G. No signs shall be erected on the Land except for the following purposes:
   1. to state the name of the property and the name and address of the occupant;
   2. to advertise any use or activity consistent with the agricultural or open space uses as herein defined; or
   3. to advertise the property for sale or rent.

IV. Restriction on Use of the Land to Satisfy Open Space Requirements for Development or Use of Other Real Property. Except as is otherwise provided below, in the event that an application is made at any time to a federal, state, or local governmental authority for permission to make use of any other real property including, but not limited to, real property that is contiguous to any of the Land hereby restricted, which proposed use is conditioned by such government authority on the existence of a specified quantity of open space or other restrictions on development, the Land shall not be used to contribute toward the satisfaction of any such open space requirement. This restriction shall not apply if the proposed use of the other real property is an agricultural or open space use, as defined herein.

Additional Covenants and Agreements

The Grantors and Grantee further agree as follows:

Covenant Against Encumbrances. The Grantors covenant that they have not done or executed, or allowed to be done or executed, any act, deed, or thing whatsoever whereby the Development Rights hereby conveyed, or any part thereof, now or at any time hereafter, will or may be charged or encumbered in any manner or way whatsoever.

Remedies. If the Grantors, their heirs, successors, assigns, agents, or employees violate or allow the violation of any of the terms, conditions, restrictions, and convenants set forth herein, then the Grantee will be entitled to all remedies available at law or in equity, including, but not limited to, injunctive relief, rescission of contract, or damages, including attorneys' fees and court costs reasonably incurred by the Grantee in prosecuting such action(s). No waiver or waivers by the Grantee, or by its successors or assigns, of any breach of a term, condition, restriction, or covenant contained herein shall be deemed a waiver of any subsequent breach of such term, condition, restriction or convenant or of any other term, condition, restriction, or covenant contained herein.

No Alteration or Amendment. The terms, conditions, restrictions, and covenants contained herein shall not be altered or amended unless such alteration or amendment shall be made with the written consent of the Grantee, or its successors or assigns, and any such alteration or amendment shall be consistent with the purposes of King County Ordinance No. 4341, as heretofore or hereafter amended.

Restrictions Binding on Successors. The Grantors and Grantee agree that the terms, conditions, restrictions, and covenants contained herein shall be binding upon the Grantors, their agents, personal representatives, heirs, assigns, and all other successors in interest to the Land and possessors of the Land, and shall be permanent terms, conditions, restrictions, covenants, servitudes, and easements running with and perpetually binding the Land.

Transfer of Rights by Grantee. The Grantee agrees that the Development Rights to the Land shall not be sold, given, divested, transferred, or otherwise reconveyed in whole or in part in any manner except as provided in King County Ordinance No. 4341, as heretofore or hereafter amended. The Grantors, their personal representatives, heirs, successors, or assigns, shall be given the right of first refusal to purchase the Development Rights in the Land provided such disposition and reconveyance be lawfully approved.

Condemnation. If the Land is subject to any condemnation action, and if a mutually acceptable agreement as to the compensation to be provided to the Grantee is not reached between Grantee and Grantors within a reasonable period of time, the Grantors will request that the Grantee be made a party to such action in order that it be fully compensated for the loss of, or devaluation in, the Development Rights hereby conveyed.

No Affirmative Obligations; Indemnification. Grantee, in purchasing the Development Rights and related interests described herein, assumes no affirmative obligations whatsoever for the management, supervision or control of the Land or of any activities occurring on the Land. Grantors shall indemnify Grantee and hold Grantee harmless from all damages, costs (including, but not limited to, attorneys' fees and other costs of defense incurred by Grantee), and other expenses of every kind arising from or incident to any claim or action for damages, injury, or loss suffered or alleged to have been suffered on or with respect to the Land. This provision shall be binding upon the Grantors for so long as they hold fee title to the Land, and shall bind their successors in interest to the fee title to the Land.

Grantee's Right to Enter onto the Land. After giving reasonable notice to the possessors of the Land, the Grantee or its authorized representative shall have the right to enter from time to time onto the Land and into structures located thereon for the sole purposes of inspection and enforcement of the terms, conditions, restrictions and covenants hereby imposed.

Severability. If any section or provision of this instrument shall be held by any court of competent jurisdiction to be unenforceable, this instrument shall be construed as though such section or provision had not been included in it, and the remainder of this instrument shall be enforced as the expression of the parties' intentions. If any section or provision of this instrument is found to be subject to two constructions, one of which would render such section or provision invalid and one of which would render such section or provision valid, then the latter construction shall prevail. If any section or provision of this instrument is determined to be ambiguous or unclear, it shall be interpreted in accordance with the policies and provisions expressed in King County Ordinance No. 4341.

IN WITNESS WHEREOF, the parties have hereunto set their hand and seals the day and year first above written.

Lancaster County, Pennsylvania
Agricultural Land Preservation Grant of Easement

This grant of easement in the nature of a Restriction on the use of land for the purpose of preserving productive agricultural land is made by and between _____ _____ _____, _____._____, of the Township of _____ (hereafter Grantors) and the LANCASTER COUNTY AGRICULTURAL PRESERVE BOARD, its successor, nominee or assign an agency of LANCASTER COUNTY, a third class county, created and organized under the laws of the Commonwealth of Pennsylvania, with its offices at 50 North Duke Street, Lancaster, Pennsylvania (hereafter GRANTEE).

WHEREAS, GRANTORS are the owners in fee of a farm located in _____ _____ Township, Lancaster County, Pennsylvania, more fully described in a deed recorded in the Office of the Recorder of Deeds in and for Lancaster County, Pennsylvania in Deed Book _____, Page _____; and

WHEREAS, the Legislature of the Commonwealth of Pennsylvania (hereafter LEGISLATURE) authorizes the Commonwealth of Pennsylvania and counties thereof to preserve, acquire or hold lands for open space uses, and to preserve land in or acquire land for open space uses, which specifically includes farmland; and that actions pursuant to these purposes are for public health, safety and general welfare of the citizens of the Commonwealth and for the promotion of sound land development by preserving suitable open spaces; and

WHEREAS, the LEGISLATURE has declared that public open space benefits result from the protection and conservation of farmland including the protection of scenic areas for public visual enjoyment from public rights-of-way, the conservation and protection of agricultural lands as valued natural and ecological resources which provide needed open spaces for clean air as well as for aesthetic purposes and that public benefit will result from the conservation, protection, development and improvement of its agricultural lands for the production of food and other agricultural products; and

WHEREAS, GRANTEE has declared that the preservation of prime agricultural land is vital to the public interest of the County, the region and the nation through its economic, environmental, cultural and productive benefits; and

WHEREAS, GRANTORS desire and intend that the agricultural and open space character of the Property be preserved, protected and maintained; and

WHEREAS, GRANTORS, as owners in fee of the Property, intend to identify and preserve the agricultural and open space values of the Property; and

WHEREAS, GRANTORS desire and intend to transfer those rights to the GRANTEE in perpetuity; and

WHEREAS, GRANTEE is a public agency of the County of Lancaster, qualified under Pennsylvania Acts and the Internal Revenue Code, whose primary purposes are the preservation and protection of land in its agricultural and open space condition; and

WHEREAS, GRANTEE agrees by accepting this grant of easement to honor and defend the intentions of GRANTORS stated herein and to preserve and protect in perpetuity the agricultural and open space values of the Property for the benefit of this generation and the generations to come; and

NOW THEREFORE, in consideration of the foregoing and intending to be legally bound, the undersigned GRANTORS grant and convey to GRANTEE an easement on the heretofore described real estate for which the purpose is to assure that the Property will be retained forever in its agricultural and open space condition and to prevent any use that will impair the agricultural and open space values of the Property. To carry out this purpose the following deed restrictions are recorded.

Deed Restrictions

GRANTOR declares, makes known, and covenants for himself/herself, their heirs, successors and assigns, that the land described in the deed book and page mentioned above shall be restricted to agricultural and directly associated uses as hereafter defined. However, more restrictive applicable State and local laws shall prevail in the determination of permitted uses of land subject to these restrictions.

1. Agricultural uses of land are defined, for the purposes of this instrument, as:
   (a) The use of land for the production of plants and animals useful to man, including, but not limited to forage, grain and field crops, pasturage, dairy and dairy products, poultry and poultry products, other livestock and fowl and livestock and fowl products, including the breeding and grazing of any or all such animals, bees and apiary products, fruits and vegetables of all kinds, nursery, floral and greenhouse products, silviculture, aquaculture, and the primary processing and storage of the agricultural production of the Property and other similar and compatible uses.

2. Directly associated uses are defined as customary, supportive and agriculturally compatible uses of farm properties in Lancaster County, Pennsylvania, and are limited to the following:
   (a) The direct sale to the public of agricultural products produced principally on the farm;
   (b) Any and all structures contributing to the production, primary processing, direct marketing and storage of agricultural products produced principally on the farm;
   (c) Structures associated with the production of energy for use principally on the farm including wind, solar, hydroelectric, methane, wood, alcohol fuel and fossil fuel systems and structures and facilities for the storage and treatment of animal waste;
   (d) The provision of services or production and sale, by persons in residence, of incidental agricultural goods, services, supplies and repairs and/or the conduct of traditional trades and the production and sale of home occupation goods, arts and crafts, so long as these uses remain incidental to the agricultural and open space and character of the farm and are limited to occupying residential and/or principally agricultural structures of the Property;
   (e) Structures and facilities associated with irrigation, farm pond impoundment and soil and water conservation;
   (f) The accommodation of tourists and visitors within principally residential and/or agricultural structures of the farm Property so long as this use is incidental to the agricultural and open space character of the Property;
   (g) Religious uses including the conduct of religious ceremony on the Property and family cemeteries.

(h) Other similar uses may be considered upon written request to the Lancaster County Agricultural Preserve Board.

3. Residences permitted on the land subject to these restrictions are only those pre-existing dwellings, the replacement of pre-existing dwellings, and an additional dwelling or dwellings intended for use and occupancy by a person who or a family, at least one member of which, earns a substantial part of his or her livelihood from the farm operation, or is a parent or child of the owner of the farm. Such permitted dwellings may be constructed either on the original parcel or on lots subdivided from the original parcel at a density not to exceed 1 dwelling per 25 acres of the original parcel. When permitted dwellings require subdivision, combined lot areas associated with dwellings shall not exceed a rate of $1/2$ acre per 25 acres of the original parcel. Minor exceptions may be considered and are subject to approval by the GRANTEE in the event that these restrictions conflict with State or local requirements. Other residential subdivision and uses are prohibited.

4. All permitted non-agricultural structures shall, when feasible, be located in the immediate vicinity of existing structures, described as the homestead or curtilage, as reasonable expansions of the homestead or curtilage or on the area(s) of the Property of least productive capability. Such permitted structures shall, when feasible, utilize existing or common driveways, lanes or rights-of-way.

5. Institutional, industrial and commercial uses other than those associated uses described in restrictions 1 and 2 are prohibited.

6. The commercial extraction of minerals by surface mining and the extraction and removal from the Property of topsoil are prohibited.
    The extraction of subsurface or deep-mined minerals, including natural gas and oil, and the non-commercial extraction of minerals including limestone, shale and other minerals for on-farm use shall be permitted, but may occupy, at any time, no more than one percent (1%) of the total surface acreage.

7. Use of the Property for dumping, storage, processing or landfill of non-agricultural solid or hazardous wastes generated off-site is prohibited.

8. Signs, billboards and outdoor advertising structures may not be displayed on the Property except that signs, the combined area of which may not exceed 25 square feet, may be displayed to state only the name of the Property, the name and address of the occupant, to advertise an on-site activity permitted herein and to advertise the Property for sale or rent.

9. Commercial recreational development and use, involving structures or extensive commitment of land resources (i.e., golf courses, racetracks, and similar uses) shall be prohibited.

10. Agricultural lands shall be managed in accordance with sound soil and water conservation practices in a manner which will not destroy or substantially and irretrievably diminish the productive capability of the Property. However, there shall be no limitations or prohibitions on any agricultural production or farming methods.

11. No right of public access is provided for, nor will result from, the recordation of these restrictions.

12. The GRANTEE, its successors and assigns, shall have the right to enforce these Restrictions by injunction and other appropriate proceedings. Representatives of the GRANTEE, its successors and assigns, may at reasonable times and after appropriate notice to the GRANTORS and any persons residing on the Property, may enter the Property from time to time for the purposes of inspection and enforcement of the terms of the easement.

13. The Restrictions contained herein shall apply to the land as an open space easement in gross in perpetuity.

14. This grant of easement in the nature of a restriction is intended to be an easement in gross so as to qualify for a Qualified Conservation Contribution under the applicable provisions of the Internal Revenue Code.

15. GRANTEE agrees that it will hold this easement exclusively for conservation pur-

poses and that it will not assign its rights and obligations under this easement except to another organization qualified to hold such interests under applicable State and Federal laws and committed to holding this easement exclusively for conservation purposes.

IN WITNESS THEREOF, the parties have set their hands and seals this _____ day of _____, 19 ____.

Galveston Historical Foundation
Historical Preservation Covenants

STATE OF TEXAS, COUNTY OF GALVESTON

This Agreement ("Agreement") is made and entered into this the _____ day of
_____, 1978, by and between the Galveston Historical Foundation, Inc., a Texas
non-profit corporation ("Foundation"), and _____ ("Owner").

Recitals

A. The Strand Area (as herein defined) has been designated and is listed as an Historic
District in the National Register of Historic Places, a register maintained by an agency of
the government of the United States.

B. The Foundation seeks to encourage, control and promote the restoration, maintenance, preservation and development of The Strand Area, and particularly the
architectural features of the improvements in The Strand Area. The Foundation has acquired and will acquire land and improvements in The Strand Area in order to insure the
preservation of the improvements and thereafter will convey the land and improvements
subject to obligations to repair, restore and preserve the improvements. Further the Foundation will negotiate with other owners of improvements in The Strand Area for the
purpose of obtaining from said owners agreements of a nature similar to those included
herein. The land presently owned by the Foundation is described in Exhibit "A", attached
hereto and made a part hereof for all purposes.

C. The Owner is the owner of a tract of land and improvements located within The
Strand Area, which land and improvements are described in Exhibit "B", attached hereto
and made a part hereof for all purposes.

D. The Owner and the Foundation seek to enter into a mutual agreement, as evidenced
by this Agreement, to assure the objectives of the Foundation, to-wit: to restore, preserve,
maintain and develop The Strand Area, will be carried out.

THEREFORE, FOR AND IN CONSIDERATION of the premises and the covenants herein
contained and in the further consideration of valuable consideration in hand paid by
Foundation to Owner, the receipt and sufficiency of which are hereby acknowledged,
Owner and Foundation agree as follows:

1. Owner has agreed to subject, and does hereby subject, the land and improvements
described in Exhibit "B" to the covenants, restrictions and conditions contained in Paragraph 5 hereof. Owner has agreed and hereby agrees to abide by and perform all
obligations imposed on him as the owner of property subject to such restrictions, covenants and conditions. Further, Owner will convey said land and improvements subject to
such restrictions, covenants and conditions.

2. The Foundation has agreed and by these presents does agree that at such time as the

170

land described in Exhibit "A" is sold, transferred or further conveyed in such a manner that ownership of said land is vested in any person other than the Foundation, the tract so conveyed will be made subject to the restrictions, covenants and conditions contained in Paragraph 5 hereof. It is the intention of the parties hereto that the Foundation will not be required to perform the obligations set forth in the restrictions, covenants and conditions contained in Paragraph 5, but that the Foundation's successors in title shall be so bound.

3. The Foundation and Owner agree the lands which are or hereafter become subject to said restrictions, covenants and conditions shall remain bound by said restrictions, covenants and conditions forever, and that said restrictions, covenants and conditions shall run with the land and shall be binding unto the successors, heirs and assigns of the parties hereto.

4. It is the intention of the Foundation to enter into similar agreements with other owners of lands in The Strand Area so as to restore, maintain, preserve and develop The Strand Area, and particularly the architectural features of the improvements in The Strand Area. The Foundation and Owner agree that this Agreement shall be deemed to include all future agreements between the Foundation and any owner of property in The Strand Area, and as such shall be construed to be a single plan or agreement for the maintainance, restoration, preservation and development of The Strand Area, and shall be enforceable as one agreement.

5. The covenants, restrictions and conditions agreed to by the parties hereto to be binding on the land described in Exhibit "B" as of the execution hereof, and on the land described in Exhibit "A" at the time stated in paragraph 2 hereof, are as follows:

(a) No improvements, herein defined to mean buildings, driveways, sidewalks, curbs and exterior lighting, may be demolished, damaged or destroyed by or on behalf of any owner of property in The Strand Area without the prior written consent of that Architectural Committee hereafter designated.

(b) Every improvement shall be maintained in a good state of repair, but with reasonable wear permitted. The term "good state of repair" includes, but is not limited to, considerations of historical accuracy, structural soundness, safety, and freedom from public or private nuisance. Determinations by the Architectural Committee made pursuant to the standards herein contained as to what constitutes a good state of repair shall be final. If applicable, a copy of any restoration contract entered into by the Foundation and made the basis of advancement or payment of funds by the Foundation, or a condition of sale of property by the Foundation, may be introduced into evidence in any court proceeding wherein good state of repair is at issue as prima facie evidence of what state of repair is required to be maintained. Provided, however, that good state of repair does not require historical accuracy as to the interior spaces of any building and does not permit the Architectural Committee to control the interior spaces of any building except as to safety and structural soundness.

(c) Every exterior surface of any improvements, including, but not limited to exterior walls, windows, doors and roofs of any building (the "Facade") and all other portions of land, including, but not limited to sidewalks, parking lots, driveways, curbs, fences, exterior lighting, landscaping and plantings (the "Grounds") shall be maintained in an attractive condition. The term "attractive condition" includes, but is not limited to considerations of historical accuracy, texture, choice of colors, choice of materials, cleanliness and other purely aesthetic considerations. Determinations by the Architectural Committee of what constitutes attractive condition shall be final. If applicable, a copy of a restoration contract entered into by the Foundation and made the basis of advancement or payment of funds by the Foundation, or a condition of sale of property by the Foundation, may be introduced into evidence in any court proceeding wherein attractive condition or good state of repair is at issue as prima facie evidence of what condition is required to be maintained.

(d) The written consent of the Architectural Committee must be obtained before the appearance or condition (including, but not limited to, the color) of the Facade or Grounds, or any part thereof, is changed, altered or in any other manner modified, and before any exterior sign is erected, constructed or altered. Provided, however, that no consent shall be required solely to repaint or refinish without change of color or with change of color to a combination of colors from a list of approved combination of colors maintained by the Architectural Committee. Any change or modification must be built according to plans and specifications submitted and approved by the Architectural Committee. Neon, animated, revolving or sequentially lighted signs shall not be installed, maintained or used. Choice of signs, appearance and condition involve aesthetic, historical and architectural considerations over which the judgment of the Architectural Committee shall be final. The Architectural Committee may require removal of a previously existing exterior sign, or when exterior repainting is done, that colors be changed.

(e) (1) Any and all damage to the grounds and any minor damage to the Facade shall be promptly repaired to a condition and appearance satisfactory to the Architectural Committee. The term "minor change" shall herein be used to mean (i) damage that affects the condition or appearances of 25% or less of the square footage of the exterior walls or the roof of any structure, computing damage to the roof and to each wall separately excluding damage to windows and doors or their coverings from numerator and denominator, and (ii) any damage to windows and doors or their coverings.

(2) Any major damage, meaning any damage greater than minor damage as above defined, and any combination of major and minor damage shall likewise be promptly repaired unless (i) without any wrongful act of the owner, the damage was caused by an instrumentality for which casualty insurance could not be obtained, and (ii) an undue economic burden would be imposed on said owner to preserve the architectural and historical significance of the structure.

(f) Upon five (5) days' written notice, the Architectural Committee may enter onto or in lands or improvements covered hereby at reasonable times and intervals to insure compliance with these covenants.

(g) Plans and specifications for construction of any new or replacement improvement must be submitted to the Architectural Committee for its prior approval. No such improvement shall be erected or constructed without such approval. All new structures (i) shall have a masonry, or better exterior, (ii) shall be attractive and of a design, style and finish that will compliment other improvements in The Strand Area, and (iii) shall be furnished with sidewalks, curbs, and gutters, and with storm sewers as required. All construction shall conform to the approved plans and specifications. Refusal to approve plans and specifications by the Architectural Committee may be based upon choice of materials, unattractive exterior, nonconforming architectural style or any other ground, including purely aesthetic grounds. Determination of the Architectural Committee shall be final.

(h) Whenever there is a "common" or "party" wall, the owner of the property on which such wall is in part situated shall, at the written request of the Architectural Committee, be willing to enter into the "Party Wall Agreement" set forth in Exhibit C attached hereto and made a part hereof for all purposes.

(i) Violations of these covenants may be enjoined by exparte and temporary and/or permanent injunction after reasonable notice, not to exceed thirty (30) days, or without notice if the violation jeopardizes the status quo of the improvements, Facade or Grounds as it existed immediately prior to the alleged violations. Alternatively, designees of the Architectural Committee may enter upon the land or improvements covered hereby, correct any such violation, and hold the owner thereof responsible for the costs thereof, including reasonable attorneys' fees, and such entry shall not be deemed a trespass.

(j) The Architectural Committee shall have the exclusive right to enforce these covenants through judicial proceedings. The Architectural Committee shall not be liable for the enforcement or the failure to enforce these covenants.

(k) The Foundation or its designee committee, as the Foundation shall elect, is hereby denominated the Architectural Committee until such time as a majority of the owners of property in The Strand are covered by this or a similar agreement; upon that occurrence the owners of Strand property covered by this or a similar agreement, computed by allowing one vote for each lot in The Strand Area, shall designate a committee composed of five persons as the replacement Architectural Committee which Committee shall at all times have at least two members designated by the Foundation.

(l) Lands subject to this Agreement shall not be used for any purpose of business which is considered dangerous or unsafe, or which constitutes a nuisance or is obnoxious or offensive by reason of emission of dust, odor, gas, smoke, fumes or noise.

(m) Waiver of any covenant herein or failure to enforce any covenant herein by the Architectural Committee shall not waive said covenant as to any other owner or application.

(n) The Architectural Committee shall have reasonable access to the lands and improvements affected hereby to photograph the historical attributes of any structures thereon in order to record the physical appearance and condition of said structures.

(o) In any instance that approval of the Architectural Committee is required, approval will be deemed to have been given upon failure of the Architectural Committee to respond to a request therefore within forty-five (45) days after receipt of a written request for approval.

(p) No portion of the Property shall at any time or in any way be used for any one of the following uses:
   i. an adult bookstore, an adult movie theatre or an arcade showing adult movies or films;
   ii. any business which includes nude, topless or bottomless dancing;
   iii. an art studio or other similar facility providing nude models; and
   iv. a massage parlor

   An adult movie or adult bookstore shall mean any movie or bookstore which features nudity or explicit sexual acts.

Should any covenant hereof be declared unenforceable, the remaining covenants shall not terminate thereby.

   IN WITNESS WHEREOF, this Agreement is executed this the _____ day of _____, 197_____.

Warranty Deed _____

THE STATE OF TEXAS, COUNTY OF GALVESTON

   THAT GALVESTON HISTORICAL FOUNDATION, INC., a Texas non-profit corporation, of Galveston County, Texas, (hereinafter referred to as "Grantor" and sometimes referred to herein as the "Foundation") for and in consideration of the sum of TEN AND NO/100 DOLLARS ($10.00) to the undersigned paid by the Grantee herein named, and for other good and valuable consideration, the receipt of which is hereby acknowledged, has GRANTED, SOLD and CONVEYED, and by these presents does GRANT, SELL and CONVEY, subject to the terms and conditions listed hereinafter, unto _____ _____, of _____ County, Texas (hereinafter referred to as "Grantee"), the following described real property situated in Galveston County, Texas, to-wit (the "Property"):

   subject to all the restrictions, covenants and conditions, easements, mineral interests and rights-of-way of record in the Office of the County Clerk of Galveston County, Texas, including, but not limited to those exceptions to title described on Exhibit B attached hereto and made a part hereof;

and it further and additionally understood and agreed that this conveyance is made and accepted, and the real property described herein is hereby granted, upon and subject to the covenants, conditions, and restrictions set forth in the following paragraphs, which shall run with the land conveyed, and all successors and assigns will have the same right to invoke and enforce these covenants, conditions and restrictions applicable to this conveyance as the original parties hereto:

A. Without the prior written consent of Grantor or its designee, Grantee shall not:

(1) Demolish, damage or destroy or alter any "improvements" (defined herein as buildings, structural members of buildings, driveways, sidewalks, curbs and exterior lighting now existing on the property, and all distinctive architectural features thereof).

(2) Convert the building located on the property ("building") to a multi-family dwelling structure consisting of more than _____ separate dwelling units; or

(3) In any manner alter or change the exterior appearance of the building or any of the other improvements.

B. Grantee further affirmatively covenants to perform the following undertakings:

(1) To maintain the building and every improvement, including structural members, in a good state of repair, excepting only reasonable wear and tear. The term "good state of repair" includes, but is not limited to, considerations of historical accuracy, structural soundness, safety, and freedom from public or private nuisance. Determinations by the Grantor made pursuant to the standards herein contained as to what constitutes a good state of repair shall be final. If applicable, a copy of any restoration contract entered into by the Foundation and made the basis of advancement or payment of funds by the Foundation, or a condition of sale of property by the Foundation, may be introduced into evidence in any court proceeding wherein good state of repair is at issue as prima facie evidence of what state of repair is required to be maintained. Provided, however, that good state of repair does not require historical accuracy as to the interior spaces of any building and does not permit the Grantor to control the interior spaces of any building except as to safety and structural soundness.

(2) To use the building for residential purposes only.

(3) To obtain the written consent of Grantor before altering or in any manner modifying the exterior appearance or condition of the building. Provided, however, that no consent shall be required solely to repaint or refinish without change of color. Any change or modification must be built according to plans and specifications submitted to and approved by Grantor.

(4) To submit to the Grantor for its prior approval plans and specifications for any rehabilitation of the exterior to the building. All new exterior improvements shall be attractive and of a design, style and finish that will compliment the existing improvements on the property. All construction shall conform to the approved plans and specifications. Refusal to approve plans and specifications by Grantor may be based upon choice of materials, unattractive exterior, non-conforming architectural style, or any other ground, including purely aesthetic grounds. The determination of the Grantor shall be final.

(5) To complete the rehabilitation work described on Exhibit "C" attached hereto and made a part hereof within _____ (_____) years of the date hereof.

(6) To promptly repair to a condition and appearance satisfactory to Grantor any and all damage to the property or improvements.

(7) Every exterior surface of any improvements, including, but not limited to exterior walls, windows, doors and roofs of any building (the "Facade") and all other portions of land, including, but not limited to sidewalks, parking lots, driveways, curbs, fences, exterior lighting, landscaping, and plantings (the "Grounds") shall be maintained in an attractive condition. The term "attractive condition" includes, but is not limited to considerations of historical accuracy, texture, choice of colors, choice of materials, cleanliness and other purely aesthetic considerations. Deter-

minations by the Grantor of what constitutes attractive condition shall be final. If applicable, a copy of a restoration contract entered into by the Foundation and made the basis of advancement or payment of funds by the Foundation, or a condition of sale of property by the Foundation, may be introduced into evidence in any court proceeding wherein attractive condition or good state of repair is at issue as prima facie evidence of what condition is required to be maintained.

C. (a) It is understood that Grantor, its successors and assigns, shall have the right to seek and obtain in any court of competent jurisdiction a restraining order or a temporary or permanent injunction to restrain a violation of any of the covenants contained herein. In no event shall any failure by Grantor to seek injunctive relief with regard to any one or more violations of these covenants constitute a waiver of Grantor's right to enjoin any other or further violation.

(b) Furthermore, in addition to the remedies set forth above, Grantor reserves the right to enforce any restrictions contained therein by any other appropriate action at its options.

(c) Furthermore, in addition to all other rights or remedies at law or in equity which are available to Grantor in the event of a violation of any of the covenants contained herein, Grantor may exercise one or more of the following remedies upon the occurrence of a violation, at its option:

(1) If the Grantee neglects or fails to perform any covenant to commence and complete rehabilitation of the building as provided in this deed, then the Grantor may, at any time thereafter, give the Grantee written notice specifying the default and direct the Grantee to remedy the same. If the Grantee thereafter, for a period of thirty (30) days, fails to fully and entirely remedy the default, then the Grantor shall have the privilege to repurchase the property at a price equivalent to the consideration paid by Grantee for the conveyance. Upon Grantor's election to exercise its right to repurchase by giving Grantee written notice of its intention to do so, Grantee shall exercise whatever instruments of conveyance are reasonably necessary and requested by the Grantor to effect a reconveyance.

(2) The Grantor reserves the right to enter the property at reasonable times, with five (5) days notice being considered reasonable notice of intent to enter, to inspect property to determine whether deed restrictions are being carried out.

(3) If the Grantee violates or fails to fully perform the covenants set forth herein, the Grantor may, after giving the Grantee thirty (30) days written notice specifying the Grantee's default and directing the Grantee to cure the same, enter the property and complete or remedy the undertaking of the Grantee which has been breached. In that event, the Grantee, by acceptance of this conveyance, does grant to the Grantor a lien on and against the property and all improvements thereon to secure the payment of all costs incurred by the Grantor in the performance or completion and/or performance of the covenant breached.

(4) Grantee agrees that damage to Grantor for Grantee's failure to perform Grantee's covenants herein will be difficult to ascertain or measure, and therefore Grantee agrees that in the event of failure to perform any such covenant, which failure continues for more than thirty (30) days after written notice from Grantor, Grantee shall pay to Grantor as liquidated damages for such failure the sum of _____ _____ ($_____) Dollars upon demand made by Grantor.

(d) Grantor's pursuit of any one remedy set forth herein, or any other remedy at law or in equity, shall not operate as or constitute a waiver of any other remedy or exclusive election of the particular remedy or remedies pursued. The extinguishment or invalidity of any remedy set forth herein shall in no way affect or diminish any other remedy provided herein.

(e) Grantor or its designee shall have the exclusive right to enforce the covenants herein contained through judicial proceedings, and shall not be liable for the enforcement or failure to enforce such covenants.

TO HAVE AND TO HOLD said above described premises, together with all and singular the rights and appurtenances thereto in anywise belonging unto the said Grantees, their heirs, executors, administrators, successors and assigns forever; and Grantor hereby binds itself, its successors and assigns, to WARRANT AND FOREVER DEFEND all and singular the said premises unto the said Grantees, their heirs, executors, administrators, successors and assigns, against every person lawfully claiming or to claim the same or any part thereof.

EXECUTED this the _____ day of _____, 19_____.

Exhibit "C". Required Rehabilitation

Items (__) through (__) above are herein collectively referred to as the "Work." Such Work must be done to the reasonable satisfaction of Galveston Historical Foundation. Grantee shall at Grantee's cost obtain all licenses and permits necessary to carry out any of such Work. Grantee agrees to indemnify and hold Galveston Historical Foundation harmless from any claim arising out of or in any way connected with the Work, and agrees to keep the Property free and clear of any liens or claims against the Property arising out of or in any way connected with the Work.

APPENDIX A

A Primer on Growth Management Tools and Techniques

Traditional elements in the growth management process include:

- Planning, such as preparing a comprehensive plan, which may include specific small area plans such as a downtown plan or a commercial corridor plan, and specific functional elements or plans such as housing, open space, historic preservation, recreation, and transportation elements;
- Implementing regulations and strategies, such as zoning regulations, subdivision ordinances, and land acquisition programs; and
- Capital improvements planning and budgeting, and scheduling future investments in public facilities, such as streets, sewer collection and transmission lines, and parks.

The growth management process can involve the following:
1. Determination of community goals, objectives, and policies;
2. Analysis of the community's existing or *de facto* growth policies;
3. Inventory of available growth management tools and techniques;
4. Adaptation of appropriate tools and techniques for the community;
5. Synthesis of selected tools into a system for managing growth; and
6. Continued monitoring of and refinements to the system over time.[1]

The effect of implementing growth management tools and changing market conditions creates the need to reevaluate and modify the land use plan, which in turn leads to further refinements to the various growth management tools. This process varies considerably from place to place and rarely proceeds in the orderly manner intended: growth management tools are often implemented long before plans are adopted; permit decisions are made that undermine local plans.

177

Planning _____

"Land use planning" is a broad term. According to the American Planning Association:

Planning is a comprehensive, coordinated and continuing process, the purpose of which is to help public and private decision makers arrive at decisions which promote the common good of society. This process includes:
(1) Identification of problems or issues;
(2) Research and analysis to provide definitive understanding of such problems or issues;
(3) Formulation of goals and objectives to be attained in alleviating problems or resolving issues;
(4) Development and evaluation of alternative methods (plans and programs) to attain agreed upon goals and objectives;
(5) Recommendation of appropriate courses of action from among the alternatives;
(6) Assistance in implementation of approved plans and programs;
(7) Evaluation of actions taken to implement approved plans and programs in terms of progress towards agreed upon goals and objectives; and
(8) A continuing process of adjusting plans and programs in light of the results of such evaluation or to take into account changed circumstances.[2]

Ideally, a local comprehensive plan is a product of this planning process. Additionally, a comprehensive plan is not static, but must be updated regularly in response to the effect of growth management strategies and changing community conditions.

A comprehensive plan should embody a community's vision of what it wants to become and how it intends to get there.* This vision should serve as an overall policy guide for public and private decisions that affect community development, including the implementation of land use regulations and other growth management strategies.

In fact, however, this process rarely proceeds as rationally as intended. Zoning ordinances and other growth management strategies are often revised or implemented without the benefit of prior revision to a comprehensive plan. Permit decisions that undermine community plans and goals are common. However, the degree of inconsistency between plans and other growth management techniques varies considerably from state to state and community to community.

A representative table of contents for a plan for a small community might include the following elements:

• Description of the planning process;

• Statement of community goals, objectives, and policies;

• Inventory of the community's natural and cultural assets, and assessment of possible threats to these assets;

• Description of existing community conditions, with special focus on the downtown, principal commercial corridors, and other key areas of the community;

• Description of existing and projected:
    Transportation and traffic circulation conditions;
    Public safety conditions and facilities;
    Housing supply, mix, and future housing demand;

* "Comprehensive plans" are referred to by various terms including "plan of development," "master plan," and "community plan." Traditional comprehensive plans are of the "physical" variety, i.e., they specifically identify appropriate land uses for individual parcels of land. Alternatively, some communities have adopted so-called "policy plans," which enumerate long-range objectives intended to guide future community development and serve as broad guidelines for specific land use regulations. A common approach is to merge the physical and policy approaches into a hybrid overall plan.

    Utility service conditions and facilities (water, sewer, solid waste, and energy);
    Open space and natural resource conditions;
    Recreation conditions and facilities;
    Economic conditions and assets, and economic development and redevelopment
       prospects;
    Historic preservation efforts;

- Projections of how development at permitted densities will affect the community's appearance, character, natural resources, cultural assets, economic development, fiscal conditions, and public services;
- Description of environmental constraints to development; and
- Description of future capital facilities planning and budgeting.

In many states, the minimum contents of local plans are mandated by state statute. While qualitative measures of the adequacy of local plans are difficult to legislate, evaluation of the adequacy of a comprehensive plan should focus on such questions as:

- Are planning goals, objectives, and policies clearly articulated with priorities set forth?
- Are the goals, objectives, and policies internally consistent? Is there coordination between the various elements?
- Is the plan based upon the results of a broad and meaningful public participation process?
- If maps are included, do they clearly identify land uses and the other geographic aspects of the plan? Do the maps accurately capture local geography and existing physical conditions?
- Are the economic, environmental, and public service assumptions underlying the plan clearly identified? Are they realistic?

Specific Growth Management Techniques

Planning is but one of the numerous local tools available to manage growth. The preparation and adoption of a comprehensive plan is, in fact, only the beginning of the growth management process.[3] Plans are not self-executing, they can be implemented only through land use regulations, capital facilities spending, land acquisition, and other strategies. These growth management techniques can be grouped into four basic categories:

- Land use regulations;
- Public spending and taxing policies;
- Land acquisition; and
- Private voluntary preservation and development techniques.

Although the techniques commonly appear as discrete options, most successful growth management programs, in fact, combine several separate techniques. Successful communities continually experiment with adapting various complementary strategies and techniques to meet their particular needs, which are constantly evolving.

LAND USE REGULATIONS

The authority for local land use planning and regulation is derived from the "police power" that authorizes states to enact laws to protect the public health, safety, and general welfare. States have delegated substantial portions of this broad regulatory authority to local governments. The most important and promising regulatory techniques for managing growth include zoning (in its numerous permutations); height limits; cluster zoning and planned unit development; subdivision regulations; exactions; adequate public facilities ordinances; transfer of development rights; and moratoria.

Zoning

Zoning is the most commonly used local device for regulating the use of land. Initially developed in the early part of this century basically to insulate residential neighborhoods from the negative impacts of industrial development, the essence of the traditional "Euclidian" zoning ordinance remains the physical separation of potentially incompatible land uses.*

Zoning regulates the use of land and structures—for example, commercial versus residential—and the dimensional characteristics of permitted uses, such as minimum lot sizes, the placement of structures on lots (i.e., minimum setbacks from street or property lines), the density of development, and the maximum height of buildings. In addition, zoning ordinances increasingly regulate nondimensional aspects of development such as landscaping, architectural design and features, signage, traffic circulation, and stormwater management.

Zoning ordinances consist of a text and a zoning map. The text describes permitted uses in the various districts, establishes standards for uses within these districts, and provides for administration and enforcement. The map divides the jurisdiction into districts. Changes to a zoning ordinance text or map occur through an amendment process that is initiated either by the local government, a landowner, or, in some cases, by local residents.

Conventional zoning promotes strict segregation of uses and predictable dimensional and density regulations. From this orderly and static pattern, land use regulation has evolved into a system of numerous techniques designed to balance the predictability of conventional zoning with administrative flexibility, discretionary review of individual developments, and specialized techniques to meet particular local needs.

Special Permits.   Special permits (also referred to as conditional uses or special exceptions) are the most widely used device allowing individual review and approval of proposed developments that require individual scrutiny to avoid or alleviate particular problems. In most zoning ordinances, uses are permitted within a district either "by right," with no individual discretionary review of the proposed development, or by special permit, in which case a zoning board reviews individual proposals in accordance with standards set forth in the ordinance. The special permit is available if the proposal adequately complies with the provisions in the ordinance, which typically deal with traffic and other impacts of the proposal.

A special permit should be distinguished from a variance, which is an individual exemption from zoning requirements. Variances typically are allowed when the impact of a zoning requirement would impose an undue hardship on a landowner due to unique conditions of the individual parcel. In many cases, variances may be granted from dimensional standards, but not use limitations.

Floating Zones.   Floating zones serve the same purpose as special permits, but provide the locality with more discretion. The standards for a floating zone are set forth in the text of a zoning ordinance, but the district is not mapped; rather the district "floats" above the community until a second, later ordinance amendment brings the zone to the ground. The second ordinance affixes the floating zone to a particular parcel that meets the standards set forth in the zoning text for the district.

The floating zone technique gives a locality greater discretion over a proposed use than does a special permit. A decision on a proposed rezoning to apply the floating zone is a

---

* So named because the zoning ordinance of the Village of Euclid, Ohio, was the subject of an early landmark decision from the U.S. Supreme Court that upheld the validity of zoning. *City of Euclid v. Ambler Realty Company,* 272 U.S. 365 (1926).

legislative function in most states and is rarely overturned by the courts; while a special permit application is an administrative function and must be granted if the proposed use is shown to meet the stated criteria.

Conditional Zoning and Development Agreements.   Sometimes a landowner may seek a rezoning, but the locality is unwilling to permit the whole range of uses or densities that the proposed zoning classification would allow. Instead of denying the rezoning, the local government may wish to impose conditions on the prospective rezoning. With conditional zoning, a local government may make rezoning conditional on an applicant's acceptance of concessions or conditions that are not otherwise imposed in the proposed zoning district. The applicant makes a unilateral commitment to these concessions in exchange for the rezoning; however, the local government makes no reciprocal obligation to rezone the property. Many states have upheld the use of conditional zoning, while several others have rejected its use.

Contract zoning also permits a locality to impose individual conditions on a rezoning, but—unlike conditional zoning—the municipality, in exchange, enters into an enforceable agreement to grant the desired zone change. In many states, contract zoning has been held invalid, because the locality bargains away its police power without state enabling legislation to do so.

A growing number of states (including California, Maine, Hawaii and others) have enacted legislation authorizing contract zoning or "development agreements" to regulate large-scale development. Development agreements typically are enforceable agreements between a developer and a local government, which lay out precisely the land uses and densities a developer may place on a large parcel and the public benefits the developer must provide as a condition of approval. The use of development agreements allows a single "master" approval for a large-scale, phased development. This approach provides developers and lending institutions the certainty of knowing early in the development process the amount and type of development authorized. Development agreements often also provide that the developer's right to complete all phases of a project vests earlier than it would in the absence of the agreement, which benefits developers when arranging financing. In exchange for this regulatory certainty, the local government may negotiate with the developer for a better package of public benefits than it could otherwise obtain.

Bonus or Incentive Zoning.   Bonus or incentive zoning allows a developer to exceed a zoning ordinance's dimensional limitations if the developer agrees to fulfill conditions specified in the ordinance. The classic example is when an ordinance authorizes a developer to exceed height limits by a specified amount in exchange for providing open spaces or plazas adjacent to the building.

Overlay Zones.   This zoning technique differs from conventional mapped zoning districts. An overlay zone applies a common set of regulations and standards to a designated area that may cut across several different preexisting conventional zoning districts. These regulations and standards apply in addition to those of the underlying zoning district. Two common examples of overlay zones are the flood zones created under the National Flood Insurance Program and many historic districts.

Flood zones often are described in local zoning ordinances, but are not initially mapped on the zoning map. Rather, the ordinance provides that the flood district regulations apply to areas within the 100-year floodplain, as designated in federal Flood Insurance Rate Maps. An overlay flood zone may allow the uses and densities permitted in the underlying zone, but impose additional construction and flood-proofing requirements.

Overlay historic districts often permit the uses and densities permitted in the underlying zone, but require that structures within the historic district be built or maintained in conformance with regulations to ensure historic compatibility.

Large Lot Zoning.   Large lot zoning or minimum lot size zoning—requiring that lots in a residential zone be at least, for example, 5 acres and in some cases as much as or more than 40 acres—is often used to reduce the density of residential development. The environmental and economic effects of large lot zoning vary with the specific situation. When used judiciously in areas with significant development constraints, large minimum lot size zoning can effectively reduce the negative impacts of development on sensitive landscapes or natural resources. To work effectively, large lot zoning must usually be used in combination with regulations that accommodate market demand in other more suitable areas. Overreliance on large lot zoning, however, often encourages land consuming and inefficient low-density sprawl.

Agricultural Zoning.   Agricultural zoning establishes minimum parcel sizes large enough to ensure that each parcel can sustain a viable agricultural operation. Some districts require minimum lot sizes of as much as 160 acres. Agricultural districts often also prohibit land uses that are incompatible with agriculture. (This technique is discussed in chapter 1, Agricultural Land Resources.)

Zoning Based on Performance Standards.   Zoning regulations often use performance standards to regulate development based on the permissible effects or impacts of a proposed use rather than simply the proposed dimensions. The complexity and sophistication of these standards vary widely, depending on the objectives of the program and the capacity of the locality to administer a complex program. Performance zoning may supplement or replace traditional zoning districts and dimensional standards. Under performance zoning, proposed uses whose impacts would exceed specified standards are prohibited.

   Performance standards are widely used to regulate noise, dust, vibration, and other impacts of industrial zones, and are increasingly used to regulate environmental impacts, such as the limiting of storm-water runoff resulting from development.

Point Systems.   Some communities use performance standards in combination with point systems. A proposed project must amass a minimum number of points in order to receive a permit. As opposed to the self-executing nature of conventional zoning, where a landowner can determine if a project is permissible by reading the zoning map and text, point systems require case-by-case review to determine if a specific land use is permissible. Permissible uses and densities of a parcel are determined at the time of permit application, with the applicant providing documentation that the proposal will comply with the various standards. Breckenridge, Colorado, has implemented a well-known development point system.

Height Limits
Localities limit building heights either townwide or by zoning district. In addition, height restrictions are sometimes used in conjunction with site-specific standards to prohibit structures that would be visible from scenic points or would block scenic views. (This technique is discussed in chapter 4.)

Cluster Zoning and Planned Unit Development
"Cluster zoning" (also known as "open space zoning") and the "planned unit development" (PUD) describe land use control devices that allow flexible design and clustering of development in higher densities on the most appropriate portion of a parcel in order to provide increased open space elsewhere on the parcel. These techniques, which exist in many forms, have become increasingly popular as more communities realize that conventional zoning and subdivision regulations often result in unsightly low-density sprawl with no intervening open space. These alternative clustering techniques can offer several benefits relative to conventional zoning, including:

- Limiting encroachment of development in and adjacent to environmentally sensitive areas;
- Reducing the amount of open land disturbed by development, thereby encouraging the preservation of agricultural lands, woodlands, and open landscapes;
- Reducing the amount of roads and utility lines needed for new development, which can reduce the cost of housing and public services.

Cluster development techniques typically do not allow increased overall development density, but simply rearrange development to preserve open land and improve site design. The concept can be demonstrated by a simple example of cluster development: a developer has 100 acres in an area zoned for one-half-acre residential lots, which could be developed into around 200 buildable lots, using up the entire 100 acres. Under a cluster zoning program, the developer could cluster the 200 units on 50 acres, for example, and permanently dedicate 50 acres of open space for public use.

A recent publication of the Center for Rural Massachusetts, *Dealing with Change in the Connecticut River Valley: A Design Manual for Conservation and Development* (cited at the end of the chapter), provides excellent demonstrations of clustering techniques and shows with aerial graphics how cluster development improves the landscape relative to development under conventional zoning regulations.

Subdivision Regulations

Subdivision regulations are widely used to regulate the conversion of land into building lots. In rural communities, they are often the principal or only means by which a community regulates residential development.

Subdivision regulations were originally enacted primarily to facilitate land transfer by providing a method for landowners to file a subdivision plat with numbered lots, rather than with the traditional metes and bounds lot descriptions. In the 1920s and 1930s, cities began to use these regulations to manage the quality of streets, storm drainage systems, lot layout, and the adequacy of utility services. Typically, subdivision ordinances articulate design standards and materials for streets and utility systems, site topography, sidewalks, curbs and gutters, storm-water management, landscaping, open space, and recreational facilities. More recently, subdivision regulations have been widely used not only to improve the engineering and physical design of on-site public improvements, but also to require the provision of dedicated recreational lands, off-site road improvements, and other public services.

Development Exactions and Impact Fees

"Development exaction" is a generic term that describes a variety of mechanisms by which communities require dedication of land or facilities or payment of a fee in lieu of land or facilities. Exactions are referred to by many names, including "dedications," "linkage requirements," "mandatory tithing," and "mitigation requirements." Exactions are either explicitly mandated in development regulations or imposed informally on a case-by-case basis in rezoning or special permit negotiations. Impact fees require a developer to pay an amount of money determined by a uniform formula rather than by negotiation or tradition.

Traditionally, exactions have required subdivision developers to provide on-site infrastructure such as roads, parks, sewer lines, and drainage facilities. Realizing that to require certain on-site improvements such as parks might be inefficient or inequitable, many communities began to require developers to pay fees in lieu of improvements in certain situations. These fees are then earmarked for providing those facilities to serve the development.

Recently, municipalities have begun imposing impact fees to finance an expanding variety of public facilities and services in virtually all regulatory contexts. Martin County, Florida, for example, has enacted a Beach Impact Fee Ordinance, which requires developers to contribute to a fund, based upon the projected recreational demand resulting from the proposed development, to purchase and maintain public beachfront property.

Financially strapped large cities have been most aggressive in imposing development exactions, requiring developers of large projects to pay impact or linkage fees for numerous public services. San Francisco, for example, requires developers of large-scale downtown projects to pay impact fees for affordable housing, transit, public parks, and child care. Boston imposes fees for both housing and job training. In Honolulu, developers of large projects commonly must pay for off-site sewer improvements, park land and facilities, on-site and off-site road and transportation system improvements, police and fire protection facilities, school sites and buildings, on-site or off-site affordable housing, water supply infrastructure (perhaps including reservoirs), and employment programs for area residents. San Diego finances capital facilities for suburban development through "flexible benefits assessments," which combine impact fees and special assessments. These fees finance parks, roads, libraries, schools, utilities, drainage systems, transit service, and police and fire protection.

Adequate Public Facilities Ordinances

This type of ordinance conditions development approval upon a finding that adequate public facilities are available to serve proposed development. The ordinance sets quantitative standards for required public service levels and links development approval to the ability of public services that serve the proposed development to comply with these standards. The public services that have the most significant impact on development decisions are water, sewer, and the traffic circulation network. Other public services sometimes linked to development approval are storm-water management facilities, parks and recreational lands, emergency response time, and mass transit. Florida requires all local governments to adopt adequate public facilities standards. After the state approves a local plan and development regulations, the local government cannot issue development permits unless public services can be provided for the development at the established level of service.

Transfer of Development Rights

Transfer of development rights (TDR) is an innovative growth management technique based on the concept that ownership of land gives the owner many rights, each of which may be separated from the rest and transferred to someone else. One of these separable rights is the right to develop land. With a TDR system, landowners are able to retain their land, but sell the right to develop the land for use on other property.

Under a typical TDR program, a local government awards development rights to each parcel of developable land in the community or in selected districts, based on the land's acreage or value. Persons can then sell their development rights on the open market if they do not want to develop their property or are prohibited by regulation from developing the property at a desired density. Land from which development rights have been sold cannot be developed.

There are many possible variations on TDR, but a system can work in the following way. Suppose A owns four acres of land that has been allocated two development rights. If local regulations require A to have one right per acre in order to fully develop the land, A has three choices. A can develop just two acres and expend all the development potential for the parcel; A can buy two development rights on the market and develop the entire four acres; or A can sell the two rights at a market-determined price and preclude any development of the property. If the land is in an agricultural or historic district, regulations may restrict development of the parcel, in which case A can only develop the parcel at a low density and sell the balance of the development rights for use on another site.

TDR can reduce, substantially, the value shifts and economic inequities of restrictive zoning. For example, it can allow the market to compensate owners whose land cannot be developed because of its environmental, scenic, or historic significance. By selling development rights, a landowner can receive profit from property appreciation without developing the parcel.

TDR requires a high level of staff expertise to design and administer. The novelty of the TDR concept and the sophistication required to make it work properly reduces its attractiveness and political acceptance in many communities.*

Moratoria and Interim Development Regulations

Moratoria and interim regulations are designed to substantially restrict development for a limited period. They can impose a complete temporary moratorium on all development or on specific types of intensive development. A moratorium can apply to zoning approvals, subdivision approvals, and building permits.

Restrictive interim regulations must generally relate to one of two permissible goals. Either they must relate to planning—used to restrain development until a plan can be developed or a permanent growth management program implemented—or necessary to protect public safety, health, or the environment by preventing potentially hazardous overburdening of community facilities (such as a sewage treatment facility). The duration of a moratorium should be specified when enacted, and should be tied to the time period necessary to develop a plan, implement a growth management program, or upgrade public facilities related to the relevant safety or environmental problem.

LOCAL SPENDING AND TAXING POLICIES

Although not traditionally viewed as methods of managing development, local expenditure and property taxation policies may have significant impacts on land use. Public facilities such as roads, water systems, sewers, and public transit can especially influence the level and characteristics of development in a community. A local growth management strategy is incomplete unless it accounts for these influences.

Capital Improvements Programming

The provision of municipal services is an important local tool for managing development. A municipal decision whether to extend or expand public utilities or facilities strongly influences the economic feasibility of most large private development projects. The extension of municipal services is generally governed by a city's capital improvements program (CIP), a timetable by which a city indicates the timing and level of municipal services it intends to provide over a specified duration. Generally, the CIP covers a five- to ten-year period, although it may be shorter or longer depending upon the municipality's confidence in its ability to predict future conditions.

Capital programming, by itself, influences land development decisions. By committing itself to a timetable for expansion of municipal services, a locality influences development decisions to some extent, especially in areas where on-site sewage disposal or water supply is unusually expensive or infeasible. A capital program may also be used effectively as part of a more comprehensive program to manage development. By properly coordinating its utility extension policy with its planning and growth management program, a community can control the direction and pace of development. Using a comprehensive plan to delineate the location and type of development desired and a capital program to schedule the provision of services, a locality can inform developers when development of a particular parcel will be encouraged and the type of development that will be allowed. In addition, a municipality can regulate the pace of development to coincide with the availability of adequate public services.

Preferential Assessment

Most states have enacted preferential or use-value property tax assessment programs for farmland and open space land. With use-value assessment, property taxes for a parcel are based upon the value of the parcel only considering its current use, rather than its value based upon the property's development potential. Use-value assessment can reduce the property tax assessments for lands whose value for development purposes exceeds its

---

* Montgomery County, Maryland, has implemented perhaps the most successful TDR program with approximately 20,000 acres preserved for farmland due to the program.

value for agricultural or forestry uses. Reduced property tax assessments can lessen the need to sell or develop sometimes caused by high property taxes.

Special Assessments

The special assessment is the local taxation technique that has the greatest potential impact on growth management policy. A special assessment, while not technically a tax, is a method of raising revenue in which all or part of the cost of a facility is charged to a landowner who derives a special benefit from the facility. Special assessments are often used for road improvements, street lighting, off-street parking, sewers, and water systems. The fee is usually proportionate to the distance the facility abuts a parcel, the area of the land served by the facility or improvement, or the value added to the land served.

Improvement Districts

Special improvement districts have been created in many forms to raise revenue for traffic circulation improvements, aesthetic improvements, or other public improvements within a limited area. Landowners within a specified district are levied a special tax or assessment (sometimes through tax increment financing), which is used to make public improvements that benefit that district.

LAND ACQUISITION

Local governments enjoy broad authority under state enabling legislation to acquire real property interests, either through voluntary sale or condemnation, for any legitimate public purpose. Land acquisition is an important supplement to land use regulations as a means of managing growth and protecting critical resources. Although localities generally use land acquisition to directly control the use of the specific parcel acquired, several communities have used land acquisition to influence the community's general growth policies. For example, Boulder, Colorado, has used the proceeds of local bond issues and a local sales tax to acquire a large amount of land in the foothills and farming districts surrounding the city to prevent environmentally destructive and fiscally unsound development of these areas.

Local land acquisition programs are generally funded either by local property taxes, sales taxes, or real estate transfer taxes. Bond issues backed by one of these taxes are commonly used. Nantucket, Massachusetts, and Block Island, Rhode Island, for example, impose a 2 percent conveyance tax on most transfers of real estate to fund local open space acquisition programs. (The federal Land and Water Conservation Fund and, more recently, state land acquisition programs have also been important revenue sources for recreational land acquisition and improvement programs.)

Fee Simple Acquisition

The ownership of land is often analogized to ownership of a "bundle of rights," including, for example, the right to control access to the land, the right to develop property, the right to mine coal from beneath the land, the right to hunt on the land, and so forth. (Each of these are subject to reasonable police power regulations.) When one person owns all the rights associated with a parcel (the entire bundle), this person is said to own the land "in fee simple"; however, these rights can be owned separately, in which case an owner is said to own a "less-than-fee interest."

Local governments generally acquire fee simple ownership for parks and other property needed for municipal uses, such as for schools or landfills. Fee simple acquisition provides the greatest level of control over the use of a parcel; however, it is also usually the most expensive method of land acquisition. In addition to the substantial acquisition costs, fee simple acquisition removes property entirely from local tax rolls and can result in significant maintenance costs. For these reasons, localities and land trusts often prefer alternative land protection techniques to full ownership in fee.

Acquisition of Easements

The acquisition of easements constitutes a particularly useful tool for many local governments and land trusts. Easements are effective devices for preserving sensitive lands, providing public access along rivers or greenways, and allowing landowners to obtain income, estate, and property tax benefits for land stewardship while they continue to live on their land.

Easements are among the distinct property rights that may be sold separately from the other rights (in other words, "separated from the fee"). Easements can be divided into two categories: affirmative or negative. The owner of an affirmative easement has the right to do something with or on property belonging to someone else. An affirmative easement, for example, may authorize a utility company to place electric lines across someone's property or may authorize the public to pass over property to a riverside fishing spot.

The owner of a negative easement has the right to prohibit certain activities on property belonging to someone else. A negative easement may prohibit a landowner from constructing a building that would interfere with a scenic view from a neighboring parcel. A negative easement—for instance, an easement that prohibits development but allows a landowner to continue to farm and live on a parcel—may provide many of the same public open space benefits as full fee acquisition, but can generally be acquired at a substantially lower cost than a fee interest. In addition, management costs are usually assumed to a large degree by the private landowner, rather than by the public agency or land trust that holds the easement. Another fiscal advantage of easements is that the land remains on the tax rolls, albeit at a reduced value. Negative easements, however, may create long-term administrative, enforcement, and maintenance costs.

Easements may also be characterized as "appurtenant to the land" or "in gross." An appurtenant easement benefits one parcel of land (the "dominant estate") at the expense of another parcel (the "servient estate"). Usually these parcels are adjacent. For example, an appurtenant easement may grant the owner of the dominant estate access over an adjoining parcel to a county road. An easement in gross exists for the benefit of the person who owns the easement, regardless of whether that person owns any nearby land that is benefited. There is a strong presumption that if an easement is not clearly in gross, it is appurtenant.

The rules governing conveyance of appurtenant easements often differ from those governing easements in gross. When a parcel benefited by an appurtenant easement is sold, the benefits of the easement pass with the land to the new owner, even if the deed does not mention the easement. The benefits created by an easement in gross do not, by comparison, pass automatically to a new owner when the property is transferred. In some states, easements in gross are not recognized or are not transferrable to another person. Under traditional legal doctrines in many states, easements, and especially easements in gross, were difficult to enforce for various reasons. Because of these difficulties, almost all states have passed specific statutes authorizing conservation easements.

Conservation Easement Statutes.   Conservation easement statutes clarify the ambiguities and remove the barriers to enforcement of certain easements. These statutes set forth rules governing the definition, creation, transfer, and enforcement of easements created to conserve land or buildings. Although conservation easement statutes vary from state to state, some of the more important provisions typically found in conservation easement statutes include the following:

• <u>Definitions</u>. Most states define conservation easements to include a broad spectrum of property interests that restrict the development, management, or use of land. Typically, easements may be created to retain land in its natural condition, to provide recreational access, or to preserve and maintain the land's historic or architectural character.

• <u>Creation and Transfer</u>. Conservation easements must be created in writing. Some states require that conservation easements must be held by governmental agencies or be approved by a central authority (for example, the secretary of environmental affairs in

Massachusetts) and that conservation easements held by nonprofit corporations or trusts be approved by the relevant local government.

- Permitted Holders. Many states authorize only certain types of entities to hold conservation easements. These entities usually include governmental agencies, land trusts, corporations, and other entities whose purposes include conservation or preservation.

- Enforcement. The most important benefits of conservation easement statutes involve granting clear validity to conservation easements and eliminating most of the technical barriers to enforcement of conservation easements.

- Relation to Nonstatutory (Common Law) Easements. Some statutes are more comprehensive than others. If a state statute does not address a common law defense to enforcement, a conservation easement would still be subject to the defense, such as the defense that an easement in gross cannot be transferred.

PRIVATE VOLUNTARY LAND PROTECTION TECHNIQUES

Land acquisition and conservation techniques available to local governments or private nonprofit organizations can provide an important complement to local regulatory and public spending measures. A public or private land trust can use a range of land acquisition and conservation techniques, singly or in combination, to meet local conservation and growth management objectives. In towns such as Nantucket, Massachusetts, Block Island, Rhode Island, and Davis, California, municipalities have established local land trusts as municipal or quasi-municipal entities. These land trusts participate in the private real estate market as representatives of the public interest and use the range of voluntary land conservation techniques available to private land trusts.

The two most important private land protection techniques used by land trusts to protect land or historic buildings are fee simple acquisition and acquisition of easements.

Although land or easement acquisition are the conservation techniques most commonly employed by land trusts, there are many other private voluntary land protection tools to consider.*

A common factor in these tools is that they provide land trusts a method to control or influence the use of valuable parcels with limited expenditures of money.

Other than acquisition at full market value, the principal private tools available to preserve land include:

- Donation or bargain sale of fee simple interests, conservation easements or other less-than-fee interests in land;

- Options to buy;

- Rights of first refusal;

- Leases and management agreements;

- Preacquisition;

- Limited or controlled development; and

- Conservation investment.†

Donation or Bargain Sale
In addition to purchasing land for conservation purposes at its full fair market value, land trusts often acquire property, whether fee or less-than-fee interests, through donation or bargain sale. Full-value purchase is rarely the approach of first preference because of the expense of acquisition and management.

———————

* This section is comprised, in part, of material reprinted by permission of the California State Coastal Conservancy, from Stephen F. Harper, *The Nonprofit Primer: A Guidebook for Land Trusts* (Oakland, CA: California State Coastal Conservancy, 1984).

† Many land trusts have compiled descriptions of these alternatives in a succinct brochure to be used in building landowner interest and confidence. This type of brochure can introduce landowners to conservation techniques, and to the income and estate tax benefits accruing from donations and bargain sales. The Land Trust Exchange in Alexandria, Virginia, can provide sample brochures.

Donation, when available, is the option of choice for obvious reasons. Donation also offers the conservation-minded landowner the greatest potential tax benefits.

In between full-value purchase and donation lies the bargain sale approach. A bargain sale involves a combination of donation and purchase, in which a landowner transfers property at a price below fair market value. The landowner may thus obtain tax benefits as well as a direct cash payment.

Options

An option is a widely used real estate contract device that provides a party with a temporary right—but not obligation—to purchase property. An option is the exclusive right to purchase a property at a specified price within a specified time. The party is not obligated to purchase the land; however, the landowner is prevented from accepting offers from other potential purchasers during the term of the option. Options can generally be acquired at a fraction of the ultimate purchase price, or they may be donated by the landowner. The deadline imposed by an option may be useful to a land trust in marshaling the funds necessary to purchase a parcel or finding a suitable private purchaser. The land trust can purchase the property during the option period; if not, the option interest expires.

Rights-of-First-Refusal

A right-of-first-refusal is an agreement between a landowner and a second party in which the landowner agrees that if he receives a legitimate offer from a third party to buy the property, he will notify the second party and give the second party a specified period of time in which to match the third party offer under similar terms, before the landowner will accept the offer from the third party. Land trusts can acquire such rights, by purchase or donation, in order to tie up a parcel without having to buy it immediately. If a potential purchaser with conservation objectives makes an offer on the property, the land trust may decide not to exercise the right-of-first-refusal. Although both an option and a right-of-first-refusal can be donated, the land trust's legal position will be improved if the interest is created in a written contract, a minimal amount is paid for the contract interest, and the contract is recorded in proper form in the appropriate land records office.

Leases and Management Agreements

These tools provide a land trust with temporary control or influence over a parcel without the expense of acquisition. Leases and management agreements are flexible instruments that can be drafted to implement any number of desired relationships between a landowner and a land trust. Leases generally give a land trust the right to manage and occupy property for a certain time, while management agreements specify the terms and restrictions under which the landowner continues to manage the property. Generally, both devices are recorded in the land records and remain in force for their full term even if the land changes hands.

Preacquisition

Land trusts may acquire property to hold and manage in perpetuity. In other cases, land trusts serve as an intermediary for a public land management agency. A public agency may wish to work with a private land trust for preacquisition because a private organization can often negotiate and undertake other necessary steps for acquisition faster and more adeptly than the public agency. After land is acquired by a land trust and turned over, public land management agencies can often manage additional adjacent land more economically than could a private trust. Ownership by a public agency also confers more protection against condemnation by other public agencies, such as a state highway department, than does private land trust ownership.

Even when a land trust intends to retain ownership of a parcel, it may be wise for its deeds and other title documents to provide for transfer of the title to a public agency or to a larger local, regional, or national land trust if the trust itself ceases to exist or is unable to manage its holdings.

Limited or Controlled Development

Increasingly employed by innovative land trusts, this technique typically entails clustered development or other limited development of a portion of a parcel in order to finance acquisition and preservation of the balance of the parcel. Development is generally limited to nonsensitive or previously disturbed portions of a parcel. Limited development (also called "controlled development" or "creative partial development") can permit land stewardship and substantial resource protection in situations when donation is not possible and acquisition for full preservation is not financially feasible. Limited development is often feasible because building lots or houses adjacent to restricted open space are frequently more valuable than otherwise.

This tool often lends itself to the formation of a partnership for joint development between the trust and a landowner. In such partnerships, the latter provides the land and the land trust provides planning and land protection expertise, community goodwill, assurance that the open space portions of the property will be permanently protected from development, and development capital.

When considering limited development, a land trust should obtain professional assistance from bankers, builders, real estate agents, and other development professionals to determine whether development at the density necessary to finance the acquisition is feasible from a financial perspective. This tool is only appropriate for parcels of sufficient size and with appropriate conditions to allow creative partial development without endangering the resources that are worthy of protection. Finally, before undertaking limited development, a land trust should ensure that its proposed actions will not endanger its mission and public reputation as a conservation organization. The public that volunteers time and donates money may not readily accept the limited development concept, especially without an educational effort by the land trust.

Conservation Investment

Many real estate development ventures are financed through syndications, in which numerous individuals or entities join together to finance a project. In return, the investors receive some combination of periodic income, capital gain upon resale, and, perhaps, significant tax benefits. This technique can be adapted for land conservation. Although the Tax Reform Act of 1986 reduced the income tax advantages of most types of real estate investments, creative tax-saving arrangements are still possible.

In some cases, a land trust may sell property subject to appropriate deed restrictions or conservation easements to a buyer looking for an aesthetically pleasing place to live or own a vacation home. In other cases, "charitable investors" may be persuaded to invest in a working farm, fishing preserve, or ranch with deed restrictions to allow only agriculture, forestry, or other open space uses. Investors would receive a percentage of the operation's income and tax benefits (for example, through depreciation of capital assets, deductions for business expenses, or deductions for mortgage interest payments) as well as the satisfaction of knowing they have helped conserve open land.

Information Resources _____

Babcock, Richard F., and Charles L. Siemon. *The Zoning Game Revisited.* Boston: Lincoln Institute of Land Policy, 1985.
   Updated version of a classic book on zoning and the land use regulation process. Provides case studies of 11 local and regional land use programs, their origins, development, legal aspects, and political history.

Brower, David J., Candace Carraway, Thomas Pollard, and C. Luther Propst. *Managing Development in Small Towns.* Chicago: American Planning Association Press, 1984.
   Provides a comprehensive overview of the use of growth management measures in small towns, including techniques based upon local land acquisition, public spending, taxation, and regulatory

powers. Provides tangible guidance in assessing the need for growth management and in implementing specific techniques.

Chapin, F. Stuart, and Edward J. Kaiser. *Urban Land Use Planning*. 3d ed. Urbana: University of Illinois Press, 1979.
A leading land use planning textbook.

Clark, John. *The Sanibel Report: Formulation of a Comprehensive Plan Based on Natural Systems*. Washington, D.C.: The Conservation Foundation, 1976.
Explains the process leading to the development of a performance-based comprehensive planning process and overlay zoning program for Sanibel Island, Florida. The basis for the program is mitigating the impacts of development on vegetation, wildlife, coastal process, geology, or hydrology of the barrier island.

Conservation Foundation. *Groundwater Protection*. Washington, D.C.: The Conservation Foundation, 1987.
This book contains the final report of the National Groundwater Policy Forum and a guide to problems, causes, and government responses to groundwater pollution.

Diehl, Janet, and Thomas S. Barrett. *The Conservation Easement Handbook: Managing Land Conservation and Historic Preservation Easement Programs*. Trust for Public Land and Land Trust Exchange 1988. Available from Land Trust Exchange, 1017 Duke Street, Alexandria, VA 22314.
Authoritative and well-written book that provides solid information about establishing and managing easements programs.

Hoose, Phillip M. *Building an Ark: Tools for the Preservation of Natural Diversity Through Land Protection*. Covelo, CA: Island Press, 1981.
Provides an overview of private techniques to preserve open space and important wildlife and plant resources. Includes chapters on conducting natural heritage inventories, private land protection techniques, and lobbying state government to protect our natural heritage.

Kusler, Jon A. *Regulating Sensitive Lands*. Washington, D.C.: Environmental Law Institute, 1980.
This thorough book discusses regulatory programs to protect floodplains, lake and stream shores, coastal zones, wetlands, rivers, areas of scientific interest, and similar sensitive areas. It discusses state resource protection programs and cases.

Land Trust Exchange. *Organizing a Land Trust: Starting a Land Conservation Organization in Your Community*. Available from Land Trust Exchange, 1017 Duke Street, Alexandria, VA 22314.
The Land Trust Exchange publishes this handout and others about land trusts.

McHarg, Ian. *Design With Nature*. Garden City, N.Y.: The Natural History Press, 1969.
A pioneering introduction to regional land use planning based upon the development constraints and opportunities presented by natural systems. Contains case studies showing how environmental and scenic inventories can be combined to indicate where development should be directed.

Meshenberg, Michael J. *The Administration of Flexible Zoning Techniques*. Planning Advisory Service Report No. 318. Chicago: American Society of Planning Officials, 1976.
Provides an introduction to and analysis of flexible zoning techniques, including PUDs, special permits, floating zones, overlay zoning, tract zoning, incentive zoning, exactions, and TDR.

Sanders, Welford. *The Cluster Subdivision: A Cost-Effective Approach*. Planning Advisory Service Report No. 356. Chicago: American Planning Association, 1980.
Provides detailed guidance on the design of cluster subdivision ordinances. Includes legal guidance and excerpts from several local zoning ordinances.

Smith, Herbert H. *The Citizen's Guide to Planning*. Chicago: American Planning Association, 1979.
A lay person's general introduction to planning written by a veteran planner. Provides overviews of the planning process; the role of the local planning commission; the relationship between plans and regulations; and the connection between capital improvements and planning.

Smith, Herbert H. *The Citizen's Guide to Zoning.* Chicago: American Planning Association, 1983.
    Provides a basic primer on all aspects of zoning and zoning administration, the citizens' role in zoning hearings, frequent problems with zoning, and emerging zoning techniques.

Thurow, Charles, William Jones, and Duncan Erley. *Performance Controls for Sensitive Lands: A Practical Guide for Local Administrators.* Planning Advisory Service Report Nos. 307, 308. Chicago: American Society of Planning Officials, 1975.
    An early, comprehensive discussion of the use of performance standard regulations to protect environmental resources, including streams and lakes, aquifers, wetlands, woodlands, and hillsides. Includes excerpts of illustrative performance control ordinances.

Whyte, William H. *The Last Landscape.* Garden City, New York: Doubleday and Company, 1970.
    An early, but still valuable look at both the politics of planning and land use regulation and how specific techniques can be employed to protect specific resources.

Yaro, Robert D., et al. *Dealing with Change in the Connecticut River Valley: A Design Manual for Conservation and Development.* Amherst, Mass.: Center for Rural Massachusetts, University of Massachusetts, 1988.
    This valuable publication discusses the advantages of clustered development, provides practical planning standards for preserving distinctive local character while accommodating economic development, includes sample ordinance language for clustered development, and includes excellent aerial graphics showing various landscapes before development, after conventional development, and after creative site-sensitive development. This book builds a convincing argument for clustered development regulations.

Notes

1. Brower, David J., Candace Carraway, Thomas Pollard, and Luther C. Propst. *Managing Development in Small Towns.* Chicago: American Planning Association Press, 1984: 1–2.

2. American Planning Association, Planning Policies, APA Action Agenda, APA News (in *Planning*), 24B (July 1979); quoted in Donald G. Hagman, and Julian C. Juergensmeyer. *Urban Planning and Land Development Control Law*, 2d ed. (St. Paul: West Publishing Company, 1986): 25.

3. Although professional planners define "planning" to include steps to implement plans, the means by which local governments can manage growth are broader than what many people think of as planning. Therefore, the term "growth management" is used to describe the process and techniques available to influence the characteristics of community growth.

APPENDIX B

Open Space Protection: An Overview of Strategies

Government and Nonprofit Open Space Acquisition _____

GOVERNMENT FINANCING OPTIONS

Bond Act
Explanation: Borrowing money through issuance of bonds is a common way to provide funds for open space. Usually approved through referendum on a local or statewide basis.

Advantage: Availability of funds allows for immediate purchase of open space. Distributes cost of acquisition.

Disadvantage: Needs approval of general public. Can be expensive—interest charges are tacked on to cost of project.

Examples: In 1987, Florida issued $200 million in bonds for acquisition of oceanfront and beachfront lands. And a 1987 Rhode Island bond act provides $65.2 million for park acquisition and improvements.

General Fund Appropriation
Explanation: Appropriation from general state or local government fund.

Advantage: Avoids interest and debt service cost.

Disadvantage: Unpredictability of budget allocations. Might not provide sufficient funds and competes with other programs.

Real Estate Transfer Tax
Explanation: Acquisition funds obtained from a tax on property transfers, which is a small percentage of purchase price. Percentage and amount exempted varies with locality.

Advantage: Growth creates a substantial fund for open space acquisition. Enables local communities to generate their own funds for open space protection, reducing reliance on scarce state funds.

Disadvantage: Discriminates between new and existing residents. Can inflate real estate values. Works effectively only in growth situations.

193

Examples: Between 1983 and 1986, Nantucket has used the 2 percent transfer tax to generate over $6 million. Florida, Vermont, Maryland, Tennessee and Block Island, Rhode Island, also have successful programs.

Land Gains Tax

Explanation: Capital gains tax on sale or exchange of undeveloped land held for a short period of time. Tax rate varies depending on holding period.

Advantage: Discourages speculative development. Has a regulatory and revenue impact.

Disadvantage: Can inflate real estate values and slow market.

Example: An established tax in Vermont on land held for six years or less. Tax rates range from 5 to 60 percent.

Tax Return Checkoff

Explanation: On state income tax forms, a filer may appropriate a small amount of taxes owed toward revenues for natural lands acquisitions.

Advantage: Convenient and successful means of generating significant financial resources for acquisitions.

Disadvantage: Vulnerable to competition from other equally worthwhile programs.

Examples: Over 30 states use the checkoff as a source of open space acquisition revenue.

Other Fund/Tax

Explanation: Taxes on cigarettes, sales, gasoline, and natural resource exploitation as well as revenue from fees and licenses can be used toward park acquisitions.

Advantage: With income from fees and licenses for boat, off-road vehicle and snowmobile use, park entry, and hunting, users pay for resources they use.

Disadvantage: Revenues from taxes can be diverted easily for other uses unless firmly dedicated to park and recreation purposes. Fees create pressures for money to be spent on special interest uses.

Examples: Florida and Michigan successfully use revenues from severance taxes on exploitation of nonrenewable resources. Many states use revenues from cigarette and gasoline taxes, fees, and licenses.

State Grant

Explanation: States can provide matching grants for municipalities to acquire open space.

Advantage: State funding encourages localities to preserve important open space by leveraging limited local funds. Donated lands may be used as a match.

Disadvantage: Localities must compete for limited funds and be able to match state funds.

Examples: In Indiana, state appropriates up to $5 million in 50 percent matching funds for acquisition and management of natural areas as private contributions are raised. Similar programs in Delaware and Alabama.

Sale or Transfer of Tax Default Property

Explanation: Sale of tax default property can provide a fund for open space acquisition. Also, if meets criteria, it can be transferred to appropriate agency for park use.

Advantage: Funds for acquisition are acquired with little cost to taxpayers.

Disadvantage: Need to assure that sale proceeds are specifically allocated to open space acquisition. Might not provide a significant income. Very political process.

Example: In Oregon, State Law 271.330 allows a public agency to transfer title of foreclosed land to another public agency as long as the land continues to be used for a public purpose.

Payment in Lieu of Dedication

Explanation: Local government requires developers to pay a fee to a municipal trust fund for open space acquisitions.

Advantage: New construction pays for its impact on open space.

Disadvantage: Acquisition funds dependent on development. May be lack of accountability for funds.

Example: In California, *Associated Home Builders v. City of Walnut Creek* upheld use of payment in lieu of dedication if money is used for acquisitions serving the subdivision.

Special Assessment District

Explanation: Special tax district for area benefited by an open space project.

Advantage: Users finance acquisition and management.

Disadvantage: Increases taxes. Timely and costly to implement.

Examples: Between 1962 and 1982, the number of special districts in the United States increased by 57 percent. Commonly used in California due to Proposition 13 reduction in local property tax revenue.

Land and Water Conservation Fund

Explanation: Federal funds are provided to local governments for acquisition and development of outdoor recreation areas.

Advantage: Cost of acquisition for local government is lowered by subsidy.

Disadvantage: Receipt of funds is dependent on federal approval. Limited funds available. In 1987 and 1988, no funds were provided for state and local acquisition.

Examples: Through 1984, 31,955 state acquisition and development projects have been aided with this fund.

GOVERNMENT OWNERSHIP ENTITY OPTIONS

Federal Techniques

Explanation: Acquisition by National Park Service, Forest Service, U.S. Fish and Wildlife Service, or Bureau of Land Management.

Advantage: Acquisition is at federal level, eliminating financial obligation for locality.

Disadvantage: Acquisitions are limited due to agencies' specific criteria for acquisition. Needs congressional authorization.

State Techniques

Explanation: Acquisition by state agency.

Advantage: Statewide bond acts can provide significant funding resources for important open space acquisitions throughout a state. Provides revolving loan funds to leverage nonprofit activity.

Disadvantage: Government may miss acquisition opportunities due to long time-frame for acquisition approval.

Local Techniques

Explanation: Acquisition by county or municipality.

Advantage: Local government can be more flexible about the type of open space it acquires.

Disadvantage: Limited local funds and expertise limit the number of acquisitions.

NONPROFIT PURCHASE AND OWNERSHIP ENTITY OPTIONS

Nonprofit Acquisition/Conveyance to Public Agency

Explanation: A nonprofit can help to implement government programs by acquiring and holding land until a public agency is able to purchase.

Advantage: A nonprofit can enter the real estate market more easily than government, and can often sell to the government at under fair market value if property was acquired through a bargain sale.

Disadvantage: Must have a public agency willing and able to buy within a reasonable time frame.

Nonprofit Acquisition/Conveyance to Land Trust

Explanation: A national or regional nonprofit can acquire and hold land until a local land trust has been established or is able to finance acquisition.

Advantage: A nonprofit can finance an immediate acquisition and hold property until a land trust has been established or has acquired funds.

Disadvantage: If a land trust does not exist, a community must establish one. A land trust needs solid support, funding, and ability to manage land.

Nonprofit Acquisition/Management

Explanation: A national/regional nonprofit or local land trust retains ownership and assumes management responsibilities.

Advantage: Local land trusts allow for ownership within community; local citizens can provide responsible care and management of site.

Disadvantage: Land must fit criteria of acquiring organization, which must be prepared to assume long-term management responsibilities and costs.

Nonprofit Acquisition/Saleback or Leaseback

Explanation: A nonprofit can purchase property, limit future development through restrictive easements or covenants, and resell or lease back part or all of property.

Advantage: Acquisition is financed by resale or leaseback. Resale at less than fair market value (because of restrictions) makes land affordable for buyer. Sale can finance preservation of part of site.

Disadvantage: Complex negotiations. If leaseback, nonprofit retains responsibility for land. Finding a buyer for restricted property may be difficult.

TYPE OF OWNERSHIP OPTIONS

Fee Simple

Explanation: Outright purchase of full title to land and all rights associated with land.

Advantage: Owner has full control of land. Allow for permanent protection and public access.

Disadvantage: Acquisition can be costly. Removes land from tax base. Ownership responsibility includes liability and maintenance.

Conservation Easement/Development Rights

Explanation: A partial interest in property transferred to an appropriate nonprofit or governmental entity either by gift or purchase. As ownership changes, the land remains subject to the easement restrictions.

Advantage: Less expensive for purchaser than fee simple. Landowner retains ownership and property remains on the tax rolls, often at a lower rate because of restricted use. Easement may allow for some development. Potential income and estate tax benefits from donation.

Disadvantage: Public access allowed only upon landowner approval. Easement must be enforced. Restricted use may lower resale value.

Fee Simple/Leaseback

Explanation: Purchase of full title and leaseback to previous owner or other, subject to restrictions.

Advantage: Allows for a comprehensive preservation program of land banking. Income through leaseback. Liability and management responsibilities assigned to leasee.

Disadvantage: Leaseback would not necessarily provide public access. Land must be appropriate for leaseback (e.g., agricultural land).

Lease
Explanation: Short- or long-term rental of land.

Advantage: Low cost for use of land. Landowner receives income and retains control of property.

Disadvantage: Lease does not provide equity and affords only limited control of property. Temporary nature of lease does not assure permanent protection.

Undivided Interest
Explanation: Ownership is split between different owners, with each fractional interest extending over the whole parcel. Each owner has equal rights to entire property.

Advantage: Prevents one owner from acting without the consent of the other(s).

Disadvantage: Several landowners can complicate property management issues, especially payment of taxes.

TRANSFER OF TITLE OPTIONS

Outright Donation
Explanation: A donation by landowner of all or partial interest in property.

Advantage: Allows for permanent protection without direct public expenditure. Tax benefits to seller since property's fair market value is considered a charitable contribution.

Disadvantage: A receiving agency or organization must be willing to accept donation, and capable of management responsibilities.

Other Donations
Explanation: By devise: landowner retains ownership until death. Reserved life estate: landowner donates during lifetime but has lifetime use.

Advantage: Reserved life estate: landowner retains use but receives tax benefits from donation. Management responsibility for acquiring entity deferred until donor's death.

Disadvantage: By devise: donor does not benefit from income tax deductions. Date of acquisition is uncertain with either option.

Bargain Sale
Explanation: Part donation/part sale—property is sold at less than fair market value (FMV).

Advantage: Tax benefits to seller since difference between fair market value and sale price is considered a charitable contribution. Smaller capital gains tax.

Disadvantage: Seller must be willing to sell at less than fair market value. Bargain sale price may be high.

Fair Market Value Sale (FMV)
Explanation: Land is sold at a price equivalent to its value at highest and best use.

Advantage: Highest sale income (cash inflow) to seller.

Disadvantage: Can be expensive to acquire.

Land Exchange
Explanation: Public agencies or nonprofits can exchange developable land for land with high conservation value.

Advantages: Relatively cost-free technique if trade parcel is donated. Reduces capital gains tax for original owner of protected land.

Disadvantage: Property owner must be willing to accept exchange. Property must be of comparable value. Complicated and time-consuming transaction.

Restricted Auction (Nonprofit)

Explanation: Government can restrict the future use of their sale property to open space.

Advantage: Property still sold to highest bidder, but restriction lowers price and competition.

Disadvantage: It may be difficult for nonprofit to convince government that a restriction will serve to benefit the general public. Purchase price may still be expensive.

Eminent Domain (Government)

Explanation: The right of the government to take private property for public purpose upon payment of just compensation.

Advantage: Provides government with a tool to acquire desired properties if other acquisition techniques are not workable.

Disadvantage: High acquisition costs. Can result in speculation of target properties. Potentially expensive and time-consuming litigations.

Tax Foreclosure (Government)

Explanation: Government acquires land by tax payment default.

Advantage: Limited government expenditure.

Disadvantage: Land acquired from tax foreclosure might not be appropriate for public open space; however, can be sold to provide funds for open space acquisition. Cumbersome process.

Agency Transfer (Government)

Explanation: Certain government agencies may have surplus property inappropriate for their needs that could be transferred to a parks agency for park use.

Advantage: Agency transfer eliminates the need for any expenditure on parkland acquisition.

Disadvantage: Surplus property available may not be appropriate for park use or the owning agency may want to sell to a private party to generate revenues.

NONPROFIT FINANCING OPTIONS

Institutional Lender

Explanation: Conventional loan from bank or savings and loan.

Advantage: Less time-consuming process than fund-raising.

Disadvantage: Long-term financial commitment for nonprofit. Higher interest costs than owner financing. Mortgage lien.

Installment Sale

Explanation: Allows buyer to pay for property over time.

Advantage: If seller-financed, can lower taxes for seller. Buyer can negotiate better sale terms (lower interest rates).

Disadvantage: Long-term financial commitment for nonprofit. Mortgage lien.

Fund-raising

Explanation: Through foundations, corporations, and local community. Program-related investments (foundations), nonstandard investments (corporations), or charitable creditors (community) can provide no- or low-interest loans for acquisition.

Advantage: Fund-raising creates publicity and support throughout community. Low- or no-interest loans can make an acquisition possible.

Disadvantage: Obtaining grants and contributions is a long, uncertain, and time-consuming process.

Revolving Fund/Loans or Grants

Explanation: A public or private organization makes grants to localities or nonprofits for land acquisition based on a project's revenue-generating potential.

Advantage: Encourages projects with revenue-generating potential. An alternative funding source.

Disadvantage: Projects with low revenue-generating potential have lower priority.

Partial Development/Saleback or Leaseback

Explanation: A nonprofit can purchase property, limit future development through restrictive convenants, and resell or lease back part or all of property.

Advantage: Acquisition is financed by resale or leaseback. Resale at less than fair market value (because of restrictions) makes land affordable for buyer. Sale can finance preservation of part of site.

Disadvantage: Complex negotiations. If leaseback, nonprofit retains responsibility for land. Finding a buyer for restricted property may be difficult.

Development Regulatory Techniques

GROWTH CONTROL

Preferential Assessment

Explanation: Under state laws, agricultural and forest districts can be established to assess land as farmland or forestland rather than at its highest and best use.

Advantage: Reduced property assessment encourages preservation. Particular benefits to landowners near areas with development pressure. Tax base loss can be reclaimed through penalty tax (a tax on landowners who terminate enrollment in district).

Disadvantage: Voluntary participation. Does not provide long-term protection. Minimum acreage for entry. Strength of program depends on penalty from withdrawals. Local government bears burden of reduced tax base.

Examples: At least 16 states have preferential assessment programs. In use since 1965, the California Williamson Act, which allows assessment of open land at its use value, has protected 15 million acres.

Phased Growth

Explanation: Phased growth permits a limited amount of growth each year.

Advantage: Phased growth is effective as a comprehensive planning strategy.

Disadvantage: Under phased growth, there must be an equitable system to approve developments.

Examples: Amherst, Massachusetts, recently enacted a point system for rating new development, which limits new units to 250 every two years.

Moratorium

Explanation: A moratorium is a legal postponement or delay imposed upon land development.

Advantage: Moratoriums are often useful as an interim measure during the formulation of a master development plan.

Disadvantage: A moratorium provides only a temporary solution and can create a rush on land development prior to it taking effect.

Examples: A model moratorium ordinance from Dover, New Hampshire, can be found on page 143.

Transfer of Development Rights (TDR)

Explanation: Under an established program, a landowner wishing to preserve property can sell development rights to other landowners whose property can support increased density.

Advantage: Cost of preservation is absorbed by property owner who purchases development rights.

Disadvantage: Difficult to implement. Preservation and receiving areas must be identified. Development pressure must be sufficient to make a TDR program workable.

Examples: At least 15 states have communities with TDR programs. Montgomery County, Maryland, initiated a program in 1981 that by 1987 had protected 10,300 acres.

ENVIRONMENTAL REVIEW

Local Environmental Ordinances
Explanation: Often, under mandate of federal or state legislation, localities must regulate development in sensitive areas. Includes floodplain, wetland, watershed, and tree-protection ordinances.

Advantage: Development in protected areas requires permit. Permit issued only if proposed development is within ordinance guidelines.

Disadvantage: Ordinances do not always prohibit development (e.g., in floodplains). Regulatory guidelines are often broad enough to allow subjectivity in permit application approval.

Examples: National Flood Insurance Program requires floodplain ordinances.

Critical Environmental Area Designation (CEA)
Explanation: Any development proposed in a CEA (designated by the local government) requires an environmental assessment or environmental impact statement (EIS).

Advantage: An effective tool for preventing or mitigating the impact of development on sensitive natural areas.

Disadvantage: Does not assure preservation since determination of environmental impact is discretionary.

Examples: Florida's 1972 Environmental Land and Water Management Act authorizes the governor to establish critical areas, and a 1984 Chesapeake Bay Critical Area Protection Law protects a 1,000-foot buffer in Maryland.

Conservation Council/Board
Explanation: Commission members are appointed to oversee the community's natural resources and advise the planning board on development applications.

Advantage: The commission can advise the planning board on ways of mitigating development's impact on natural resources.

Disadvantage: Usually advisory capacity only. Strength of board depends on members and influence on governing body.

Examples: In Massachusetts, a local conservation commission implements the State Wetland Act (issues permits, enforces regulations, and conducts open space plans).

Federal/State Review
Explanation: Through legislation, government agencies can require mitigation measures to reduce the environmental impacts of specific developments or can restrict development through permit review.

Advantage: Encourages preservation of significant natural areas and allows for objectivity and creative solutions to development conflicts.

Disadvantage: Environmental impact review can be a time-consuming and complicated process that can stall development, adding to project costs.

Examples: Vermont's Act 250 is an effective state development permitting process.

FINANCIAL INCENTIVES

Purchase of Development Rights
Explanation: Local government, under state program, purchases development rights (PDR) to maintain land in farm use.

Advantage: Under PDR program, landowner can derive income from selling development rights and continue to own land. Lower property value should reduce property taxes.

Disadvantage: Acquisition of development rights can be costly, particularly in a community with high real estate values.

Examples: Many states—including Washington, Pennsylvania, North Carolina, California, and Massachusetts—have enacted PDR programs.

Land Conservation Grants

Explanation: State programs pay landowners to preserve land, enhance wildlife, and provide public access.

Advantage: Landowners derive revenues from preserving land without selling interests in land.

Disadvantage: Preservation of land or provision of public access requires public expenditure.

Examples: North Carolina has a program that pays landowners for public access, and programs in Michigan and Nebraska pay landowners for habitat enhancement.

ZONING/SUBDIVISION PROVISIONS

Large Lot Zoning

Explanation: Large minimum lot sizes restrict the density of development.

Advantage: An established land use control used as part of a comprehensive plan. Effective at maintaining low densities and protecting water resources, particularly in rural areas.

Disadvantage: Since zoning is subject to change, not an effective device for permanent preservation. Can increase real estate values and infrastructure costs, and can foster urban sprawl.

Performance Zoning

Explanation: A zone is defined by a list of permitted impacts (based on natural resource data and design guidelines) as opposed to permitted uses.

Advantage: Directs development in appropriate places based on a comprehensive, environmentally based plan. Can be implemented through cluster development.

Disadvantage: Difficulties in implementation since environmental impacts can be hard to measure and criteria are hard to establish. Plan can be expensive to prepare.

Examples: Bucks County, Pennsylvania, adopted performance zoning in 1973.

Carrying Capacity Zoning

Explanation: Based on the ability of an area to accommodate growth and development within the limits defined by existing infrastructure and natural resource capabilities.

Advantage: Zoning is based on an area's physical capacity to accommodate development. Can be implemented through cluster development.

Disadvantage: Requires a comprehensive environmental inventory for implementation. Determining carrying capacity can be a difficult process, subject to differing opinions.

Examples: Petaluma, California, and some counties in Florida have a time growth plan that considers future strains on physical capacity.

Cluster Zoning/Planned Unit Development

Explanation: Maintains regular zoning's ratio of housing units to acreage but permits clustered development through undersized lots, thus allowing for open space preservation. A PUD provision allows clustering for a large, mixed-use development.

Advantage: Flexibility in siting allows preservation of open space areas within development site. Can reduce construction and infrastructure costs.

Disadvantage: Open space often preserved in small, separate pieces, not necessarily linked to a comprehensive open space system. May increase processing time for development approval. Lack of infrastructure can inhibit use of technique.

Examples: In Concord, Massachusetts, an increase in density is allowed for conformance to stringent requirements.

Preservation Overlay Zoning

Explanation: At discretion of municipality, overlay zones with development restrictions can be established to protect agricultural and natural areas, scenic views, and historic neighborhoods.

Advantage: Special zones have regulations specific to the needs of a unique area and may be subject to mandatory clustering, performance standards, special permits, and site plan and architectural review.

Disadvantage: Language in special district ordinance must be specific enough to avoid varying interpretations.

Examples: Nantucket, Massachusetts, has established a special "moorland" district zone (ten acres), and Concord, Massachusetts, a Watershed Protection Zone.

Exaction

Explanation: As a condition of obtaining subdivision approval, local government requires developers to pay a fee or dedicate land to a municipal trust fund for open space. Also, the state can require open space set-asides as part of environmental review.

Advantage: New construction pays for its impact on open space.

Disadvantage: Acquisition funds dependent on residential development. Commercial development often not subject to exaction fees. Difficult to calculate developer's fair share of costs.

Examples: Commonly used in many states. California's Subdivision Map Act also requires public access to be provided to publicly owned water bodies.

Conservation Density Subdivisions

Explanation: Permits developers the option of building roads to less expensive specifications in exchange for permanent restrictions in number of units built.

Advantage: Increases open space and reduces traffic. Discourages higher densities to pay for the high costs of road building.

About the Authors

Michael A. Mantell is the general counsel of World Wildlife Fund and The Conservation Foundation where he oversees legal and congressional affairs for the two affiliated organizations. He directed the Successful Communities Program and the Land, Heritage and Wildlife Program of the foundation in Washington, D.C., and managed its State of the Environment and National Parks Projects. A principal author of *National Parks for a New Generation* and *A Handbook on Historic Preservation Law*, he has also been involved in foundation work on wetland and floodplain protection, industrial siting, and environmental dispute resolution. Before joining the foundation in 1979, he was with the city attorney's office in Los Angeles, where he worked on various environmental matters. Michael Mantell is a graduate of the University of California at Berkeley and Lewis and Clark College Law School, and serves as chairman of an American Bar Association Subcommittee on Federal Land-Use Policy.

Stephen F. Harper is a Washington-based environmental policy and planning consultant and writer. He formerly directed the Nonprofit Organization Assistance Program of the California State Coastal Conservancy and served as assistant director of the American Farmland Trust. He has also served in staff capacities with the U.S. Environmental Protection Agency, the Colorado State Legislative Council, and in several state agencies in New Jersey. He authored *The Nonprofit Primer*, a guidebook to management of citizen conservation organizations, published by the California State Coastal Conservancy. Stephen F. Harper has a master's in public affairs from Princeton University's Woodrow Wilson School of Public and International Affairs, a B.A. from the University of Colorado, and has completed additional graduate planning studies at the University of Pennsylvania.

Luther Propst is the field director for The Conservation Foundation's Successful Communities Program in Washington, D.C., where he oversees the delivery of technical assistance in land use matters to communities nationwide. Before joining The Conservation Foundation, he was an attorney in the Land Use Group with the Hartford, Connecticut, law firm of Robinson & Cole, where he represented governments, developers, and local environmental organizations in land use matters. Luther Propst received his law degree and master's of regional planning from the University of North Carolina at Chapel Hill. He coauthored *Managing Development in Small Towns*, published in 1984 by the American Planning Association, and has taught land use law as an adjunct professor at the Western New England College School of Law.

Henry R. Richmond
1,000 Friends of Oregon
Portland, Oregon

Richard J. Roddewig
Clarion Associates
Chicago, Illinois

James W. Rouse
The Enterprise Foundation
Columbia, Maryland

Joseph L. Sax
University of California
Berkeley, California

Susan E. Sechler
The Aspen Institute
Washington, D.C.

William H. Whyte
Street Life Project
New York, New York

Also Available from Island Press

Americans Outdoors: The Report of the President's Commission: The Legacy, The Challenge, with case studies
Foreword by William K. Reilly
1987, 426 pp., appendixes, case studies, charts
Paper: $24.95 ISBN 0-933280-36-X

The Challenge of Global Warming
Edited by Dean Edwin Abrahamson
Introduction by Senator Timothy E. Wirth ,
In cooperation with the Natural Resources Defense Council
1989, 350 pp., tables, graphs, bibliography, index
Cloth: $34.95 ISBN: 0-933280-87-4
Paper: $19.95 ISBN: 0-933280-86-6

The Complete Guide to Environmental Careers
By The CEIP Fund
1989, 300 pp., photographs, case studies, bibliography, index
Cloth: $24.95 ISBN: 0-933280-85-8
Paper: $14.95 ISBN: 0-933280-84-X

Creating Successful Communities
By Michael A. Mantell, Stephen F. Harper, and Luther Propst
In cooperation with The Conservation Foundation
1989, 350 pp., appendixes, index
Paper: $19.95 ISBN: 1-55963-014-0
Cloth: $34.95 ISBN: 1-55963-030-2

Crossroads: Environmental Priorities for the Future
Edited by Peter Borrelli
1988, 352 pp., index
Cloth: $29.95 ISBN: 0-933280-68-8
Paper: $17.95 ISBN: 0-933280-67-X

Natural Resources for the 21st Century
Edited by R. Neil Sampson and Dwight Hair

In cooperation with the American Forestry Association
1989, 350 pp., index, illustrations
Cloth: $34.95 ISBN: 1-55963-003-5
Paper: $24.95 ISBN: 1-55963-002-7

The Poisoned Well: New Strategies for Groundwater Protection
By the Sierra Club Legal Defense Fund
1989, 400 pp., glossary, charts, appendixes, bibliography, index
Cloth: $31.95 ISBN: 0-933280-56-4
Paper: $19.95 ISBN: 0-933280-55-6

Reopening the Western Frontier
Edited by Ed Marston
From *High Country News*
1989, 350 pp., illustrations, photographs, maps, index
Cloth: $24.95 ISBN: 1-55963-011-6
Paper: $15.95 ISBN: 1-55963-010-8

Rush to Burn
From *Newsday*
Winner of the Worth Bingham Award
1989, 276 pp., illustrations, photographs, graphs, index
Cloth: $29.95 ISBN: 1-55963-001-9
Paper: $14.95 ISBN: 1-55963-000-0

Shading Our Cities: Resource Guide for Urban and Community Forests
Edited by Gary Moll and Sara Ebenreck
In cooperation with the American Forestry Association
1989, 350 pp. illustrations, photographs, appendixes, index
Cloth: $34.95 ISBN 0-933280-96-3
Paper: $19.95 ISBN: 0-933280-95-5

War on Waste: Can America Win Its Battle with Garbage?
By Louis Blumberg and Robert Gottlieb
1989, 325 pp., charts, graphs, index
Cloth: $34.95 ISBN: 0-933280-92-0
Paper: $19.95 ISBN: 0-933280-91-2

Wildlife of the Florida Keys: A Natural History
By James D. Lazell, Jr.
1989, 254 pp., illustrations, photographs, line drawings, maps, index
Cloth: $31.95 ISBN: 0-933280-98-X
Paper: $19.95 ISBN: 0-933280-97-1

These titles are available from Island Press, Box 7, Covelo, CA 95428. Please enclose $2.00 shipping and handling for the first book and $1.00 for each additional book. California and Washington, D.C., residents add 6% sales tax. A catalog of current and forthcoming titles is available free of charge.